Money on the Line

Workers' Capital in Canada

MONEY ON THE LINE | Workers' Capital in Canada

Edited by Isla Carmichael and Jack Quarter

National Library of Canada Cataloguing in Publication
Money on the line: Workers' capital in Canada / Isla Carmichael and Jack Quarter, editors.
Includes bibliographical references.
ISBN 0-88627-287-4
1. Pension trusts—Canada—Finance. I. Quarter, Jack, 1941-
II. Carmichael, Isla III. Canadian Centre for Policy Alternatives.
HD7105.45.C3M65 2003   331.87'35'0971   C2002-905257-2
Printed and bound in Canada

Cover design by Studio 2 studio2@rogers.com

Book layout by Nadene Rehnby www.handsonpublications.com

Index by Jorge Sousa

Canadian Centre for Policy Alternatives
Suite 410, 75 Albert Street
Ottawa, ON K1P 5E7
Tel 613-563-1341 Fax 613-233-1458
www.policyalternatives.ca
ccpa@policyalternatives.ca

Dedication

To Bill Clark, trade unionist, labour educator

BROTHER CLARK SAW THE POWER OF WORKERS' PENSION capital some forty years ago. Since then he has worked unceasingly to achieve worker control of pension funds in his Local, his union and his province of British Columbia. As modest as he is, Bill understands the power of what he and his co-workers have achieved as a model for trade unionists everywhere. He has happily, generously and enthusiastically shared his experience with others.

Acknowledgements

FIRST, WE WOULD LIKE TO THANK ALL CONTRIBUTORS for their excellent and timely work and their patience as this edition unfolded. We thank both the Canadian Labour Congress and the Canadian Labour and Business Centre for their support of pension fund investment issues and for their innovative conferences. Both provided a stimulus to the work in this volume. Arlene Wortsman's support as Labour Director of the CLBC was particularly invaluable. We are indebted to the Shareholder Association for Research and Education for their support of some of the work in this volume and—overall—for their invaluable work in support of pension trustees.

We thank the Social Sciences and Research Council of Canada for funding and the Canadian Centre for Policy Alternatives for publishing this edition. We also thank Jorge Sousa for his work in producing the index.

Finally, we are indebted to Larry Brown, President of the Canadian Centre for Policy Alternatives and Secretary-Treasurer of the National Union of Public and General Employees for providing the foreword. He has provided the hands-on leadership that union trustees and pension activists have so desperately needed.

— *Isla Carmichael and Jack Quarter, October 2002*

Contents

List of tables and figures

Investing in a better world?

The union role in joint trusteeship of pension plans

EARLY IN JANUARY 2001, I CHAIRED A MEETING OF PENSION PLAN trustees from the National Union of Public and General Employees (NUPGE). A new group, these people represented every pension plan where the National Union has joint trusteeship. Over $60 billion in pension fund assets were represented in the room. That's a really large number, so large that it's hard for many of us to even fully comprehend the amount of money associated with that figure.

One week later, I was at a meeting of Public Services International on pension trusteeship. There was $1 trillion in pension fund assets represented around that table. This is an enormous amount of money, representing a potentially huge amount of economic power.

The road to joint control has been long one, and it hasn't always been a straightforward route. Pensions were originally put into place so employers could keep workers loyal. If you left a job or were dismissed, you wouldn't get a pension, so you stayed. These early pensions weren't paid out for too long a time, because life expectancy was shorter, and workers therefore didn't live too long after retirement. As more pensions became contributory, workers regarded pensions as their deferred wages—an entitlement that is earned when working, but paid out after retirement.

Unions in the public and private sector worked hard to win better benefits for their members, whether or not they had the right to negotiate. For a long time the focus was on the actual amount of the pension: that is, on the level of benefits that an individual worker was entitled to under his or her plan. The 'administration' of the pension fund itself was left to employers. In fact, in respect of public sector employees, most governments operated these pension plans on a "pay as you go" basis.

This meant that there was no need for a fund, per se, because the benefits were guaranteed. In other words, there would always be a government in place to ensure that the benefits promised were actually paid.

Within the last two decades there has been a huge shift. The focus has shifted from the benefit entitlements under the plan to one where the health of the pension fund is considered the major factor in attaining one's pension benefits. There were a number of reasons for that shift, and I don't really want to go into any real detail about them here. However, included in the factors was the imposition by the financial profession of the concept of an "unfunded liability" into the public pension system. Another was the deficit hysteria that we saw all too often in so many facets of government operations, and the resulting cuts in pensions and benefits, along with contribution "holidays" by employers.

The result is a good example of the law of unintended consequences: if, as a result of these events, workers are now more aware that the health of the pension fund is critical to their pension entitlements, then control over that fund becomes a critical issue. When workers know that the health of the fund is such a critical factor in pension payments, then they become far more aware of the fact that it really is *their* money in the fund. The reason, of course, is that the fund determines the pension benefits available. To put this another way, the balance in the fund determines the deferred wages our members are entitled to. An added factor is that, in the public sector, most often half of the money in the fund has been contributed by public service employees themselves.

There are several models of how employees exercise effective control over the health of their pension funds, including sole trusteeship by worker representatives. But it's safe to say that joint trusteeship is the most common model, and the fastest growing model.

All of this begs a very fundamental question: for what purpose do we want effective control? Is it simply to do a better job in maximizing returns? Or is it to make more fundamental changes in the financial system, a system that up until now has not had a "worker-friendly" agenda?

As an important example, our financial system includes the stock market, where stock values have often been known to fall when unemployment comes down. In the perverted logic of financial markets, too many workers with jobs may not be "good news," because that could possibly result in inflation. In companies that make their money from privatizing government services, cutting government jobs is an investment with instant payoffs for their shareholders—even though this is bad for public sector workers, and *very* bad social policy.

Slavery, sweatshops, environmental negligence, *maquiladora* factories— all can be very profitable for companies. They all reduce corporate costs, and augment the corporate bottom line. Short-term profits become the be-all and end-all, even if they result from violating human or labour rights, polluting the environment, or irretrievably damaging the long-term wellbeing of our families and communities.

The question is whether we have to use workers' money in an investment system that is anti-worker. Is there no choice but to play by *their* rules?

Before answering that, let's make something quite clear. Whatever we do, we need to be responsible with our members' money. We have our fiduciary responsibilities to meet, under the law, duties that we would want to meet anyway, whether the law required it or not. The law demands that we earn investment returns as Priority No. 1, so that our members have decent pensions, and of course that would be our goal even without the legal requirement. When we have joint control, or *any* kind of control, we are exercising important responsibilities that relate to our members' retirement incomes, in some pretty direct ways.

But remember this: the trade union movement is responsible for our members' retirement incomes in almost everything we do. Bargaining a collective agreement with higher wages affects the retirement income of our members. Higher wages while working equals higher pensions on retirement. Winning job security affects our members' right to a pension, because without a job there is no pension to look forward to. If we win an arbitration on unfair dismissal, or a wage improvement grievance, or even a grievance on basic discipline, we are affecting our members' retirement income.

Sometimes we allow ourselves to be put into a financial straightjacket, based on the fact that we have particular responsibilities towards our members through managing their pension funds. Yes, we do have that responsibility. But it's not the only area where we're responsible for our members' financial security. In reality, that responsibility is the very essence of the union's role in almost *every* activity, not just trusteeship on a pension board. Trusteeship may differ in its *details*—but it's part of the same fundamental concept of what we do as unions. We can and must exercise control over our money—our members' money—in ways that promote the financial *and broader* interests of our members. We must also challenge the financial industry where it does not meet the interests of workers, their families and communities.

We are learning quickly how to do this. We know some of the tools, and we are rapidly expanding our ability to use them. Our efforts focus on three areas.

First is the use of ethical screens. While they are an important tool, ethical screens are most often a 'passive' intervention, involving a decision *not* to invest in companies that operate outside some acceptable limits. For example, ethical investing may be behind a decision not to invest in companies that do business in Burma.

Secondly, there is the growing field of shareholder activism, where we exercise the votes our shareholdings in particular companies give us. For example, we might use our votes to change a company policy that says that a bank vice-president should get paid $14 million per year in salary and bonuses. Or we might vote against a policy that says that a corporate CEO should get paid 400 times the salary of the average worker in a company. Or we might vote for a new policy that ties management salaries to independent surveys of worker satisfaction; or the promotion of environmentally conscious workplaces.

Finally, there are economically targeted investments, where we invest in activities that provide our workers with returns on their pension fund investment, but also provide what are known as "collateral benefits." These include jobs, affordable housing, local development, the promotion of local businesses, and a range of other economic and social priorities. Earlier on, I said that the National Union's own pension trustees sit on pension boards that are responsible for some $60 billion of workers' pension money. If we used a percentage of a percentage of a percentage of that money to invest in things that were socially useful, and if every other union trustee could accomplish the same thing, it would result in a significant investment in a better world.

The union movement is drawing attention from others for our work in pension fund trusteeship. They are giving us strong hints that we may not yet fully grasp the enormous potential that is in front of us. I quote from *The Ambachtsheer Letter*, in an article with the ominous title, "Public Pension Fund Power in Canada: For Good...Or For Evil?". The article says the following:

> *By almost any standard, this massive accumulation of public pension fund assets, managed by only a handful of agencies, represents a significant concentration of economic power in this country. The implication is that just eight investment agencies could lock up effective control of all of corporate Canada over the next decade if they chose to do so. Thus, if used for the wrong purposes, these eight agencies could wilfully distort business decision-making in Canada, and seriously damage its economic prospects for decades to come.*

"Wilfully" distort business decision-making? We have seen huge examples of distorted business decisions recently. The fact is that others see more clearly than we yet do how huge an impact we might have, if we harness this awesome economic power effectively in the interests of our members.

Of course we need to act responsibly. We can't reasonably exercise this kind of power carelessly. We have to learn the ropes. The problem is that much of the information about the responsibilities of pension plan trustees comes from the industry. Together with the technical and legal jargon, it also contains a lot of biased advice aimed at telling trustees what they can and can't do—mostly what they can't do.

Let's take a different approach. Part of this whole process is for unions to recognize their responsibilities to trustees. We need to recognize that being a trustee can be a lonely job. Trustees are too often kept isolated within their individual plans, and perhaps the whole process is designed that way: to keep trustees isolated from each other. We need to overcome that separation, to provide ways for trustees to get together and work in concert.

Unions need to provide support to the work our trustees are asked to do. We don't ask our bargaining committees to go off on their own without backing them to get good agreements. We don't ask union staff to handle arbitrations without giving them backing and resources. So we shouldn't send our trustees off to do such important work without providing the resources necessary, either.

We also need to establish clear *objectives:* we need to be very clear about what we want as a movement. What we want in the area of pension funds must be both transparent and consistent with our broader objectives.

We need to provide education, at two levels. We need to provide our own technical tools and education, to counter the current model where the technical issues are used by "experts" and the system to build walls and chains around our trustees, used to emphasize what they can't do. We need to provide a balance to all the attempts to muzzle and intimidate our trustees with the heavy weight of 'responsibility.' But we also need to provide education on the broader issues: not just the tools, but also the analysis, the broader perspective, the union perspective.

We need to link our work on pensions fund investment to our work in other portfolios. For example, one of the possible tests for investment within our pension funds is adherence to the core labour rights established by the International Labour Organization (ILO). This is also a very significant factor in debates about the World Trade Organization (WTO), the Free Trade Area of the Americas (FTAA), and so on. It is important that the trade union movement be consistent in these positions and in our arguments, whether our work relates to our pension funds, international trade agreements, or other areas.

Another example: we know that so-called public-private partnerships are a bad deal for many reasons. We've done the economic analysis, and we know this is bad public policy. But we also know this kind of investment can be very profitable. That's one of the problems with the idea: private companies are practically guaranteed a profit at great expense to the public purse. It is important that we take our broader analysis back to our pension trustees so they are armed with this information in the face of the pressure to make "good" investments in such schemes.

Unions need to provide a place for debate about the current limits, the rules faced by trustees in the system. All of us—unions and trustees—need to work on parallel tracks. We need, at one and the same time, to work within the current rules, while also challenging them, pushing the limits back, breaking the chains that put narrow, short-term corporate needs ahead of those of our members, their families, and our communities.

We can find an analogy in the way unions deal with bad labour law. We always need to understand it, and we mostly work within it, while fighting to improve the legislation. But we sometimes have to confront the rules, to actively and openly challenge them. Or course we accept in general the principle that trustees act in a fiduciary capacity. That doesn't for a moment answer all of the questions. Where exactly is the line between proper and improper behaviour? Are we just going to accept the lines drawn for us by the financial industry? Why would we assume that their rules are designed for the benefit of those same workers?

Let me give you some examples of why even apparently good mandates don't fully answer the real questions. One of the large progressive funds in Europe has the following objectives, to ensure:

1. long-term viability of the plan with low and stable premium/contributions;
2. maximum return at preferred risk; and
3. acceptance of general constraints (human rights, weapons, etc.).

If you think about it for a moment, there are some intriguing questions that arise from this set of guidelines. The most obvious is this: what happens when there is a direct conflict between goal No. 2 and goal No. 3—maximum returns vs. human rights concerns?

Another big progressive fund has as its principles to act solely in the interests of the stakeholder/pensioner; to achieve maximum return with reasonable risk; and not to invest where socially unacceptable. Again, what if there is a contradiction between the second and third principles?

And what exactly does "solely in interests of the stakeholder" mean? A major South African pension plan has the articulated goal of improving social conditions in the country. How could this *not* be in the interests of the stakeholder/member?

We usually insist that ethical investment is actually better investment by the rules of maximum return. There is ample evidence that ethical plans earn greater returns, on average, than non-screened investments. But there *will* be times when to be truly ethical, to be truly operating in the best interests of the members, requires lesser returns. The most profitable way of operating can be the most damaging to society. In that case, do we reserve the right not to invest ethically? After all, the opposite of ethical investment is unethical investment. Do we want to reserve the right to act unethically if it means higher returns for our members?

Why is the *sole* definition of "best interests" limited to the financial aspect? Is it somehow in the *sole* interests of our members to have a good pension in a bad society? Is it in their interests to have private (but profitable) hospitals? Private (but profitable) jails? This is a strange and company-friendly system. We should be prepared to challenge it. We have a responsibility to learn what the financial industry and the current law *say* the rules are, and a responsibility to challenge and re-define those rules.

We need to find our own limits, our own rules, our own answers to the difficult conundrums that will face us in this area. And I don't just mean that our trustees have to do this. We need to work together to come up with our own collective answers as to what we think is in the best interests of our members, their families and communities.

Let me make one observation about the responsibility of international trade union organizations. In our discussions about the use of our pension funds, we are asked to take account of the needs of the developing world, and quite properly so. To do this, we must connect with workers in the countries we are discussing, so we aren't put in the position of making decisions *about* workers in other countries—our own form of enlightened colonialism—but rather so we can make decisions *with* the workers of those countries.

Finally, trustees have a responsibility to make pension plans more friendly to members. In financial language, the members of a plan are called liabilities. In practice, many plans treat them that way, with obscure information about their plans and their entitlements, with difficult and complex processes. In those plans, it seems that the *fund* comes first, the members second.

Union trustees can bring a new sense and a new fairness to the process, to the administration of the plan, to members' access to their plan and their rights under it.

We had to fight out way into joint trusteeship. We weren't welcomed, we weren't invited, until we forced the issue—until we crashed the party. Now that we're inside, the next level of defence is to tell us what we can do, and what we can't. In essence, they're saying to us: "You got here too late, the rules are all defined, the culture is established, and you can only stay if you behave."

We'll behave, all right. We'll behave the way we always do: in the interests of working people. It's *our* money, and we and our members will decide how to use it.

I remember the old call to "do something: lead, follow, or get out of the way." Well, we're here, and we're not leaving, not getting out of way. We shouldn't just follow rules we didn't set, rules that don't work for us or our members. That gives us only one choice: to lead the way to a better system—a system where workers' money acts in workers' interests. Isn't that what we're all about?

— *Larry Brown, Ottawa, October, 2002.*

Introduction

by Isla Carmichael and Jack Quarter

ALTHOUGH THERE IS A GROWING BODY OF RESEARCH ON SOCIAL investment, this research is predominantly from the U.S. and does not relate social investment to the involvement of unions. The papers in this book, by comparison, are predominantly Canadian and focused around funds that have union sponsorship: that is, union-based pension funds and labour-sponsored investment funds. The latter are a different type of fund than a pension fund, but in the context of this study have the common feature of labour involvement. The growth of union interest in the investment of pension funds and their participation in labour-sponsored investment funds reflects a change of attitude on the part of labour (Quarter 1995). That change is an important component of the context for this book.

The context

By the late 1970s, unions began to show an increased interest in how pension funds were being invested. The context for that interest was rising unemployment, stagnant wages, restrictions of the rights of public sector workers to strike, and the internationalization of finance. Within the Canadian Labour Congress, earlier discussions culminated in a resolution at the 1986 convention that "endorse[d] the goal of organized Canadian workers achieving greater control and direction of the investment of pension funds" (cited in Baldwin et al., 1991; p. 10). This resolution was reinforced by a similar one adopted at the 1990 convention.

To assume greater control, unions have taken two types of initiatives. One is the direct sponsorship of pension funds, involving about 14% of the membership of pension plans in Canada, largely in the building trades and in industries such as textiles (O'Grady, 1993). The other is joint trusteeship, typically in the public sector, the building trades, forestry, transportation, and some retail industries.

The Ontario Federation of Labour argued for co-determination of pension funds in a 1988 brief to the Rowan Commission (Task Force on the Investment of Public Sector Pension Funds, 1987). In Ontario, the Ontario Public Service Employees' Union (the large public sector union) has achieved joint trusteeship of its major pension plans (Carmichael 1996; 1998). The Canadian Union of Public Employees, which represents the employees in 30 of the top 100 plans in Canada, is also pushing for that objective, having also achieved joint trusteeship in some of its plans and having succeeded with other unions in winning co-trusteeship of the large Hospitals of Ontario Pension Plan).

The most recent data from Statistics Canada (2002) indicate that the assets of trusteed pension funds for the third quarter of 2001 were $541.6 billion. However, in addition, these vast pools of capital are a primary source of equity for the largest corporations in Canada, and internationally for the largest corporations in the world. As of 1994, pension funds in the U.S. controlled 47% of all U.S. equities; in Canada, the comparable figure was 35%, with 40% of pension fund assets invested in equities (Patry and Poitevin, 1995). The Caisse de Dépôt et Placement du Québec and the Ontario Teachers' Pension Plan, both with in excess of $50 billion of assets, are among the largest pools of capital in Canada.

In addition to pensions, organized labour has also become involved in the provision of venture capital through labour-sponsored investment funds. Unlike pension funds that are invested predominantly in government bonds or blue chip equities, labour-sponsored investment funds represent risk capital that is designed to meet gaps in markets for small- and medium-sized firms in particular provinces, as defined by the fund, and possibly in particular sectors of the market, if the fund is specialized (Quarter, 1995). For that reason, labour-sponsored investment funds are also referred to as venture capital funds. In general, these funds make long-term investments that bear a greater risk than the equities purchased by pension funds. However, labour-sponsored investment funds, like pension funds, are required by law to diversify their investments and to minimize the risks. To encourage participation in labour-sponsored investment funds, participants receive tax credits (federal and provincial) of 30% cent of their investment.

From 1983, when the Quebec Federation of Labour started the Solidarity Fund (Fonds de Solidarité des Travailleurs du Québec), an increasing number of unions have set up labour-sponsored investment funds. A 1995 study found there were 17 funds with more than $1.8 billion of assets, $582 million of investments, and 362,350 investors (Canadian Labour and Business Centre, formerly the Canadian Labour Market and Productivity Centre, 1995).

Most provinces have one labour-sponsored investment fund organized by the central labour federation. However, in Ontario, the Ontario Federation of Labour was split over whether or not to support such a fund because of the opposition of one union, the Canadian Autoworkers' Union (CAW). Therefore, a legislative model was developed that spawned many labour-sponsored investment funds without genuine labour involvement. Moreover, some of these are sponsored by organizations that have a questionable status as a union (for example, the Canadian Football League Players Association). These have been labelled as "rent-a-union funds" to denote the fact that the so-called labour associations that have organized them serve as a front for a conventional investment firm that wants to take advantage of the tax assistance available to labour-sponsored investment funds.

The CAW maintains its historic opposition to both labour-sponsored investment funds and union involvement in pension fund investment through joint trusteeship. According to the CAW, first, this 'muddies' the 'traditional understanding' (Stanford, 1999, p. 372) between unions and employers, and undermines the role of unions in representing their members through collective bargaining. Bargaining flat pension benefits has worked well for the CAW, but not so well for other unions, whose members—these days—must also make contributions to their pension plans and demand a stronger say in the administration of their plans.

Secondly, the workings of the market dictate losses in the rate of return of investments made in the benefit of a broader social good. Unions therefore would be obliged to make trade-offs between the interests of their members and the broader interests of a social investment (Stanford, 1999). This concern has been shared by other unions and is discussed later in this introduction.

Taken as a group, it is estimated that labour-sponsored investment funds are now providing nearly one-half of the venture capital in Canada. As with the investment of pension funds, organized labour's interest in such funds is based upon dissatisfaction with how capital is being invested. A report prepared for the Canadian Labour Congress in 1991 states: "A strong common current that has animated both the direct involvement of trade unionist in investing...is a strong sense that capital investment markets, left to their own devices and operating under the direction of traditional managers, have not served the interests of working people adequately" (cited in Baldwin et al., 1991; p. 11).

The social investment movement

At the same time as the labour movement was increasing its interest in how capital was being used, there was a parallel movement regarding the socially responsible investment of capital (Ellmen, 1989; Quarter, 1992; Reder, 1995). Although this phenomenon was not specifically tied to the labour movement and had a broad base of support that included religious organizations, social investment groups as well as businesses (for example, The Body Shop and Ben and Jerry's [Quarter, 2000]), the social investment movement has interacted with strategies of the labour movement.

Although there are differing manifestations of social investment, all involve the inclusion of social standards in investment decisions (Bruyn, 1987; Carmichael, 2000; Ellmen, 1989; Kinder, Lydenberg and Domini, 1998). In other words, investment decisions are not simply based on the rate of return (the typical standard), but also social criteria (for example, impact on the community) that may interact with the rate of return. The problem with this definition is that it also allows for the inclusion of right-wing criteria such as the anti-gay screens used by some U.S. funds. Therefore, this study utilizes the additional criterion suggested by some researchers (Bruyn, 19897; Carmichael, 2000; Lowry, 1991; Zadek, Pruzan and Evans, 1997) that social investment should challenge conventional corporate behaviour. Social investment is also referred to as ethical investment; for the purposes of this book, these two terms are used interchangeably.

There are at least three distinct forms of social investment that shall be discussed in turn. In general, all address methods of handling the assets of a fund and may be called: asset screening, asset targeting, and asset managing. The first, asset screening, involves the application to an investment of social screens, either negative or positive. Negative screens or sanctions occur where the funds prohibit particular investments. South Africa prior to the move to majority rule was one of the earliest examples; tobacco and armament companies are more current targets. The prohibition of investments in South Africa was utilized by a number of unionized pension funds and other labour investment vehicles prior to majority rule. Some labour-sponsored investment funds (e.g., the Working Opportunity Fund sponsored by the British Columbia Federation of Labour, the Crocus Fund of the Manitoba Federation of Labour, and the Solidarity Fund) have applied social screens to the firms that they evaluate for investment.

Where asset screening is positive, investment is directed to a fund with a positive social goal; for example, to encourage the quality of the environment (Desjardins Environment Fund) or with more general ethical objectives (for example, the Summa Fund). One difficulty with this approach is that it is based on normative criteria within a particular industry, and the overall standard within an industry might not be very positive. In general, unions have not been the sponsors of investment funds with positive objectives. However, there is a union-screened fund (MFS Standard Trust) in Washington that is channelling its investments to firms with a positive labour record. Moreover, CalPERS (the California Public Employees' Retirement System), with assets of about (U.S.) $170 billion, has recently instituted a more comprehensive screen based on the Global Sullivan Principles (Sullivan, 1999), which emphasize a broad range of environmental and social justice criteria.

A second form of social investment is asset targeting or economically targeted investment (Carmichael, 2000; Jackson, 1996). In this strategy, a fund targets 1% or 2% of its assets for specific social goals (affordable housing for low-income earners). In Canada, unions in British Columbia have engaged in economically targeted investment by establishing a development company to which they channel a small portion of their investments (Concert Properties). Some of these unions employ their own members through this strategy, thereby increasing the pay-in to the pension plan. In the U.S., the AFL-CIO has set up a housing trust for a similar purpose.

The third form of social investment—asset management or shareholder activism—involves both individuals and funds that are concerned about issues typically involving the governance of companies in which the fund invests. Activist shareholders raise these issues for discussion and propose strategies for change. In Canada, the impetus for shareholder activism has come largely from religious organizations (Hutchinson, 1996), although individuals also engage in such actions; for example, lawyer Yves Michaud's campaign to force the banks to address issues of executive compensation as well as issues related to governance. In the U.S., some of the large public sector pension plans (for example, CalPERS) have established a reputation for using this practice (Smith 1996). Labour-sponsored investment funds often insist on participating in a company's governance as a condition for investment.

Even though there are examples of labour involvement in social investment strategies, unions have also been reluctant to engage in such practices. There appears to be at least two major reasons for this reluctance. First is a concern that applying social criteria to investment can adversely affect the rate of return. Second is the tendency on the part of labour trustees to defer to management. Each of these issues shall be discussed in turn.

Rate of return

This concern is most pronounced with respect to pension plans because the so-called "prudent man" rule suggests that the trustees are required to seek the best possible rate of return for the beneficiaries. Canadian legal opinion on this matter has been heavily influenced by the 1984 decision of the Court of the Queen's Bench of England, the widely cited Cowan v. Scargill case, in which union trustees for the coal miners' fund insisted that there not be investments in energy industries in direct competition with coal. Justice Megarry, writing for the court, ruled against the union trustees, stating: "When the purpose of the trust is to provide financial benefits for the beneficiaries, as is usually the case, the best interests are normally their financial interests...the trustees must not refrain from making the investments by reasons of the views they hold." (Cowan v. Scargill, 1984; p. 760).

As a result of the Megarry ruling, which has been cited in Canada as well, trustees of pension funds have been very cautious about making investments that do not maximize the return to beneficiaries. In summarizing Canadian legal opinion on the issue, Waitzer, (1990; p. 10-11), the former chair of the Ontario Securities Commission, issues a warning that probably reflects the norm for social investment of pensions in Canada: "If ethical choices do not lower investment returns, the practical (and legal) reality is that trustees are unlikely to face judicial interdiction, regardless of their motivation. If investment returns are lowered, trustees are in trouble."

Unions in Canada have struggled with this issue. The policy statement passed at the 1992 convention of the Canadian Labour Congress hedges a bit on the rate-of-return issue when it states that: "Unions which achieve greater control of pension fund investment should seek to broaden the range of criteria involved in investment decisions, consistent with securing an *adequate* [emphasis added] rate of return." (Canadian Labour Congress, 1993; p. 9).

Andrew Jackson, a senior economist at the Canadian Labour Congress, takes the point further and suggests that a fund "invest for a positive rate of return but that [it] does not have to compete with best rate of return." (Jackson, 1993; p. 2). CUPE refers to a "good rate of return" (Beggs, 1993; p. 3), whereas the OPSEU Pension Trust, a jointly trusteed pension plan for Ontario government employees, stipulates a 'reasonable' rate of return (OPSEU Pension Trust, 1996). In legal circles, there are also some who argue that a broader range of benefits for the participants of a plan than the rate of return should be considered in determining appropriate investments (Ravikoff & Curzan, 1980).

In addition to legal considerations, there are also practical and political considerations. Evidence that pension plans are yielding a lower rate of return than RRSPs, for example, would provide justification for employers already eager to rid themselves of the responsibilities associated with pension plans and also create dissatisfaction among plan members. With respect to labour investment funds, there isn't the same legal prohibition, but the practical concerns mentioned above do apply. If the funds are not yielding a competitive rate of return to investors, they will eventually lose their appeal. This type of criticism has already been directed at labour-sponsored investment funds, both from labour critics (Gindin, 1989; Stanford, 1999) and from business critics (Suret, 1993).

An implicit assumption in the argumentation regarding social investment strategies is that they are likely to reduce the rate of return. Yet there does not appear to be evidence to support this point of view. In the U.S., there is some systematic research related to shareholder activism (one type of social investment strategy). A comprehensive review of the U.S. literature on pension fund activism and firm performance suggests that there is no substantial effect (Wahal, 1996). That review suggests that the firms targeted by CalPERS experience a small increase in stock values, whereas non-CalPERS targets do not change significantly. Wahal suggests, therefore, that there might be an effect associated with that particular fund rather than funds in general. There is some evidence that suggests that public funds that are subject to political interference may be forced to make investments that do not yield the best rate of return (Romano, 1993).

In Canada there is one study—recently released—done over a five-year and a ten-year period (Asmundson and Foerster, 2002). The study compares returns of ethical funds with the TSE 300. There were no statistically significant differences in results. Therefore, they conclude, screened ethical funds do not have lower returns.

Managerial control

Even though unions have been increasingly assertive in assuming the trusteeship and sponsorship of investment capital, their role in management has been limited. Few unions take a direct role in the management of their pensions. Control over investment can only be a reality once trusteeship of pension plans is won. Unions in 18 of the top 23 funds in Canada are in the process of winning, or have won some form of joint trusteeship (Carmichael, 1998). These struggles have been achieved largely in isolation from one another, from the early 1990s until fairly recently. Therefore, trusteeship models vary considerably and do not always include effective control over the investment arm of the fund (Carmichael, 1998). For example, teachers' unions in Ontario have very little control over the investment of their pension fund.

In cases where union representatives are either sole or joint trustees, they often do not assert themselves or they choose to defer to management. Deaton (1989) argues that trustees of pension funds, including union trustees, often defer to management's advice and fail to assume the level of independence in decision-making that they have the right to exercise. The reasons for this are not entirely clear. It could be a lack of confidence in their abilities, particularly where a fund involves large amounts of money. Other possible explanations are: a lack of training;

acceptance of the view that introducing social criteria is likely to reduce the return on investment; or lack of interest in the importance of social criteria in selecting investments.

Union pension trustee education as contested terrain

Undermining union trustees is not unusual, where fund managers stress their own professionalism and objectivity in contrast to the lack of expertise and supposed bias of most 'lay' or union trustees. William Dimma, chairperson of several Canadian companies, in a report presented to the House of Commons Standing Committee on the Governance Practices of Institutional Investors, said that:

> *While many plans are managed professionally, their boards are sometimes stocked with persons whose principal merit is that they are members...[who] have been elected by their fellow employees. While this is laudably democratic, it does not always produce the quality of direction and oversight necessary in today's bewildering world* (Report of the Senate Standing Committee on Banking, Trade and Commerce, p. 6).

This paternalistic attitude towards union trusteeship pervades the financial industry. Invariably, trustee education is delivered by representatives of the financial industry, who stress the high levels of accountability expected of union trustees compared to that of employer trustees. Union trustees are expected to set aside the interests of their members and communities to employment security, pension protection, environmental safety, and workplace standards in the interests of the "maximum rate of return." This generally means investment in large trans-national corporations that are already highly capitalized.

Hegemonic approaches to pension fund investment education and training are reinforced by existing training programs delivered primarily by the financial industry and its representatives through the Institute for Fiduciary Education, an American educational institution. This institute is corporate and anti-worker in its focus. The argument is made that training is 'neutral' and that a training program supported by unions will be biased. But union trustees have complained that training received from the financial industry tends to map out 'the way it is always done' uncritically, emphasizing dependence on fund managers. There is often not enough information supplied to allow trustees to pursue a critical learning path on their own. Instead, the presentations tend to mystify participants (Carmichael, 1998). Furthermore, existing training takes no account of policy discussions on economics and the behaviour of stock markets, gives few alternatives on different approaches to asset allocation, and fails to discuss gaps in the market caused by over-capitalization of the top 100 companies.

The results of a recent Canadian study (Carmichael, Quarter and Thompson) confirms anecdotal reports that existing opportunities for trustees are minimal and serve mainly to consolidate existing investment practice. Unions and trustees wishing to take a broader perspective towards investment are receiving little support from their pension funds. This is unfortunate because Canada needs new sources of capital to encourage emerging businesses. Pension funds are ideal for this purpose because they can be invested for the long term. However, this will not happen unless there are radically different approaches towards pension fund investment, a strategy that requires a transformative educational agenda developed by the trade union movement.

The need for educated trustees has been recognized as well among conventional business leaders and politicians. For example, Senator Michael Kirby, chair of the Standing Senate Committee on Banking, Trade and Commerce, has referred to the need for "highly knowledgeable people" who can "effectively monitor fund managers" (Canada, Standing Senate Committee on Banking, Trade and Commerce, 1998, p. 6). However, its proposal to deal with this is to replace lay trustees with professionals to be selected from the financial industry, as is legislated for the Ontario Teachers' Pension Plan. This would, in effect, cement control over workers' pension funds by the financial industry.

There are indications that union trustee education is critical to the informed, productive use of pension funds. Carmichael (1998) found through anecdotal reports that union trustees complained about the lack of support and resources from their unions, and suggested that education could be a critical factor in preparing union and other employee representatives to take an active role in pension fund investment. Rudd and Spalding's (1997) ground-breaking research indicates that, if trustees receive an appropriate education, they are encouraged to place pension funds in economically targeted investments which have the added benefits of creating jobs for working people.

Union pension education has traditionally been limited to equipping rank-and-file members to understand their rights to pension benefits when they retire. Freire (1973) refers to this type of training as involving a semi-transitive consciousness, where the union might take credit for gaining benefits for its members, but there is little historical context for struggle and few connections made between individual experience and social systems. In fact, until recently, unionists (including some trustees) for the most part have remained unaware of the notion that their pensions constitute vast capital funds.

However, it is clear that unions must develop their own body of knowledge on capital markets and pension fund investment strategies, providing impetus to a more collective discussion of investment in the interests of working people (Habermas, 1972; Comstock and Fox, 1993). At present, even where trade unions have a role in investment, it is not recognized. For example, an article on labour-sponsored investment in *The Globe and Mail* bore no mention of union involvement (Won, 2000). Through education, this silence can be broken (Reinharz, 1992; Hooks, 1988; Schrjivers, 1991).

Central to such an educational approach must be an "unmasking" of the power dynamics of the capital markets, the self-interest of the financial industry, and the development of a union agenda based on the perspectives and interests of working people and their communities. This approach is particularly important since, in some cases, unionists—who have been trustees for many years—agree with the financial industry that they cannot 'wear a union hat' when making investment decisions for fear of being subjective.

This belief has been bolstered by the *Cowan v. Scargill* case (1984) in the British courts, which had a chilling effect on union involvement in investment decisions and union support and training of union trustees in North America, as well as the U.K. Such education therefore needs to examine how participants are socially and historically located (Smith, 1987; Harding, 1992) as workers, trade unionists, community members, and future beneficiaries. Some union trustees are beginning to argue that fiscal prudence in the trusteeship of pension funds may be impossible in the absence of training that promotes critical reflection. Critical learning is needed to expose dominant thinking and show how alternative approaches may be initiated; and critical reflection is central to a transformative approach to adult learning (Mezirow, 1991).

Transformative learning may be liberatory at a personal level, or it may also be the outcome of education for radical social change through challenge to hegemonic ideology (Mojab & Gorman, 2002; Schugurensky, 2001; O'Sullivan, 1999). Critical reflection then becomes the process of revealing oppressive power dimensions in society (Brookfield, 2000).

There is some anecdotal evidence that some employer trustees may also believe that responsible trusteeship requires more comprehensive training and that they would like to work with union trustees jointly on training issues. Obviously, both union and employer trustees need training that will enable them together to make prudent decisions based on a critical approach to their trustee work. Indeed, developing a prudent approach involves deciphering disparate interests in investment decisions.

This approach to transformative education is influenced by Paulo Friere's work on conscientization (1970), as well as the development of critical theory where critical reflection is a means of unmasking hegemonic ideology as a liberatory step (Habermas, 1972). This direction is also supported by literature on socialist pedagogy (Youngman, 1986), popular education (Freire, 1970; Freire & Faundez, 1989), participatory research (Hall, 1993), social action (Newman, 1995), critical teaching (Shor, 1992), feminist theory (Smith, 1987; Harding, 1992), and labour education (Wertheimer, 1981; Martin, 1995; Taylor, 2001). This social activist approach has also been central to the practice of adult education by such educators as Freire, Tomkins, and Coady.

In British Columbia, in the 1960s, concerns about regional development drove Bill Clark, the local president of the Telecommunication Workers' Union, to negotiate joint trusteeship of his members' pension plan and administration of the fund assets. His leadership, together with the support of the B.C. Federation of Labour and its President, Ken Georgetti, and the work of several union-sympathetic professionals, led to the birth of Concert Properties, a real estate development company, and its sister investment vehicle, Mortgage Fund One. Their success was due to dynamic, informal learning processes which occurred between experts outside the trade union movement and leaders and supporters within the Federation of Labour. Their goal was investment in their provincial economy. The experience of these unionists in B.C. can be replicated through effective education for union trustees in pension fund investment.

There are indications that active involvement of the trade union movement in initiatives that may be broadly called social investment are on the increase in Canada. The CLC has held a conference on pensions, a large portion of which was devoted to trusteeship and investment issues; and it is extremely active in the international movement on corporate social responsibility. It has also endorsed the Shareholder Association for Research and Education (SHARE), a national organization sponsored by the trade union movement to help pension funds "build sound investment practices."

The Shareholder Association for Research and Education (SHARE) is a non-profit agency established by Working Enterprises, a company which provides travel, insurance, and investment services to the trade union movement and is wholly-owned by the B.C. Federation of Labour. SHARE works with pension trustees, plan administrators, and plan members to provide shareholder research, education, and policy. It is a relatively new initiative, fully supported by the CLC, that aims to work as part of the international movement to hold the corporate sector accountable through shareholder proposals. So far, SHARE has drafted and circulated proposals to be filed with the Hudson Bay Company and Sears concerning the use of sweatshop labour by suppliers. It has also developed critical research papers on fiduciary responsibility and investment policy.

The National Union of Public and General Employees has now instituted regular meetings of its union trustees and activists across Canada, and recently held a first pilot educational for trustees to establish a union agenda for investment strategies. The Canadian Union of Public Employees has held similar week-long workshops for trustees.

The CLC is also supporting a new trustee education initiative to provide training to union trustees. This new initiative is sponsored by Carleton University and the Ontario Institute for Studies in Education of the University of Toronto, and aims to design and deliver, through workshops and web-enabled methods, focused, practical training on fund investment for trustees with public-sector and private-sector pension funds across Canada. This group is supported by an advisory committee that includes representatives from the CLC, the National Union of Provincial Government Employees, CUPE, and other leading labour organizations.

Another new initiative is a proposal for Social Science and Humanities Research Council funding for a research/education program to be developed by and for union trustees. Still in its early stages, every federation of labour in Canada has indicated an enthusiastic interest in playing a partnership role. This is startling support for a project which is still in its infancy and, furthermore, based in academic institutions. Whether or not this proposal is successful, indications are that the trade union movement is clearly ready to work on pension fund investment issues and a comprehensive research/education program reflecting a union perspective on investment. More importantly, federations of labour are preparing to play a leadership and coordinating role in working with union trustees and pension activists on investment issues.

There are many resources close at hand to support the research needed for educational programs, including academic institutions such as the Ontario Institute for Studies in Education, the Centre for the Study of Training, Investment and Economic Restructuring at Carleton University, as well as the Canadian Labour and Business Centre, SHARE, the Social Investment Organization, labour-sponsored investment funds, church-based organisations such as the Task Force for Churches on Social Responsibility, economically targeted investment vehicles (such as Concert Properties), unions such as NUPGE, the Ontario Public Service Employees Union, and other components of NUPGE and CUPE. All of these are in Canada, but there is also a wealth of expertise in the U.S., such as the George Meany Labor Center and the Center for Working Capital at the AFL-CIO.

We are witnessing a change in organized labour's attitude to dealing with investment matters, and a growing recognition that education—a transformative education—must play a central role in supporting trustees. While we know that training for trustees is dominated by the financial industry, there is a vacuum to be filled by unions and academic institutions that may stress a more transformative, holistic approach to pension fund investment, taking account of benefits to working people, their families, and their communities.

This book

We intend this book to contribute to this process of education. We anticipate that it will be read by union activists, trustees, and other groups interested in progressive approaches to the social investment of pension funds and labour-sponsored investment funds. We hope that it will be a valuable educational tool as a walk-through of the critical issues facing pension trustees who want—through their work—to make a difference.

The first chapter, by Richard Minns, provides a political analysis of the damaging consequences for workers and communities of the prevailing international investment practices of pension funds. He argues that pension funds are too massive to be evaluated by a financial rate of return only. Their social-economic impacts must be assessed. In that regard, pension funds contribute to financial speculation, often with negative results for productive investment, economic growth, employment, and incomes. This affects millions of people world-wide. New approaches are needed, providing new measures of economic and social welfare in contrast to a narrow rate of return index. Any change to the status quo, he says, depends on unions.

The second chapter, by Isla Carmichael, challenges conventional interpretations of fiduciary responsibility, and argues that the "prudent man" rule has been used by the financial industry to bolster its control of workers' pension funds and to prevent any union involvement. Through an examination of the leading cases in North America and Britain, it assesses the legal opportunities for union trustees to develop social investment strategies. It highlights recent Canadian legal opinion, encourages trustees to work with their unions on economic development policy, and calls for a much stronger role for unions on pension investment education, investment policy, and economic development projects.

The third chapter, by Gil Yaron, Legal Director of SHARE, provides practical, legal guidance to trustees on the development of statements of investment policy (SIPs)—the first step in responsible trustee activism. The product of extensive research in North America, Yaron's chapter provides the legal context, fiduciary checklists, models of general provisions, proxy voting guidelines, investment screening and economic development provisions, conflict of interest guidelines, questions for fund managers and lists of on-line resources. The chapter is a unique and critical resource for those interested in pension fund investment issues.

The fourth chapter, by Jack Quarter and Isla Carmichael, provides the results of a study to understand the dynamics that lead pension funds in the direction of social investment. It builds on an earlier study that found that pension funds in Canada have minimal social investment initiatives. Through an organizational analysis, it identifies leadership as a critical factor in the adoption of social investment strategies, prompted—in one example—by grassroots pressure from members. The authors caution that this is a fragile base for social investment strategies. Furthermore, size appears to be a complicating factor; can pension funds sustain social investment practices as outside management becomes more likely?

The fifth chapter, by Isla Carmichael, provides a case study of Concert, a real estate development company in British Columbia, set up by a group of jointly trusteed pension funds. The impetus for Concert and its sister investment vehicle, Mortgage Fund One, came from the union trustees. This case study of Concert provides a model of a Canadian ETI for trustees. It tells a story of trade unionists and their friends who, in spite of numerous legal and practical obstacles, built a real estate development company that is a leader in affordable housing in Canada. It shows the structure of VLC, the two Concert companies as well as its sister investment vehicle, Mortgage Fund One. This chapter points the way for trustees and trade unions in assessing the collateral value of investment vehicles to their members and the general community. There are no generally accepted measuring tools available to trustees. Yet there are generally accepted measurement tools commonly used in soci-economic analysis. Research in the area of social accounting needs to continue to support the social investment initiatives of trade unions and their trustees.

The sixth chapter, by Tom Croft and Tessa Hebb, tells the story of the development of the Heartland Network, which evolved from a small "grievance committee" into an important part of the growing labour-capital movement in the U.S. A collaboration of labour and community leaders and academics can create opportunities for public and labour education, mobilize leadership, rally expertise, and create the momentum for major social change.

In the seventh chapter, we learn about our Canadian experience growing out of labour sponsored investment funds. Sherman Kreiner describes some of the most recent cutting- edge directions being taken by Crocus, Manitoba's fund. Kreiner defines LSIFs as examples of economically targeted investment in Canada in that they fill capital gaps in the market, provide collateral benefits to the community and risk-adjusted rates of return to investors. As such, these funds may provide leadership and expertise to Canadian pension funds in more progressive investment practices such as the establishment of new venture capital pools, real estate development funds, sports, and entertainment facilities and other downtown amenities and enterprise development corporations in low-income communities.

The last chapter takes us to California. Sean Harrigan, Chair of the Investment Committee, describes the well-established experience of the California Public Employees' Retirement System (CalPERS) in economically targeted investment. He gives concrete examples of benefits to working people in rural and urban communities in mortgages, supportive housing, and affordable housing development. He describes venture capital investing in the retail foods industry, biotechnology, communications, and merchant banking—all worker-friendly.

Canadian trade unions and their pension funds are on the threshold of developing more innovative investment practices of long-term benefit to members as well as the broader community. Indeed, it can be argued that the country itself will benefit from more productive approaches to investment with goals of job creation, community development, corporate accountability, and long-term sustainable growth. The trade union movement can only benefit, as well, through a more pro-active, holistic approach to the interests of their members and communities. With such large interests at stake, and with such enormous amounts of money, the trade union movement may become a more significant player in the Canadian economy.

Canadian Centre for Policy Alternatives

CHAPTER 1

Collateral damage

The international consequences of pension funds

by Richard Minns

IT MIGHT SOUND OBVIOUS, BUT THERE IS A SERIOUS QUESTION about the role of private pension funds which continues to go unanswered. What do these funds actually *do*? These enormous stocks of investments which have been accumulated in private pension plans are not anonymous, passive pools of capital earning their rates of return for future pensioners. They have far-reaching ramifications for what happens in the world generally, affecting investment and economic development for future beneficiaries and their families, and millions of people in many countries, inside and outside the country of origin of the funds.

Governments, financial institutions, academics, corporations, the World Bank, 'social reform' bodies, *and* trade unions continue to create or support further private pensions throughout the world, while largely ignoring or dismissing the economic and political implications of their actions. Perhaps the most culpable are academics who take privatization as the *sine qua non* for addressing the alleged problems of paying for the aged. For those who think that pensions are just about 'pensions' and value-free fiduciary responsibilities which provide maximum returns for pensioners, I suggest that it is time to think again about *who* actually benefits from these flows of national and international funds.

The growth in pensions and financial markets

First, we have to churn through a number of statistics before we get to the more important political and economic points. But if you bear with me, I will try to establish the role that pension funds—our savings for retirement—play in the sometimes esoteric world of 'finance.'

'Pension dollars' have helped to fuel the world's financial markets, following Eurodollars and petro-dollars during the first 30 years after the Second World War. They began their significant take-off in the 1970s. They were often seen by unions and employers as ways of 'deferring' wages in the 'stagflation' period following the post-World War II period of economic growth.

The OECD puts the figure for total pension assets at $8.7 trillion (thousand billion) (all dollar figures are U.S.) for the OECD countries for 1996—an annual average growth rate of 10.9% since 1990 (OECD, 1998). It estimates that pension funds comprise 28% of all institutional finance in the OECD (insurance companies, investment companies, pension funds and others for 1995).

Growth rates for the financial assets of these institutions reveal the relative significance of pension funds (Table 1). But these figures for pension funds exclude the pension-related activity of insurance companies, which is included in separate figures for insurance and mutual funds, and other similar institutions elsewhere in the OECD. Their inclusion in the figures would probably increase the figure to nearer $10,000 billion, or

Table 1: Average annual rate of growth of assets held by institutional investors in OECD regions, 1990-1995 (%)

	Europe (20 countries)	North America	Asia and Pacific
Insurance Companies	11.4	7.9	9.2
Pension Funds	6.8	10.1	11.1
Investment Companies	16.5	18.7	7.6
All	11.3	10.9	8.3

Source: adapted from OECD, 1998, p. 30

over 40% of the OECD total for investment assets. The addition of non-OECD countries would increase the absolute monetary amount again. I estimate that the total for world-wide pension assets is over $12,000 billion for the end of the 1990s.

In contrast, U.S. GDP for 1998 was $7,000 billion. Total world stock market capitalization for 1997 was $23,000 billion and total world GDP for 1998 was $28,000 billion. So we have a possible $10-12,000 billion of global pension fund assets versus a world GDP of only two to two-and-a-half times that much. Thus, global pension fund assets amount to nearly 43% of world GDP. The relationship between the two, and whether the former represents realistic claims on the latter, is central to some of the arguments and counter-arguments about the real 'value' of pension funds and economic growth, and whether this value is based on anything 'fundamental.'

I doubt that it is. This is based on my understanding of recent financial 'bubbles,' stock market fluctuations, and the fact that millions of future pensioners in the UK, at least, are apparently not going to receive what they had predicted unless they pay an extra $4,000 GBP per year into their pension plans.

International pension flows

Now we come to the international aspect of all this. Pension fund assets alone amount to over 10 times the size of all the foreign currency reserves of the 15 largest 'Western' economies (most of EU plus U.S., Australia, Canada, Japan, Switzerland). In the U.S. and the UK, they own over 30% of their respective stock markets (the market capitalization of the companies quoted on those markets) and are the largest institutional holders of company shares. They are followed in the UK by insurance companies and in the U.S. by mutual funds, both of whose official statistics include private pensions.

The cross-border presence of these funds reveals the internationalization of pension financial flows. Although various sources provide different figures, it can be reasonably concluded that, in total, over 12% of *all* pension fund assets are invested outside their country of origin. In G-10 countries, the figure is 17%. The UK and Netherlands are in the lead among the countries with large pension funds. They have around 30% invested outside their home countries. Australia has 24%.

The private capital is not for the most part 'direct investment'—the provision of finance for new capital investment in infrastructure, production or services. It is mainly a trade in existing stocks and securities—the 'portfolio' markets of secondary stocks, shares, and associated currencies, along with the purchase of newly issued stock, especially privatized companies. In any case, foreign direct investment (FDI) is said to be smaller as a proportion of world output than before the First World War, whereas gross international financial flows are much bigger and have recently increased exponentially. Cross-border sales and purchases of bonds and equities by U.S. investors have risen from the equivalent of 9% of GDP in 1980 to 164% in 1996.

'Flight capital,' as opposed to long-term fixed capital or dedicated investment, is an essential part of the increase in capital mobility and the ending of capital controls. For instance, flight capital amounted to one-third of Latin America's external financing by 1992 (Cordery, 1994). Other countries and regions, whether 'developed,' 'developing,' or 'in transition,' are increasingly affected by flight capital—funds that are not tied into specific investment projects. The problem is to measure their significance and, for our purposes, to assess the role of pension investment.

I calculate that the international holdings of shares by pension funds are up to three times the official figures for new equity issues alone, and therefore their participation in international capital market activity is considerably larger than thought.

Excessive Third World lending by Western banks created its own problems of repayment. Corporate investment and lending to governments has also been subject to defaults caused by changes in regime or ability to repay. But flight capital is 'liquid' investment, and protects against the risks of non-payment and default by being able to withdraw at short notice (or so it hopes), creating financial 'shocks' with enormous knock-on effects for other countries, markets, and asset values as the rush for cash or some other haven commences in a subsequent panic.

My point is that something rather novel has occurred. International financial flows emanate not solely from the financial transfers arising from trade or corporate surpluses. They also spring from how we pay for the maintenance of a large and growing proportion of the population as defined by a certain stage in life.

Indeed, the role of pension funds suggests a new paradigm of economic analysis whereby 'social' provision through flows of finance for income security has augmented international financial flows. 'Social security capital' is now as important as other sources of capital, if not more so. It is a key element in fuelling the expansion of financial markets.

So what, then, has happened over the last few years to the international flows of this social security capital?

Financial flows to developing countries

Let us first take their contribution to global economic development by way of investment in so-called developing countries, or 'emerging markets.' This is again important because of the theory of international economic development based on liberalized markets.

'Emerging markets' of interest to institutional investors grew significantly over the 10 years to 1998. There are 166 'developing countries' referred to by the World Bank, a group of which constitute the International Finance Corporation (IFC) Emerging Markets Index (IFCI) (World Bank, 1997, pp. 11 & 15). Reflecting the fluidity of the situation, sometimes the words 'developing countries' and 'emerging markets' are used interchangeably in official publications (IFC, 1998, p.8, and World Bank, 1998, p.3, use a similar table to portray financial flows to 'emerging markets' in the former case and 'developing countries' in the latter).

Although institutional investors for the most part assess their investment policies for developing countries by using the IFCI smaller group, the countries included in this index have nevertheless grown over the 10 years in which it has operated. This is a response to the increase in the number of stock markets throughout the world (by 1997, 75 emerging markets were covered by the IFC reports - IFC, 1998) and a growing interest amongst institutional investors themselves in a broader investment and geographical coverage (by 1997, 32 countries were included in the ICFI, compared to 18 in 1996).

Bearing these differences in mind, private capital flows to 'developing countries' rose to $240 billion in 1996 (World Bank, 1997, p. 9) and to $256 billion in 1997 (World Bank, 1998, p.3) from $33.3 billion in 1985. In 1985, official development finance (funding through grants and loans from government and intergovernmental bodies) was higher than private flows. But by 1997 private flows were nearly six times greater (Table 2).

Foreign direct investment (FDI) comprises the largest category of private flows. (FDI includes corporate investment in overseas subsidiaries through the increase in fixed capital investment, or the establishment or purchase of ventures and plant). But portfolio flows (investment mainly in equities and bonds) have risen 10 times between 1990 and 1997, for example, while FDI has risen five times.

By 1997, portfolio equity flows were similar to bank loans and official development finance in size. Moreover, total portfolio flows (bonds and equities) made up more than one-third of total private financial flows (World Bank, 1998, p. 9, IFC, 1998, p.8, World Bank, 1997, p. 11). But, '(u)nlike FDI flows, portfolio flows to the emerging markets have been volatile' (IMF, 1997, p. 63). Developing countries now receive 30% of

Table 2: Net long-term resource flows to developing countries (selected years) (US $billion)

Type of Flow	1985	1990	1997
All Developing Countries	82.5	98.3	300.3
Official Development Finance	37.8	56.4	44.2
Total Private Finance	33.3	41.9	256.0
Debt Flows	21.8	15.0	103.2
Bank Loans	8.5	3.8	41.1
Bonds	5.6	0.1	53.8
Other	7.6	11.1	8.3
Foreign Direct Investment	11.3	23.7	120.4
Portfolio Equity	0.1	3.2	32.5
Official Development Finance as % of Total Flows	45.8	57.4	14.7
Equity, Bonds as % of Total	6.9	3.3	28.7
Equity as % of Total	0.1	3.3	10.8

Source: adapted from IFC, 1998, p.8, World Bank, 1998, p.9

global portfolio capital, compared to only 2% before 1990 (World Bank, 1997, p.15).

This international investment activity has increased substantially in geographical scope over only 10 years, with greater 'financial integration' as defined by the World Bank (1997), while, at the same time, the speed of reaction by international investors has also increased. The share of world stock market capitalization represented by emerging markets (the market value of securities on their stock markets) increased to 9% of world capitalization by 1997 (IFC, 1998, p.18). This should be contrasted with just over 4% in 1988. Despite ups and downs in the meantime, this growth is another indicator of the increase in the numbers of markets and the increase in investment in those markets, thereby enhancing their relative proportion of global stock market capitalization.

One of the major factors driving this growth has been the increase in the investment of pension funds and related institutional pension provisions, and their search for an increase in diversification of investments. The returns on investments in domestic markets are deemed to be flattening, or they are predicted to reduce as the increase in private funds from ageing populations flows into a relatively fixed stock of tradeable assets, pushing prices up (rise in stock market indices in the U.S. and the UK—the U.S. Dow Jones and London 'FTSE' indices of stock market prices), with an associated decline in relative income which can be received as a result of the rising asset prices.

Emerging markets appear as a way of buying low-priced assets in high-growth economies, producing higher rates of return. There was deemed to be a low correlation between returns in developed markets and those in emerging markets. The increase in risk incurred by the investment in emerging markets is supposed to be at least equalized by the increase in the relative return.

As a result, pension funds held $70 billion of investments in emerging markets by 1997, representing around 1% of their total assets (World Bank, 1997, p.22). In the U.S., pension funds held around 2% of their total assets in emerging markets (3.75% according to one source for 1996), while in the UK, surprisingly given the significantly higher proportion of total overseas holdings, the figure has hovered around 1%, with the larger pension funds holding a larger percentage (IFC, 1996 and World Bank, 1997 for the U.S.; for the UK, IFC, 1996).

I conclude—what may be fairly obvious to some—that what amounts to a small relative figure for the substantial pension funds of the developed world has enormous implications for the smaller markets of the developing world. Indeed, what may be a small portfolio adjustment for one large institutional investor may have a major influence on an emerging market or markets, especially if other large institutions with their similarly small investments follow suit, as they seem to have done.

Indeed, '(t)he sheer size of institutional investor assets in the mature markets has meant that small changes in their portfolio allocations to emerging markets could have enormous effects on flows to those markets' (IMF, 1997, p. 88).

Financial integration

The result of pension fund and other institutional investment in emerging markets is said to include greater 'financial integration,' a supposedly benign development which will help in the free flow of institutional finance throughout the world and thereby promote higher economic growth for the benefit of us all. Believe the rhetoric if you will, but let us examine the argument.

Financial integration is measured by the World Bank (1997) as comprising;

1. access to international financial markets, as measured by 'country risk' ratings according to international risk assessment agencies;
2. the ratio of private capital flows to GDP, with a higher weighting given to portfolio investment and commercial bank lending (as opposed to FDI, for example); and
3. the diversification of a country's financing generally.

The Top Ten emerging markets in terms of financial integration for 1992-1994 were: 1) Thailand, 2) Turkey, 3) Brazil, 4) Argentina, 5) Korea, 6) Indonesia, 7) Malaysia, 8) Mexico, 9) Hungary, and 10) Ghana. This list of the most integrated markets is particularly interesting in the light of the financial crises of 1997-1999. The crises started with No. 1 on the list and subsequently spread to numbers 6, 7, and 3, followed by the Philippines, No. 13 of the total number of 13 countries rated '*high*' (compared to only two with such rating for 1985-87) on the scale of low, medium and highly integrated countries out of the 65 developing countries assessed by the World Bank (World Bank, 1997, pp. 17-18).

The 'push' factor for portfolio diversification is set to continue, it seems (IMF, 1997, OECD, 1998). One argument is that, if pension funds and mutual funds have between 1-2% of their assets invested in emerging markets, then they are 'underweight' in emerging markets because, as noted above, the market capitalization of those markets equals 9% of total world market capitalization. About 60% of total world assets are outside the U.S., but the average U.S. pension fund allocated only 16% of its equity assets, and 8.8% of total assets to foreign stocks in 1995 (*Institutional Investor*, 1997, p.106). Diversification, in other words, should allow for a closer matching of regional values within the global total.

In quantitative terms, relative to some other institutions, pension fund investment in these markets will increase anyway, because of the number of countries considering reforms to their state pension systems. This applies to all areas of the world. In Latin America, the private market response to pension reform exemplified by Chile in the early 1980s is being followed by reforms in Peru, Uruguay, Bolivia, Mexico, El Salvador, Colombia, and Argentina. In Central and Eastern Europe, the process includes Hungary, Poland, Czech Republic, Latvia, and Romania, among others.

Most important, however, are the continuing reforms in the developed world, including the possibility of the major privatization of U.S. Social Security pensions, and the extension of additional private solutions in the UK—the two countries which dominate the world's league tables of private pension provision as measured by the size of pension funds and pension-related financial assets. Privatization also continues in other countries such as Germany and Ireland. This is accompanied by the relentless and predictable arguments, from academics in particular, about the demographic and public pensions' "crises" which are about to overwhelm us all.

The increase in private pension assets may continue, but the OECD points out that investment in emerging markets is not the solution to ageing problems in the developed world (OECD, 1998). Recall that this theory suggested that greater returns could be obtained from the emerging markets in order to offset the decline in returns in developed stock markets as a result of increasing demand causing rising prices from a fixed stock of assets. Through international diversification, future pensioners could thereby claim a greater share of world economic growth to compensate for the growing relative claim of ageing populations on more limited domestic economic growth.

Essentially, the contrary argument suggests that the overall returns will equalize or correlate as money leaves the low-return, high-asset-priced developed world and flows to the high-return, low-asset-priced developing world. Asset prices in the latter will go up and returns fall in relative terms, so levelling out the initial global variances. This even takes into account the downward pressure on returns relative to capital invested in developed markets as more people enter private plans for retirement savings invested on 'mature' or developed country stock markets. Indeed, the World Bank points out the inflationary implications of the increased demand for emerging market securities and views it as a negative local factor which should be countered by what remains of local economic policy discretion.

Following another strand of argument, the World Bank argues that financial integration, as described above, can, however, promote better macro-economic policies:

> *Although integration increases the costs of policy mistakes in the short term, and increases the constraints on the conduct of macroeconomic policy, the market discipline that comes with integration can be a powerful force in promoting prudent and stable macroeconomic policies, with large benefits over the longer term. For instance, Indonesia's decision to open its capital account almost three decades ago has been an important element underpinning its track record of prudent and responsive economic policies* (World Bank, 1997, p. 24).

How unfortunate, one might comment, in the light of subsequent problems in 1997-8 for economies like Indonesia's, which had introduced such open policies leading to greater financial integration. Indonesia was No. 6 out of 65 on the World Bank list of integrated financial markets. Where does this leave World Bank economic theory?

The advocates of greater portfolio flows, however, acknowledge certain inherent risks. The first problem concerns 'surges' in private capital flows, with considerable variations between countries in the timing, magnitude, and duration of the surges (World Bank, 1997, p. 26). How do these surges arise?

The surge in flows in the 1990s initially reflected the 'strong economic performance' of the Asian countries, "including rapid growth, sustained improvements in macroeconomic balances (public sector balances, inflation), and structural changes that have fostered a market-led, outward orientation since the late 1980s. The cyclical downturn in international interest rates in the early 1990s provided the initial impetus for the surge in flows (particularly portfolio flows); continued increases reflected structural changes that have increased the responsiveness of capital to cross-border investment opportunities' (World Bank, 1998, p. 31).

The surges are extremely large in relation to the size of the economies affected by them, with possible inflationary consequences. The World Bank lists 20 developing countries, half of which received annual inflows averaging more than 4% of GDP during inflow episodes in the 1990s: Chile at a cumulative 25.8% of GDP by the end of the inflow period, Malaysia at 45.8%, Thailand, 51.5%, and Mexico 27.1%, experienced the earliest and cumulatively the largest surges. South Asian countries experienced the surge after 1992, along with Eastern Europe where the flows were very large. Low interest rates were a factor in these surges during 1990-93, but there were also changes in perceptions of creditworthiness. The consequent adjustments to institutional investment portfolios 'mean that surges in private capital are a likely feature of the early stages of integration' (World Bank, 1997, p. 26).

The World Bank suggests that the next issue concerns the threat of major reversals of these flows. It notes that the reversal of flows in the case of Mexico triggered reversals in several other countries, notably in Argentina and Brazil. As well as the problem of major reversals, there are concerns about volatility and 'herding' in relation to private capital flows, especially the portfolio flows. Countries can become exposed to 'new sources of shocks' in the international economy, and the effects of domestic shock can be magnified. This becomes even more important,

> *because the degree of policy autonomy declines with growing financial integration......Investor herding and contagion effects may change investment in a country even if fundamentals are unchanged......Financial and capital markets in developing countries suffer more from incomplete and asymmetric information, and from other institutional weaknesses, than in industrial country markets. In this environment, the potential for investor herding is greater, and domestic investors may be influenced by foreign*

investors, leading to even greater volatility (World Bank, 1997, pp. 27, 28 and 29).

Unlike foreign direct investment, 'portfolio investors can divest themselves easily of their stocks of equities or bonds.' Moreover, while volatility has tended to come down in the majority of countries, "or at least not increase," the absolute magnitude of variation is now much greater, since the average level of flows is higher. "Financial integration can therefore magnify shocks or the cost of policy mistakes, leading to greater instability" (World Bank, 1997, p. 143).

Next, if we can take these points in turn, 'herding' is a result of problems arising from what is euphemistically described as 'asymmetric information.' What this means in everyday language is that fund managers will follow the investment decisions of others. If the investment goes wrong, they are more likely to be judged as unlucky rather than incompetent, because others acted likewise. Given that such a large proportion of personal and pension fund assets is handled by a small group of 'professional' managers, the World Bank concludes that the potential for this behaviour 'clearly exists' (World Bank, 1997, p. 126-7). Some may ponder the dissembling posture of this public institution.

The risk of financial institutions themselves

There are two other factors to consider in the assessment of the instability of financial markets, in which pension funds and pension-related investment play a crucial part.

Financial innovation and technical capacity has produced a significant range of new financial instruments and 'vehicles,' especially the financial derivatives (including 'swaps,' 'forwards,' 'options' for foreign exchange, interest rates, equities, and commodities) and hedge funds (private investment partnerships and offshore funds with wide flexibility to invest in securities and derivatives, and with wide powers to 'leverage,' or borrow against their assets). These can change the risk profile of investment institutions very quickly. The growth of the global derivative markets has been phenomenal (IMF, 1997, p. 120). When we also consider the concentration of investment management in relatively few organizations, along with the combinations of different financial activities within one particular institution or financial conglomerate, and the connections between the institutions, then a further issue concerning risk appears.

Investment activity is concentrated in the hands of relatively few institutions. The IMF itself points out that in the United States the 10 largest institutional investors managed assets of $2.4 trillion in 1995 (IMF, 1997, p, 120). This is exactly 10% of all the financial assets of institutional investors within the OECD area, according to OECD data for total assets for the same year. The IMF further adds that it is widely held that there will be considerably more concentration through consolidation in the fund management business, as well as geographically (as indeed has been happening). This could give rise to the scenario of 'a relatively small number of very large global companies each managing assets well in excess of $150 billion, and a number of smaller management companies surviving in regional niche markets' (IMF, 1997, p.121).

By 1998, a mere 20 financial institutions individually managed assets in excess of the $150 billion benchmark—with cumulative total assets amounting to $6 trillion (calculations from *Institutional Investor*, 1998)—25% of all the attributed world financial portfolio assets for 1995.

The combination of complex financial instruments, the potential for rapid changes in risk profile, the enormous concentration of funds in institutions, or financial conglomerates with a range of financial and banking functions, along with the financial integration of institutions within the developed markets, all give rise to an important issue. This issue concerns the cumulative implications, or knock-on effects, of policy mistakes *within and among the financial institutions themselves.*

Hedge funds are interesting in this context because, although they appear relatively small in the panoply of financial institutions, the implications of their activity for that broader panoply can be startling. Some estimates put their total size at $100 billion, others at $400 billion (*Banker*, 1998). The overseas, or non-domestic, investment assets of pension funds alone are many times these figures, with pension fund and pension-related investment assets of other institutions in emerging markets approaching the lower figure for the total assets of hedge funds. Emerging market hedge funds amounted to $7.1 billions of assets in 1997, from $0.7 billions in 1992 (World Bank, 1998, p. 17). Pension fund assets in emerging markets were 10 times the 1997 figure for specialist emerging market hedge funds.

However, when we consider the situation more closely, we can see some aspects of the institutional risk factor described above. The IMF itself observes that the financial institutions have been an important source of funds for emerging markets, 'but they have also led to the growth of highly leveraged hedge funds and proprietary traders [institutions trading with their own capital], who are prepared to tolerate significant risk in their search for weaknesses in foreign exchange arrangements...It is estimated that the total assets of hedge funds, proprietary traders, and speculative-type mutual funds have grown to well above $100 billion,' but 'these funds have at times undertaken investments that involved leveraging their capital by between five and 10 times' (IMF, 1997, p.33).

We are warned of problems with financial institutions in developing countries (World Bank, 1997 & 1998, and IMF, 1997). There should perhaps be a similar concern for the financial institutions of the developed world. As a result, and in conclusion, alongside the risks of volatility, surges, reversals and contagion, we should also add the cumulative risk of a) institutional concentration, b) the complexity of financial instruments and investment vehicles, c) the dangers inherent in the technical ability of investment institutions to amass enormous risk at enormous potential cost to institutional savers and banks depositors, and d) the lack of 'transparency' of risk profiles in a wide range of financial institutions in 'mature' markets. Pension funds are complicit in all of this.

Institutional investment and economic growth

We now have to assess whether a lot of the foregoing adds up to very much at all in terms of economic growth and general social benefit. Again we have to indulge in some esoteric language and more statistics. But the argument will, in general, direct us towards a critical view concerning the role of financial markets.

The World Bank suggests that financial integration, whether on the national or international level, severs the link between local savings and local investment, and allows savings to gravitate towards the most rewarding projects regardless of location, so enhancing the productivity of global capital, increasing world production and reducing the cost of capital for the most productive economies. Integration is said to encourage an acceleration of investment by augmenting local savings and increasing local growth rates. All this, in turn, will lead to domestic financial deepening, leading to higher investment and faster productivity growth (World Bank, 1997, pp. 154-157). As we have noted, the increase in private pension investment flows have been an important part of the general increase in international financial flows.

Now for the bad news. Some have argued that the increase in private pension provision and associated contractual savings arrangements will not have the positive effects on economic growth locally within one country's savings and investment market, or internationally through diversified portfolio management which the advocates of increasing financial integration and liberalized investment markets suggest (Singh, 1996, Singh and Weisse 1998). Even the IMF now concludes that there is no significant relationship between capital liberalization and economic growth (IMF, 2001).

We noted the surges in investment flows to developing countries earlier, along with the substantial reversals which can occur. In their case study of Mexico, Singh and Weisse noted the tendency of the capital inflows to lead to an increase in consumption rather than investment. The deteriorating macroeconomic performance of Mexico and the enormous flows of capital into the country suggest, they argue, that the primary motive of investors was speculative and not based on economic fundamentals (Singh and Weisse, 1998, p. 614).

There is also a psychological effect in liberalization that creates unrealistic expectations about growth in assets generally. Perhaps most important, Singh and Weisse note that external financial liberalization leads to an interaction between two inherently unstable markets: the stock market and the foreign exchange market. When there are economic shocks, they argue,

> the relationship between these two unstable markets can lead to a negative feedback loop and even greater instability. This, in turn, would affect other important economic variables such as investment, exports and imports (through exchange rate fluctuations), and consumption (through the wealth effects arising from stock market fluctuations)' (Singh and Weisse, 1998, p. 615).

We have already noted the surges and reversals in portfolio flows. Prices in several developing country stock markets increased significantly in the first part of 1997. The stock market in Indonesia, for instance, rose 14%, Brazil 79%, Chile 10%, Russia 129%. But the second half of the year saw major reversals of these figures, with Indonesia at minus 45%, Brazil minus 22%, Chile minus 16%, and Russia minus 3% (World Bank, 1998, p. 12). These were accompanied by associated falls in exchange rates, confirming the links between the two volatile markets. The concern noted by Singh is that world share prices do not reflect fundamental values and that markets are dominated by 'noise traders' (short-term speculation) and by whims and fads (Singh, 1996, p. 31).

International flows to developed countries

In developed countries, we have an interesting additional vocabulary for international speculation. It is described as maximizing 'shareholder value' or promoting good 'corporate governance.' This is a further dimension of the 'financial integration,' 'liberalization,' 'deepening of financial markets' philosophy. It is similar to the logic of investment in emerging markets: buying low-priced assets in potentially high-growth countries (companies in this case). I ask that anyone who can prove that this philosophy actually provides greater corporate growth, as opposed to shareholder gains, should now display the evidence (and one example will not do).

The leader in the field in this area is CalPERS—the pension fund of the State of California in the United States, which has a clear strategy of identifying companies in Europe (as well as in the U.S. itself) which appear to 'underperform' relative to the assets underlying their share price. The assets, and therefore the company as measured by share value, are deemed to be undervalued according to the criteria of stock exchange economics. Again, share prices do not reflect fundamental values. The aim is to exercise shareholder pressure and/or change voting rules in order to increase the better use of assets (including selling them off), and thereby to raise the price of the shares and prospective capital gains. As with emerging markets, the real issue is returns to shareholders.

In 1998, CalPERS joined forces with HERMES—the UK British Telecom (BT) pension fund manager—in a combined, so-called Anglo-American 'corporate governance' strategy. These funds are among the largest pension funds in the U.S. and the UK (some figures show them to be the largest in their respective countries). They were also involved in another joint venture called Hermes Lens Asset Management. By the end of 1999, this had accumulated 10 pension fund investors from the U.S., UK, Canada, and Scandinavia (CalPERS, BT, Ontario Municipal Employees Fund, among others).

What all this has to do with economic growth, increases in pension-able employment, and the promotion of real long-term investment to help realize pensioners' claims on society (especially in some European countries said to be in serious demographic crisis and facing high unem-ployment), misses the point. Indeed, *The Wall Street Journal Europe* (1999) has reported on—

> *the rising profile of buyout funds—those packs of private capital that prey on juicy assets that are prime for a quick makeover and a resale to the highest bidder. The fast-moving funds typically boast returns of 30% a year...What's driving all this? U.S. pen-sion funds and other big investors, encouraged by talk of wide-spread restructuring within Europe's sclerotic conglomerates, have been investing in private equity as never before (p. 1).*

Some pension fund representatives will argue that it is not their re-sponsibility (using the escape route of trust law and the absolution ritual of fiduciary responsibility) to promote economic growth and employ-ment. They must concentrate on the rate of return, and all else, good or bad, will follow. On the other hand, some will argue that pension fund investment will help create that economic growth from which the de-sired rates of return ensue (World Bank, 1994). The ideology of pension fund investment contains conflicting arguments, picking and choosing as seems fit. What unites the different strands is the exhortation that markets should not be 'interfered with' in their pursuit of the highest 'return' (rather dubious concepts, however, in terms of economic struc-tures, outcomes, public subsidies, state support mechanisms, and the growing need for 'regulation').

Conclusion

Pension funds are too large to be treated as if they were some 'prudent man's' personal savings account. The quantum of funds, the sum of the parts, gives them a global responsibility to account for their consequences.

(i) On emerging markets and pension fund investment

> *The globalisation of financial markets, driven in part by popula-tion ageing and other structural factors, is reflected in the quicker international transmission of short-term price movements in fi-nancial markets, as occurred in the Mexican crisis of 1994-95,*

> *the ongoing Asian crisis, and the recent Russian turmoil, and their impact on OECD financial markets. Financial integration has also increased the potential intensity and duration of the attacks. There is evidence that* pension funds *and other institutional investors* have played a crucial role *at times in determining asset prices in emerging financial markets, with shifts in institutional investor sentiment occasionally contributing to increased volatility in markets* (OECD, 1998, p.62, my emphasis).

Joseph Stiglitz (former chief economist at the World Bank, and Nobel Prize Winner, 2001) has noted that, in just a few months, some countries in Asia went from robust growth to deep recession. He points to—

> *children dropping out of school, millions of people either falling back into poverty or coping with already desperate circumstances, and poorer health* (Financial Times, 1998, p.20).

ii) On developed markets, pension fund investment and trade unions

After the hostile takeover of the German company Mannesmann in 1999-2000, by Vodafone of the UK, during the fad for technology stocks, the *Financial Times* reported that—

> *It is a deal that will throw open the doors of corporate Europe... One investment banker to Vodafone said, 'Germany's hitherto unbreachable corporate world has been finally broken and many are going to be licking their lips [no less]'* (Financial Times, 2000).

Unfortunately for some, Vodafone lost over half its value in the two years since before the bid, and even managed to under-perform the European technology sector by 18%. At least the AFL/CIO in the U.S. urged the managers of its benefit funds to oppose the takeover, on commercial grounds (in stock market terms, it proved to be right). TIAA-CREF, the teachers and college workers fund—the other contender for the position of the largest U.S. pension fund—supported the takeover, and presumably lost out along with the AFL/CIO funds. But the CEO of Vodafone was awarded $15 million by the company, and a knighthood by the British government. Financial advisers to the deal walked away with upwards of $1 billion in fees. So who are pension funds really supporting in much of this activity—whether in developing or developed markets?

The issue, however, is much larger than judging everything in stock market terms, and who gets what—shareholders, management, financial advisers. I ask that we should look at pensions in a totally different light.

Trade unionists representing future beneficiaries, and others concerned with the broader implications of money and capital for people of all ages and countries, can perhaps seriously consider where we are headed with financial provision for older people and reliance on stock market theories of economic welfare. Many academics and policy-makers take it for granted that there are 'looming crises' of public expenditure on pensions, and that privatization can address the issue. Not only is there a serious question about who really benefits from all this, but the political and economic implications stretch far beyond stock market returns and our local or national borders.

Labour should also make no mistake about the political and economic implications *for itself* which arise from its share in pension fund capital and the shallow imperative of financial returns. One ex-senior adviser from the Bank of England and other public institutions suggests that privately funded pensions may—

> *increase overall economic efficiency and flexibility by reducing the conflict between labour and capital, since with funding,* workers do not focus on high wages and safe employment (sic) (Davis, 1997, p. 37, my emphasis).

A World Bank representative has added that private pension funding—

> *sensitizes workers to financial issues and enterprise performance,* reducing the dichotomy between capital and labour (Holzmann, 1997, p. 1, my emphasis).

A possible inference is that we should simply ignore the economic and social consequences of pension funds, both for anonymous others *and* ourselves, because that recreates 'the dichotomy,' resuscitates concerns about employment and welfare, and detracts from maximizing financial returns. The circle of the singularly unconvincing stock market theory of economic development, I suppose, is complete. In criminal law, this might be called 'entrapment.'

The argument therefore suggests that trade unions (if they represent 'labour' or some alternative to what is simplistically summed up in the concept of 'capital') have a vital role to play as advocates of alternative policies to the inequalities and insecurity created by pension funds.

BY WAY OF A KIND OF ENDNOTE, OR ANTIDOTE, I SUGGEST A possible initiative to reduce the absorption of labour into capital and the narrow (and increasingly misleading) stock market criteria of prosperity. I propose an international pension initiative, led by trade unions, and even a Centre for International Pension Research and Cooperation, to conduct research and coordinate action on the vast implications of pension fund investment.

We could start with alternative measures to the infamous and counter-productive 'rate of return' concept as conventionally understood. *The Cold War in Welfare* (Minns, 2001) contains a proposal for a Human Development Index for Pension Funds, inspired by the United Nations Development Project (UNDP) Human Development Index, which contains different variables but a similar objective. The Pension Fund Index applies to holdings in companies. For countries, the UNDP Index can be used. The UNDP Index is continually refined by permanent research staff, and published annually in the *Human Development Report*. The Pension Fund Index could be compared to the normal financial return criteria, and we could then see what in fact pension funds contribute to economic development through their corporate investments, as opposed to capital gains, fees, and 'juicy makeovers.' The UNDP Index can be compared to 'returns' from emerging markets. The whole exercise will reveal the extent of the match between financial returns and socio-economic development.

What to do about it is then a matter for trade union and political consideration.

Some of this chapter is drawn from The Cold War in Welfare: Stock Markets versus Pensions, *Richard Minns, published by Verso, 2001.*

CHAPTER 2

Fiduciary responsibility

A tool to control workers or an opportunity to build community wealth?

by Isla Carmichael

THE PRUDENCE RULE IS A CENTRAL CONCEPT OF TRUST LAW and a legal requirement of the management of pension fund assets in Britain, the United States, Canada, and most other industrialized countries. The trust concept has its origins in the Middle Ages, and has a history of jurisprudence and litigation covering several centuries. The concept of the "prudent man" is central to the accumulation of private capital through the protection of family wealth.

The roots of trust law are patriarchal, lying in the remnants of feudal society where wealth was passed on through the male heads of households. In the absence of the male head of the family, the prudent man was essential in keeping the wealth of the family secure for the benefit of the male heirs (Longstreth, 1986). The trust ensured that the trustees would act only in the interests of the family (the male heirs) and not in their own interests. Trustees, in effect, control the wealth on behalf of the family, but cannot access it for their own use. Trusteeship embraces the responsibility of ownership, without the ownership itself. Trustees must not act out of self-interest or personal bias (Longstreth, 1986; Mercer Ltd. 1997; Minsky, 1988; Scott, 1987; Waitzer, 1990).

Prudence is the antithesis of speculation; according to the prudence rule, careful investments are characterized as low- risk ones. With the development of stock exchanges in the early part of the century, lists of investments were published for trustees as well as other cautious investors. Everything else was classified as speculation. However, the stock market crash of 1929 and the Depression of the '30s brought a re-examination of lists. Nevertheless, lists persisted as a prescription for investment up until the '70s.

U.S. trust law originates from an 1830 case in Massachusetts, *Harvard College v. Amory*. The ruling states that the trustee's duty is to:

> *conduct* himself *faithfully and exercise a sound discretion, observe how* men *of prudence, discretion and intelligence manage their own affairs, not in regard to speculation, but in regard to the permanent disposition of their funds, considering the probable income as well as the probable safety of the capital to be invested* (26 Mass (9 Pick) 446, 1830) (emphasis mine).

In a similar manner, the Supreme Court of Canada more recently stated:

> *Where...one party has an obligation to act for the benefit of another and that obligation carries with it a discretionary power, the party thus empowered becomes a fiduciary. Equity will then supervise the relationship by holding him to the fiduciary's strict standard of conduct* (Guerin v. The Queen, 1984).

Even more recently, the Supreme Court identified the following criteria for a fiduciary relationship:

1. The fiduciary has scope for the exercise of discretion or power.
2. The fiduciary can unilaterally exercise that power or discretion so as to affect the beneficiary's legal or practical interests.
3. The beneficiary is peculiarly vulnerable to, or at the mercy of, the fiduciary holding the discretion or power (Frame v. Smith, 1987).

British and U.S. case law to date

There has been no decision in a Canadian court addressing the issue of social investment. There have been several in U.S. and UK courts. A summary of the key cases follows.

U.S. case law supports several points. First, union trustees cannot act as union officers in the interests of the union. They must act clearly as trustees responsible for the fund, and in the interests of the fund members. Otherwise they are in a conflict of interest.

Second, the long-term interest of the fund and its members is a legitimate investment concern, even where the rate of return may be lower and risk to the investment may be higher. Third, the investment decision itself must be based on independent financial advice. If the trustees are fully informed, then they are not liable for a lower rate of return.

Finally, trustees do not violate their duties of prudence by considering the social consequences of investment, provided the costs of considering such consequences are minimal; in fact, they are encouraged to do so, given the power of pension funds (*Blankenship v. Boyle* [1971]; *Withers v. The Teachers" Retirement System of the City of New York* [1978]; *Donovan v. Walton*, [1985]; *Board of Trustees v. City of Baltimore*, [1989]).

Blankenship v. Boyle (1971) was the American equivalent in some ways of *Cowan v. Scargill* and was referred to by Judge Megarry in his decision. The United Mineworkers of America's Welfare and Retirement Fund invested in electrical utilities stock as a way of encouraging the utilities to use union-mined coal in order to maintain and increase the number of jobs in the coal industry. This was part of a larger union campaign. The shares subsequently decreased in value. The court judged that these investments were in the interests of the union, rather than the beneficiaries, and noted the close relationship between the trustees and the union.

Some commentators have interpreted this as a warning to trustees that they may not invest according to non-financial criteria (Langbein and Posner, 1980). In fact, the court required both employer and union to refrain from self-dealing. The decision enjoined "the trustees from operating the fund in a manner designed in whole or in part to afford collateral advantages to the union or the employers" (p.1113). One finding of the court was that the union conspired to benefit from the breach of trust. The case was really about conflict of interest, self-dealing and breach of trust, rather than social investment. In fact, given that investments did decline, it is notable that the decision rested on breach of trust rather than prudence. Further, the court recognized that, "in the longer view of matters, the union's strength protects the interests of beneficiaries, past and prospective" (p. 1112; in Hutchinson and Cole, 1980). Patricia Lane, a B.C. lawyer and one-time director of research at the Federation of Labour, also notes that the union's campaigns were for the benefit of its members (1991).

In *Withers v. The Teachers' Retirement System of the City of New York* (1978), a group of retired teachers sued their pension fund after the trustees, having sought independent advice, invested $860 million in New York municipal bonds to prevent the city's bankruptcy. The trustees took this extreme action to secure the assets of the fund (which were employer contributions from the City of New York) and protect the interests of all beneficiaries, given that the fund was not fully-funded. This case corroborates and relies on *Blankenship v. Boyle* in finding that the duty of trustees is to act in the best interests of all beneficiaries, even if it may mean making investment decisions that may appear on the face of it to be imprudent. The court went so far as to endorse *Blankenship* because "neither the protection of the jobs of the city's teachers nor the general public welfare were factors which motivated the trustees in their investment decision" (p. 1256). Further the court said:

> *The extension of aid to the city was simply a means—the only means, in their assessment—to the legitimate end of preventing the exhaustion of the assets of the [Teachers Retirement System] in the interests of all the beneficiaries. Notably, the importance of the solvency of the city to fund lay not only in its role as the major contributor of funds but also as the ultimate guarantor of the payment of pension benefits to participants (p. 1256).*

This decision—like *Blankenship*—addresses the intentions of the trustees in making the investment and the process by which they made the investment.

In *Donovan v. Walton*, (1985), trustees financed, built and leased out an office building with the union as principal tenant. They based the project on close research and analysis, aided by independent consultants at every step of the way. While this project benefited the union because of the reasonable leasing costs and clearly took the interests of the union into account, the court decided that trustee investment decisions were made with the interests of the beneficiaries paramount. Most clearly articulated in *Donovan v. Bierwirth* (1982), and known as the *exclusive benefit rule* under the *Employee Retirement Income Security Act* (ERISA), the rule requires trustees never to put themselves in a position of divided loyalty and always to act solely in the interests of beneficiaries, whether or not others benefit. This, of course, allows for the notion of collateral benefit so long as there is no divided loyalty.

Board of Trustees v. City of Baltimore, (1989) is the most significant of U.S. cases. Trustees opposed a city of Baltimore ordinance supporting a South African boycott on the grounds that it would impair trustee activities and performance of the funds. The ordinances—which dealt directly with the issue of rates of return of the pension funds and divestiture—were declared to be valid in not impinging on trustee responsibilities of prudence. Further, the obligation on trustees to consider social factors did not violate case law standards. Finally, prudence standards were not threatened as long as the costs of considering social consequences are minimal; in fact, the court commented that, given the power of pension funds, trustees should be encouraged to consider social consequences.

These decisions leave open a broad conception of prudent investment, encompassing the job security of pension plan members and the health of their union and communities, as long as the (union) trustees are informed, responsible, and hold the interests of beneficiaries paramount. In fact, social criteria for investment should be encouraged in the general good as long as the costs are minimal.

These decisions are supported by legal commentary from Professor Scott, a leading American scholar on trust law, who says:

> *trustees, in deciding whether to invest in, or to retain, the securities of a corporation, may properly consider the social performance of a corporation. They may decline to invest in, or to retain, the securities of corporations whose activities or some of them are contrary to fundamental and generally accepted ethical principles. They may consider such matters as pollution, race discrimination, fair employment, and consumer responsibility...a trustee of funds for others, is entitled to consider the welfare of community and refrain from allowing the use of funds in a manner detrimental to society (Scott, 1988, p. 277).*

During this period in the UK, however, one case in particular was not supportive of social investment issues. In *Cowan v. Scargill* (1984), the British Chancery Court had to decide whether the union trustees of the Mineworkers' Pension Scheme were in breach of their fiduciary duty in seeking to prohibit overseas investments and any investments supporting an industry in competition with the coal industry. The five trustees for the National Coal Board (the employer) successfully opposed union policy. The judge, Sir Robert Megarry, held that the best interests of the beneficiaries were the best financial interests:

The power [of investment] must be exercised so as to yield the best return for the beneficiaries, judged in relation to the risks of the investment in question; and the prospects of the yield of the income and capital appreciation both have to be considered in judging the return from the investment (p.760).

However, he also said that non-financial criteria could be used if alternative investments were equally beneficial to beneficiaries. In subsequent commentary, Megarry maintained that it was Scargill's uncompromising prohibition of certain types of investment and his ideological approach that made a more balanced decision difficult. It may not have been helped by Scargill's insistence on representing himself, although Megarry says in the decision that Scargill represented himself "with courtesy and competence."

This may be just one of the many confusing and contradictory details of this decision. Other commentators have also found this decision unnecessarily confusing and incomplete (Yaron, 2000; Lane, 1991; Farrar & Maxton, 1986), although the majority of U.S. commentators pay it little attention, having a very extensive case law and detailed laws and regulations.

This case has retained an undeserved influence with trustees in Canada and Britain out of proportion to its place in case law. Its ideology is fundamental to the characterization of the prudent man, and has been maintained in some academic and legal commentaries, even in the U.S., in spite of the progress in legal decisions and the practical realities of the law (Hutchinson and Cole, 1980; Langbein and Posner, 1980; Manitoba Law Reform Commission, 1993; Palmer, 1986; Romano, 1993; Scane, 1993). It has also been promoted heavily by the financial industry, as well as trustees who oppose social investment and union involvement in investment criteria.

Other legal commentators disagree with this characterization and argue that, within the context of prudent decision-making, and considering the balance of decisions, there is a right to make investment decisions based on social and political criteria (Campbell and Josephson, 1983; Farrar and Maxton, 1986; Lane, 1991; Pearce and Samuels, 1985; Ravikoff and Curzan, 1980; Scott, 1987; Waitzer, 1990; Yaron, 2000).

Decisions in the UK subsequent to *Cowan v. Scargill* have moderated Megarry"s decision. In *Martin v. City of Edinburgh District Council*, the court said that trustees may have a policy on ethical investment consistent with general standards of prudence and pursue it "so long as they treat the interests of the beneficiaries as paramount" (Trades Union Congress, 1996. p. 86). This brings British case law on trusts more into line with the U.S. cases to date. It also echoes the standard set by the Goode Committee, established in 1992 by the UK government to make recommendations on legal frameworks for pension funds, given the huge losses suffered by pension funds under the control of Robert Maxwell. The committee said:

> *This means trustees are free to avoid certain kinds of prudent investment which they would regard as objectionable, so long as they make equally advantageous investments elsewhere, and that they are entitled to put funds into investments which they believe members would regard as desirable, so long as these are proper investments on other grounds. What trustees are not entitled to do is subordinate the interests of beneficiaries to ethical or social demands and thereby deprive the beneficiaries of investment income opportunities they would otherwise have enjoyed (TUC, 1996, p. 86).*

Underlying *Cowan v. Scargill* is an outright rejection of a union's right to represent its members, as well as a denial of the relevance of workers' lives to investment practice. According to this ruling, even though the membership of the union and the union trustees may be in agreement on utilizing social criteria in investment decisions, union trustees should not represent their members' desires. Further, Megarry denies any connection between the general prosperity of the coal industry and financial benefit to the fund, calling it "speculative and remote" (p. 751). This opinion was in spite of union arguments that members of the pension plan were dependent on the coal industry for their own job security, as well as the prosperity of their communities. (Similar arguments were put forward successfully in the *Withers* case, where the welfare of New York teachers, as well as the viability of the pension fund, depended on the welfare of New York City.) In the Megarry ruling, the general prosperity of the coal industry is characterized as the "personal interests and views" of the trustees (p. 761). Based on these arguments, the Megarry case establishes the concept of the maximum rate of return as *the* principle for investment (emphasis mine).

U.S. case law broadens the concept of fiduciary responsibility to take into account who makes the investment decision, how it is made and in whose interests, as opposed to evaluating the decision solely by the rate of return. It also attempts to align workers' interests with the investment, so that the investment can actually support rather than undermine their livelihoods. Furthermore, it exhibits a tolerance of a strong role for union trustees, as long as the union is not directly represented at the trustee table and as long as the trustees seek independent advice.

Union and employer accountability

While trustee law has set a high level of accountability for union trustees, standards for employer trustees are substantially weaker. It is fully accepted that some level of (self-interested) investment of pension assets in an employer's enterprise must be permitted so that employers are not discouraged from continuing to have workplace pension plans (Scane, 1993). In fact, a pension fund may be a source of economic advantage to a sponsoring employer, in which case "the opportunity to earn exceptional returns may itself be a part of the sponsor's purpose" (Ambachtsheer and Ezra, 1998, p. 37). Employers wishing to invest fund capital in their own business have not been viewed as using personal bias, as long as they proceed under self-imposed guidelines.

Further, investments that would otherwise violate the duty of loyalty can be permitted in a trust. If an investment is made in an enterprise where a trustee is an officer of the company, or has some conflict of interest (or dual loyalties), a trustee's "independent investigation" into the basis for the investment must be "both intensive and scrupulous." In Ontario, investment in an employer's securities is lawful, where the securities are publicly traded (Scane, 1993). While pension fund capital does not belong to the employer, many employers view it as their own, and the judiciary have tended to accept this appropriation as legitimate.

Maximum rate of return and diversification

It is clear that *Cowan v. Scargill* has been responsible for promulgating the myth of the maximum rate of return. Many commentators have noted the irrationality of this notion in the context of portfolio diversification. An underlying issue is how, and over what period of time, investment returns should be measured. Asset management requires that trustees understand how asset classes behave in relation to the liabilities of pension funds. Interestingly, there is no industry agreement on the rate of return of a fund. In answer to this point, Tom Gunn, Chief of Investment for OMERS, comments:

> We see our first role as fiduciary for our beneficiaries. Social investment or any other form of investment or economic-directed activity must be subordinate to the long-term interest of the plan (Report of the Senate Standing Committee of Institutional Investors, p. 8).

In Canada, the Ontario Teachers' Pension Plan Board has as its goal to maximize rates of return. In the UK, the Trades Union Congress—clearly cowed by *Cowan v. Scargill*—concedes that the ultimate responsibility of the trustee is to maximize return, and that prudence attaches to each investment (Trades Union Congress, 1996, p. 51). However, trustees can invest ethically and still meet their legal duties.

But the maximum rate of return is not a standard for all plans. The OPSEU Pension Trust, for example, has an investment policy to achieve "reasonable rates of return" (OPT, 1996). Nor is this standard of the maximum rate of return reflected in U.S. case law. In fact, *Cowan v. Scargill* reflects the tail-end of a trend in British case law based on the old investment practice of lists where the financial rate of return was the standard by which the individual investment remained on the list. One can only assume that this was—or could be—regardless of risk. Since modern investment practice is based on the diversification of asset classes in terms of their asset class benchmark and risk/return ratios, a maximum rate of return for each investment clearly does not make sense and may encourage imprudent investment to maximize return, as well as more short-term investment strategies threatening the long-term viability of a fund.

The Department of Labor, the regulatory body for pension law in the U.S., does address the issue of portfolio diversification and returns. It stipulates that trustees must consider:

- the composition of the portfolio with regard to diversification;
- the liquidity and current return of the portfolio relative to the anticipated cash flow requirements of the plan; and
- the projected return of the portfolio relative to the funding objective of the plan.

A fourth standard compels trustees to consider expected returns. The Department of Labor states:

Because every investment necessarily causes a plan to forgo other investment opportunities, an investment will not be prudent if it would be expected to provide a plan with a lower rate of return than available alternative investments with commensurate rates of return (U.S. DOL Interpretative Bulletin 94-1 1994).

As Zanglein (2000) points out, this addresses the issue of investments within an asset class, not the level of riskiness. It is therefore neither an exhortation to be conservative nor a duty to maximize benefits. The first is not in the interests of portfolio diversification. The second would be too onerous on trustees and is not supported by American courts. Rather, it says that trustees may not select an investment with collateral benefit but lower returns than can be found with another investment in the same asset class with similar risk/return ratios. Benchmarks are therefore critical.

An often overlooked fact of *Cowan v. Scargill* is that the National Union of Mineworkers and its fund's union trustees were also seeking to promote a union policy of investing only in Britain to the exclusion of overseas investment:

Pension funds have enormous assets. If all, or nearly all of these assets were invested in Britain, and none, or few, were invested overseas, this would do much to revive this country"s economy and so benefit all workers, especially if the investments were in the form not of purchasing established stocks and shares but of "real" investment in physical assets and new ventures. For the mineworkers" scheme, the prosperity of the coal industry would aid the prosperity of the scheme and so lead to benefits for beneficiaries under the scheme

Megarry decided that this evidence on economic and investment strategy was too remote from the interests of beneficiaries and, instead, relied on the *Trustee Investments Act* (1961), which said simply that trustees should have regard for the need for diversification of investments; further, that screening out international investment might harm the fund, particularly in a downturn of the British economy (even though he had acknowledged that the fund was fully-funded). This was notwithstanding his earlier comments that, if (adult) beneficiaries had strict moral or social views about alcohol or tobacco, then trustees would be justified in not investing in these corporate sectors even if returns were lowered.

Interestingly, Megarry was thrown back on a law—predating major changes in the economy and investment practice—which actually was unclear about levels of diversification, as well as being forced to speculate about the specific interest of beneficiaries of the pension fund. This may be the fundamental weakness of his decision.

Measuring social/economic or collateral returns

Cowan v. Scargill rules out the measurement of anything but the financial rate of return. Similarly, American case law prohibits the "factoring in" of the value of collateral benefit (Zanglein, 2000). Yet this is counter-intuitive. In the United States, Barber and Ghilarducci (1993) propose the "whole participant" approach, which recognizes that pension funds rely on a strong economy to keep fund members at work so that they can pay their pension contributions. Baker and Fung (2000) argue that so-called "efficient" markets which may deliver high returns in the short term often do so at the expense of workers and the economy.

In the UK, Zadek, Pruzan and Evans (1997) have suggested approaches to monitor the evolution of social and ethical accounting, auditing and reporting. This work is broader than pension fund investment, and deals with corporate accountability and its measurement.

In Canada, Carmichael, in a later article in this book, proposes preliminary models for estimating a social/economic rate of return through examination of Concert, a real estate development company funded by union pension funds. The Canadian Union of Public Employees, in its newsletter (Vol. 1, #3) gives an example of privatization initiatives funded by the Ontario Municipal Employees Retirement System that might result in collateral damage to the fund through loss of contributions from laid-off members or members with reduced pay. This does not take account of the damage to communities of loss of public services.

It has been shown that understanding the social context for an investment provides a better perspective on the value of the investment and hence its potential rates of return (Sethi, 1995; Bruyn, 1987). It has also been shown that better reporting methods on risk-management plans and their associated costs could lead to actual prevention of oil spills and protection of shareholder rates of return (Rubenstein, 1989).

A shareholder proposal submitted in B.C by Working Enterprises Limited to Placer Dome called for stronger accountability to shareholders through better reporting in the event of disasters. First, Placer Dome had already been engaged in clean-up of a spill that happened several years ago, with costs steadily accumulating. Second, it became clear soon after the spill occurred that there was inadequate insurance to cover the damage. Third, *MiningWatch Canada* reports that studies suggest that the disaster could have been avoided had proper risk management plans been in place (MiningWatch Canada, 2000). In these cases, poor management practices with respect to environmental practice lower the rate of return.

Taking into account collateral benefits and damage must be the next step in estimating rates of return of pension funds. This is of significance, since trustees must consider the long-term interests of beneficiaries—including the viability of their pension fund. This may not need to be established in law as long as trustees are open with their beneficiaries about their methods of reporting and accounting, and incorporate new methods of accounting into their present accounting structures. More transparency—particularly in Canada—is essential.

Social investment strategies, by their very nature, should be able to maintain or promote a higher rate of return, minimizing collateral damage and taking into account interests of the beneficiaries as well as the economy. There is evidence that they do so. Given the prevalence of ethical investing in the U.S., the issue of the ethical funds' rate of return has attracted more systematic studies than in Canada. One of the earliest studies (Grossman, Blake and Sharpe, 1986) compares the returns of an unscreened New York Stock Exchange portfolio (including South African stocks) to the returns of a portfolio with South African investments screened out. The study found that the unscreened portfolio did not outperform investments free of South African holdings. Doing business in South Africa was found not to pay.

For the 1986-1990 period, Hamilton, Jo and Statman (1993) found that 17 socially responsible mutual funds, established prior to 1985, marginally outperformed traditional mutual funds of similar risk, but the outperformance was not statistically significant. In that study, mutual fund data (ethical and otherwise) are unidentified, as are the social criteria for the ethical mutual funds. Luck and Pilotte (1993), using Domini Social Index performance measures, found that the social index outperformed the Standard & Poors 500 index during the period from May 1990 to September 1992. However, as they point out, this period was characterized by the outperformance generally in the market of smaller stocks over larger stocks, and the DSI has a larger proportion of smaller stocks. Still, active returns of nine basis points per month over and above the S&P 500 remained unexplained. This was the first study to show an unexplained benefit. Kurtz and DiBartolomeo (1996), for the period from May 1990 to September 1993, found that the DSI outperformed the S&P 500 by 19 points per month, which they attributed to the higher price of the DSI stock and their higher price-to-book ratios.

In his review of 159 securities, using social data from the Council on Economic Priorities, Diltz (1995) finds no statistically significant difference, during the 1989-1991 period, between the returns of two sets of 14 screened and unscreened portfolios, with the exception of the environmental and military business screens, which had a positive impact on portfolio returns. Finally, Guerard (1997), for the period 1987-1994, finds no statistically significant difference between screened and unscreened portfolios, and further finds that, during some sub-periods, screened portfolios may have yielded higher returns.

There is one Canadian study—recently released—done over a five-year and a ten-year period (Asmundson and Foerster, 2002). The study compares returns of ethical funds with the TSE 300. There were no statistically significant differences in results. Therefore, screened ethical funds do not have lower returns.

With respect to shareholder action (or corporate engagement) CalPERS reports that corporate governance strategies improve share values dramatically. A study it commissioned (published by Wilshire and Associates of Santa Monica in 1994) examined the performance of companies targeted by CalPERS between 1987 and 1992. The stock price of these companies trailed the Standard and Poor 500 index by 66% for the five years prior to the campaign, and outperformed the index by 41% in the following five years.

Another (independent) study of CalPERS, (Smith, 1996), finds that when shareholder action is successful in changing governance structure, it also results in added shareholder value. However, when the shareholder action is directed at improved operating performance, there is no statistically significant change in value. Overall, during the 1987-93 period, shareholder action resulted in a net increase of US$19 million.

This finding is not corroborated by either Romano (1993) or Wahal (1996), who, in a study of the activism of six funds (including CalPERS) for the same period (from 1987-1993), find that, while pension funds are successful in changing the governance structure of targeted firms, their activism does not change the rate of return on investment.

Although the evidence is inconclusive as to whether either ethical screens or shareholder activism actually increase the rate of return, there is no evidence of declining returns. Therefore, union trustees are justified in considering shareholder action initiatives as well as ethical screens.

Impact of prudence rule on union trustees

Based on the case law, trustees should be mindful of the overall investment strategy and asset allocation, rather than individual investments. Broadening portfolios through the addition of more asset classes, some of which might be riskier than others, is permitted. In other words, trustees are not required to be conservative investors (whatever that may mean in the days of Bre-X, Nortel and Enron). In fact, at the time of writing there is a growing interest in private equity as reported in *Benefits Canada* (Falconer, 2002).

The interests of beneficiaries are paramount. What would beneficiaries want if they were investing this money themselves and they knew what informed trustees know? Trustees must always seek independent advice, and their process (and progress) should reflect whose interests are being considered and pursued. The interests of the union may be considered, and may even be integral to the investment project, but must not supersede the interests of beneficiaries, thus causing a conflict of interest.

Divestment, essential to union boycott campaigns, must be handled carefully because of the greater potential for lower rates of return from untimely and therefore potentially costly withdrawal of investments. (It needs to be handled as carefully as coming into the market). However, divestment can be planned with alternative investments designed to minimize costs.

This all speaks to a greater transparency on the part of union trustees so that beneficiaries gain a greater understanding of investment choices and decision points.

There are several significant legal commentators of a Canadian perspective. The prevailing and more conservative legal view in Canada is possibly reflected by Waitzer, a former Chief commissioner of the Ontario Securities Commission and a lawyer practising in both Canada and the United States:

> *If ethical choices do not lower investment returns, the practical (and legal) reality is that trustees are unlikely to face judicial interdiction, regardless of their motivation. If investment returns are lowered, trustees are in trouble (Waitzer, 1990, pp. 10-11).*

Lane (1991), while reflecting the undue influence of the British case, argues that, first, social investment can be defended even if its sole concern is not to maximize the rate of return; secondly, using financial criteria alone hurts the growth of fund assets since there is evidence that the rate of return is not damaged and may be increased by investing according to non-financial criteria; finally, unions may make the decisions about which guidelines to apply in the investment of their members' funds. She advises union trustees to amend trust documents to encourage engagement in socially responsible investment; if this is not possible, she continues:

> *[union trustees] should consider how they may be able to show that the decision they took was in the best interests of the benefici-aries. To this end, it would be wise to seek and rely on independent advice. At least one of the large investment houses in Vancouver in Vancouver now offers advice to clients interested in this invest-ment concept. More will follow as the market grows. There is no need to lose money simply because of the application of some ethi-cal guidelines to one's investment portfolio. If the decision does require a short term loss: for example, the sale of shares at a poor level because of the desire to honour a boycott or to divest from a country with a repressive regime, or to apply leverage to assist another union in a dispute. It would be a good idea to canvass the beneficiaries and potential living beneficiaries in some way. Fi-nally, there is growing indication that all trustees should estab-lish ethical guidelines because of the performance of these funds (Lane, pp. 181-182).*

Finally, Yaron, Director of Law and Policy for the Shareholder Association for Research and Education, has most recently (2000) published an extensive legal commentary where he finds that:

in the context of socially responsible investment, consideration of non-financial investment criteria does not violate the principles of prudence and loyalty, provided that the investment decision adheres to the pension plans' investment policy and independent expert advice (p. 36).

This view, he points out, is supported by the Pension Commission of Ontario (now subsumed under the Financial Services Commission). He continues by making similar points to Lane with respect to trustee knowledge of corporate social and environmental behaviour and its impact on the bottom line, the favorable rates of return associated with social investment, and, finally, consideration of beneficiaries as members of communities that rely on corporate investment and good behaviour.

Interestingly, there are few union pension funds that have social investment in their statements of investment policy (Quarter, Carmichael, Sousa and Elgie, 2001; Yaron, 2002). The Hospitals of Ontario Pension Plan (with union joint trustee representation from the Ontario Public Service Employees' Union, the Canadian Union of Public Employees, and the Service Employees International Union) and the OPSEU Staff Pension Plan are two of the few. In fact, the presence of unions as sponsors or trustees is no guarantee of socially responsible investment policies (Quarter, Carmichael, Sousa and Elgie, 2001). The Shareholder Association for Research and Education from B.C., sponsored by the CLC, has recently undertaken a study of pension fund investment policies to educate trustees on models of investment policy guidelines.

In the U.S., the AFL-CIO takes an interestingly progressive stance towards the use of independent advisors:

Process prudence assumes there is a set of objective criteria against which to measure a particular investment option; the most common and effective being historical data on risk and return...foreign securities as a class should not be ruled out as an acceptable investment under the Employee Retirement Income Security Act (ERISA) on the basis that fiduciaries engaging in international investing are somehow acting in a different manner than their peers in the community, or that there is a lack of expert independent assistance to pursue such investing (AFL-CIO, 1993 p. 4).

Many trustees still maintain that there is a scarcity of investment managers with expertise in various types of alternative investment strategies. A recent survey of pension officials in Canada, sponsored by the Canadian Labour and Business Centre (CLBC) and the Pension Investment Association of Canada (PIAC), reported that 73% complained of the shortage and cost of investment specialists. A further 69% said that there was too little expertise in private capital markets (that would enable economically targeted investment) (Falconer, 1998).

Union trustees frequently complain of the lack of union-sympathetic, progressive fund managers with experience in socially responsible investment strategies (Carmichael, 1998). Rather than a shortage, this may reflect a need for more coordination and networking between trustees and their unions, as well as education for trustees on how to deal with their fund managers (Carmichael, Thompson and Quarter, 2001). The Canadian Union of Public Employees has recently published an impressive fact sheet for trustees: *Questions for money managers.*

Union trustees, therefore, should begin to develop investment strategies more in line with the interests of their members and the general community. This approach is being facilitated by the trade union movement. Unions, union activists and trustees now have networks through a number of union educational opportunities: conferences being held by the CLC and the Canadian Labour and Business Centre; publications from SHARE and individual unions; and academic research as a basis for educational strategies being pursued by the Ontario Institute for Studies in Education of the University of Toronto and Carleton University in Ottawa.

THIS CHAPTER HAS SUMMARIZED THE SIGNIFICANT CASES IN the U.S. and the UK available as guides to union trustees. It has assessed the legal opportunities presented union trustees to develop social investment strategies as part of their portfolio management. In the absence of significant investment in social investment initiatives in Canada, it highlights recent Canadian legal opinion which encourages trustees to work on statements of investment policy as a first step in making investment practice more in line with with progressive trade union policy on economic development.

This chapter also speaks to a much stronger role for unions in working with their trustees on education initiatives, investment policy, and even joint economic development projects for the benefit of members of the pension plan.

CHAPTER 3

How to incorporate active trustee practices into pension plan investment policies

A resource guide for pension trustees and other fiduciaries[1]

by Gil Yaron and Freya Kodar

A PENSION PLAN'S STATEMENT OF INVESTMENT POLICIES AND Procedures (SIPP)[2] is one of the most important governing documents for a pension plan. It sets out the pension plan's investment philosophy, strategy and objectives, and the degree of trustee involvement and oversight in the management of plan investments. The SIPP may also be supported by other investment-related documents such as investment manager mandates.

Trustees have ultimate responsibility for all plan investments, ensuring compliance with the SIPP, and ensuring that the plan's investment policy meets the long-term interests of pension plan members and beneficiaries.[3] A SIPP is usually developed through a cooperative tripartite process involving plan trustees, investment consultants, and plan actuaries. However, trustees are ultimately responsible for the content and execution of the SIPP. Therefore, they should ensure that they are *actively* involved at *all* stages of its development, implementation and review. Both federal and provincial pension and tax laws in Canada put the responsibility on pension trustees to develop and implement a SIPP. Legislation also requires that the trustees review the SIPP on an annual basis to ensure it reflects changes within the pension plan and the economy.

The basic requirements of a SIPP are set out in provincial pension law and the trust documents establishing the pension plan. Most provinces, with the exception of Prince Edward Island and Quebec, have adopted the investment requirements detailed in Schedule III of the federal *Pension Benefits Standards Regulation* (PBSA, 1985). These requirements (detailed in Appendix A) serve to focus attention on the primary concern of plan managers to ensure that plan assets match plan liabilities over the long term.

The Office of the Superintendent of Financial Institutions, which is responsible for overseeing all federally-regulated pension plans, has established guidelines ("OSFI Guidelines") to assist in the development, implementation, and monitoring of a SIPP. (OSFI, 2000) The OSFI Guidelines are not law, but courts may still take them into consideration when reviewing the decisions of trustees. Therefore, pension trustees are strongly advised to consider them. The OSFI Guidelines are summarized in Appendix A.

Active trustee oversight is also important because of the significance of pension plans in the overall well-being of the Canadian economy, our communities, and the natural environment. Trusteed pension plans in Canada own approximately 25% of the Canadian equity market and have total assets valued at approximately $568.6 billion, the second largest pool of investment capital in Canada after the chartered banks. (Statistics Canada, 2001) Therefore, investment decisions have an effect on the health of the economy, society, and the environment, which in turn all affect the potential for sustainable, long-term financial returns.

For example, investing in companies with strong corporate governance standards, labour policies and environmental practices can meet the short-term interests of current plan members and the long-term interests of future beneficiaries, their families and communities by fostering a strong and stable workforce, reducing potential corporate liabilities, and enhancing corporate goodwill and investor confidence.

This chapter provides trustees with practical guidance on how to incorporate active trustee oversight into a SIPP in four specific areas:

1. shareholder activism,

2. proxy voting,

3. investment screening, and

4. economically targeted investment (ETI).

It also looks at three other related parts of a SIPP, including the:

5. selection and review of investment managers,

6. selection of benchmarks, and

7. provision allowing trustees to deviate from the investment policy.

The first four practices are still quite new to many trustees, and trustees can incorporate them over time as they acquire greater knowledge and comfort in each area (see section entitled "All-or-Nothing Approach".) While plans now frequently engage in one or more of these practices, many have not formalized them or incorporated them into their SIPP. Interested trustees often find it difficult to identify model precedents or determine which issues should be considered when designing policy in these areas. Accordingly, the first section of this chapter provides trustees with an introduction to each practice, recommendations on how to enhance trustee oversight, a list of issues to consider, questions to ask themselves and their investment advisors, and suggested model wording for the SIPP. The second part briefly reviews some of the key process issues that pension trustees may encounter when implementing these practices. In addition, there are a number of appendices included, with sample SIPPs, a fiduciary checklist for trustees, and questions related to these practices for trustees to pose during the selection and review of investment managers.

This chapter is the result of extensive research and consultations with pension trustees and investment professionals. During the spring and summer of 2001, samples of existing SIPPs were compiled from across Canada and the United States, and interviews were conducted with individuals involved in all facets of pension investment, including pension trustees, investment managers, and other professional advisors. The chapter went through several drafts, each reviewed by a committee of pension trustees, union pension staff, investment managers, pension consultants, and pension lawyers from across Canada.[4] The views expressed are attributable solely to the authors and do not necessarily reflect the views of the reviewers, their organizations or affiliates, or others consulted during the document's preparation.

The chapter is intended to provide general information only and does not constitute legal advice or a legal opinion. Nor does it constitute investment advice and should not be taken as an endorsement or recommendation of any particular company or individual. Trustees should consult legal counsel and investment professionals for assistance with the development, implementation, and review of their individual plan SIPP.

Incorporating active trustee oversight into the SIPP

In designing a SIPP, pension trustees must always be mindful of their fiduciary duties to plan members and beneficiaries. Fiduciary duties are reviewed extensively elsewhere (Yaron, 2001). In principle, shareholder activism, proxy voting, investment screening, and economically targeted investing are all permitted, provided they are authorized in the SIPP, and conducted in a prudent and impartial manner, in the best interests of plan members (see fiduciary checklist for pension trustees under Appendix B). Explicit reference to these practices in the SIPP also communicates the plan's objectives and investment strategy to trustees and investment professionals to ensure proper execution of and compliance with the SIPP, and educates plan members about what the plan is doing to protect their interests. More information about pension trustee fiduciary duties and these investment practices is available in a paper entitled *The Responsible Pension Trustee*, available at <www.share.ca>.

A SIPP should have *breadth*, *depth*, and *clarity* (Greifer, 2001). Investment policies should be comprehensive and provide sufficient detailed guidance to trustees, plan staff, and agents. The document should also communicate clearly and concisely the pension plan's investment strategy and objectives so that those responsible for its execution can understand it and implement it. Balancing the need for a clear and succinct policy against the need for sufficient detail (i.e., *depth*) can be achieve by developing separate procedures (e.g., investment manager mandates) and incorporating them by reference into the SIPP.

SIPPs are plan-specific. Each pension plan is unique. Consequently, it is impossible to develop model wording that addresses the needs and issues of all plans. Although this chapter provides model wording for trustees to consider, trustees must develop wording that reflects the particular administrative and financial circumstances of their plan, including:

- plan liabilities,
- risk tolerance,
- administrative resources,
- whether investment is managed in-house or externally, and
- time, financial resources, and expertise of trustees and advisors to implement and monitor these practices.

Shareholder activism

One way for pension plans to protect their investments is to engage the corporations in which they invest through shareholder activism to ensure their performance is meeting the best interests of plan members. The objective in all cases is to address issues of concern to investors, including corporate governance, corporate responsibility, and other measures to improve long-term corporate performance.

Shareholder activism encompasses a wide range of activities aimed at improving long-term shareholder value, including engaging corporate management through letters and face-to-face meetings, drafting and filing shareholder proposals, and supporting other proposals at corporate annual general meetings. Shareholder activists generally take an incremental approach, beginning with writing letters raising their concerns and followed by meetings with management. If the issue cannot be resolved satisfactorily through discussion and negotiation, shareholders may file a resolution with the corporation, which is circulated to all shareholders for consideration at the corporation's next annual general meeting of shareholders. For pension funds, the trustees or their investment managers may undertake these activities.

Shareholder activism is part of prudent trusteeship and practised by institutional investors in Canada and around the world. In Canada, the

The California Public Employees Retirement System (CalPERS), the largest public sector pension plan in the United States, incorporates shareholder activism, proxy voting on issues of corporate governance and social responsibility, investment screening based on the International Labour Organization's (ILO) "Declaration on Fundamental Principles and Rights at Work," and economically targeted investing into its SIPP and related investment policies (see Appendix E).

Kirby Report of the Senate Standing Committee on Banking, Trade and Commerce has documented the considerable evidence of shareholder activism by pension plans and investment managers in the country (see sidebar) (Canada, 1998). In 2002, more than 50 shareholder proposals submitted by pension funds, religious organizations, and other institutional investors were on the ballots of approximately 30 Canadian corporations (SHARE, 2002). More than 227 shareholder proposals addressing social and environmental issues were submitted to more than 150 American companies by American investors in the same year (ICCR, 2002). By engaging corporations through dialogue, filing proposals, and initiating litigation in extreme cases, Canadian pension plans have taken an active approach on many issues related to corporate governance and adverse social and environmental practices of corporations. Examples include the dilutionary effect of stock option plans, auditor independence, the use of unacceptable labour practices by major retailers and their suppliers, and the environmental impacts of extraction industries.

In the United States, the Department of Labour, responsible for overseeing American pension plans and administration of the *Employee Retirement Income Security Act* (ERISA), has provided guidance on this issue, stating that pension funds can, consistent with ERISA and a plan's SIPP, take an active role in the governance of a corporation:

> *"An investment policy that contemplates activities intended to monitor or influence the management of corporations in which the plan owns stock is consistent with a fiduciary's obligations under ERISA where the responsible fiduciary concludes that there is a reasonable expectation that such monitoring or communication*

"[The] dramatic growth in institutional investments has been accompanied by a steady increase in the involvement of these institutions in corporate issues. A decade ago, institutional activism in Canada was almost unheard of. Institutional investors who were unhappy with corporate management or the direction of a particular company would simply "vote with their feet" by selling their shares. Today, institutions no longer automatically follow this path; they possess considerable proxy voting power and may quietly or openly seek the changes in a corporation which they believe should be implemented."

— Report of the Standing Senate Committee on Banking, Trade and Commerce, *The Governance Practices of Institutional Investors* (November 1998) *with management, by the plan alone or together with other share-holders, is likely to enhance the value of the plan's investment in the corporation, after taking into account the costs involved."* (Department of Labor, 2001).

Such statements made by American regulators are not law in Canada, but they do provide some guidance in interpreting pension trustee fiduciary duties in Canada. The Myners Review on Institutional Investment in England also recommended that "the American ERISA principles on shareholder activism should be incorporated into UK law, making intervention in companies, where it is in the shareholders' and beneficiaries' interests, a duty" (Myners, 2001; HM Treasury, 2001). The British government has indicated that it intends to legislate such a requirement for both fund managers and trustees (HM Treasury, 2001).

The ability of pension funds to engage in shareholder activism has also become easier because of changes to the law governing shareholder proposals (CBCA; Yaron, 2002). In the case of federally incorporated corporations, both registered and beneficial shareholders may file shareholder proposals. Corporations may no longer refuse to circulate a proposal to shareholders if they deem the proposal to be "primarily for the purpose of promoting general economic, political, racial, religious, social or similar causes." Now corporations must circulate a shareholder proposal as long as it "relates in a significant way to the business or affairs of the corporation." And shareholders are now permitted to communicate with each other about shareholder proposals as long as they do not solicit proxies.

In all cases, the objective of shareholder activism must be to enhance long-term corporate performance and the interests of plan members. Recent studies suggest that shareholder activism addressing corporate governance issues have had a positive impact on corporate performance and shareholder returns (Wiltshire Associates, 1995; Opler & Sokobin, 1995; Hawley and Williams, 2000, p.123).

Pension plans take many approaches to incorporating active trustee oversight into shareholder activism. Some plans choose to incorporate authorization for shareholder activism in a general SIPP provision committing them to encouraging responsible corporate practices. For example, The B.C. Public Service Pension Plan SIPP contains a "social/ethical policy" which incorporates discussion of shareholder activism, proxy voting and ethical performance criteria (see Appendix C). Some plans address the issue of shareholder activism in their proxy voting guidelines. For example, OMERS Proxy Voting Guidelines include a section entitled "OMERS Approach to Communicating Governance Concerns" (see Appendix C). A third approach is to provide a discrete provision in the SIPP to address shareholder activism.

SIPPs also vary in the extent of information provided about how to implement a shareholder activism strategy. The SIPP should indicate that the objective of shareholder activism is to improve long-term corporate performance and to further the interests of plan members. Most plans that address shareholder activism provide a general statement that they will engage corporations on issues through corporate dialogue and, where necessary, filing shareholder proposals. It should also state who is authorized to participate in shareholder activism on behalf of the plan (i.e., trustees, investment managers, custodian, and/or a proxy voting service). These measures provide some protection to trustees against

Suggested Model Wording for Shareholder Activism Provision

The Board of Trustees, and investment managers where so delegated, are authorized to engage management of corporations in which the Plan invests to ensure corporate performance supports the long-term best interests of plan beneficiaries. Engagement may take the form of letter writing, meetings with company representatives, and where necessary, filing shareholder proposals with companies.

In all instances, such action will be taken to ensure optimal financial performance of investments, to manage risk, and to secure a sustainable economic, social and environmental framework over the long-term. The decision to engage a particular company or group of companies will be guided by the desire to achieve superior investment performance through improvements in the areas of corporate governance, social and environmental practices including, but not limited to, those practices addressed in the plan's proxy voting guidelines, thereby satisfying the long-term best interests of plan members.

All shareholder activity will be carried out by the Plan's [administrator, staff, investment managers] in consultation with the [Board of Trustees, Investment Committee]. In order to maximize efficiencies and results, the Plan may cooperate with other shareholders or organizations in this area.

possible liability and also give clear direction to investment managers and information to plan members about the plan's investment strategy.

Like proxy voting guidelines, SIPPs also differ in the criteria they apply in choosing which issues to address through shareholder activism. In some cases, pension plans use the same criteria specified in their proxy voting guidelines. Some smaller plans that do not have proxy voting guidelines in place make decisions on a case-by-case basis, using information and analysis provided by larger plans and independent advisors.

RECOMMENDATION

Pension plans engaging in shareholder activism should include a separate provision in the SIPP that outlines a systematic approach for engaging corporations. Such a provision demonstrates an appreciation of the importance of shareholder activism to investment performance, and provides a degree of protection to plan representatives and trustees engaging corporations. If shareholder activism is included in the proxy voting guidelines, the guidelines should be incorporated by reference into the SIPP to ensure they are part of the plan's overall investment policy.

The shareholder activism provision in a SIPP should detail:

- authorization for trustees, plan staff, investment managers or consultants to engage corporations and specify approaches to be used;
- the fiduciary duty of trustees to act in the long-term best interests of plan beneficiaries, with specific reference to the importance of engaging corporations in order to minimize investment risk;
- responsibilities for coordinating and implementing the plan's shareholder activism strategy;
- subject to any legal restrictions, authorization to cooperate with other shareholders in developing and supporting shareholder resolutions; and
- the criteria used to determine whether or not to engage a corporation (often reference is made to the plan's proxy voting guidelines).

Key questions for trustees in developing a shareholder activism provision in the SIPP

- What are the particular governance, social and/or environmental concerns about which the plan will be active?

- What will be the extent of the plan's shareholder activism activities?
- Who will coordinate the plan's shareholder activism activities?
- Who will be responsible for representing the plan in discussions with corporations?
- Will the plan be allowed to cooperate with other organizations and institutional investors on shareholder actions?
- What will be the process for trustees to approve a shareholder resolution if required?
- What process will be used to determine the interests of plan members with regards to specific proposals?
- How will the plan assess the long-term costs and benefits to plan members associated with carrying out a shareholder action strategy?

Proxy voting

Proxies are the voting rights attached to shares that a pension fund owns in a corporation. The voting of proxies gives shareholders the opportunity to participate in the governance of the corporation by voting on shareholder and management proposals in order to enhance shareholder value. Recent American studies suggest that proxy activities targeted at underperforming firms can lead to significant improvements in shareholder value (Hawley & Williams, 2000).

The most common items of business that shareholders vote on at a corporation's annual general meeting are the election of the corporation's board of directors and the appointment of the auditor. Shareholders are also sometimes asked to approve other items of business proposed by corporate management or to vote on proposals brought forward by shareholders. Some examples of issues include executive compensation, auditor independence, shareholder rights plans, and reporting on compliance with international labour and environmental standards.

Pension trustees have a fiduciary duty to oversee the voting of all proxies in the best interest of plan members. Furthermore, federal and provincial pension regulations require that the SIPP account for the retention or delegation of the voting rights attached to investments.[5] The OSFI

Guidelines affirm that proxies are valuable plan assets, must be delegated or retained, and voted in the best interests of plan members:

> *"Plan administrators should not ignore the value of voting rights acquired through plan investments. Shareholder votes are often most valuable when used in alliance with others. Failure to describe in the investment policy how these rights will be used leaves plan administrators open to charges of either negligence or arbitrary action, possibly in violation of the standard of care requirement. Investment policies should describe and require the use of voting rights, whether directly or through proxy.*

> *"If the power to vote proxies is delegated to investment managers, proxies should be bound by rules established in the investment policy. The administrator should receive a report showing how proxies were voted, and affirming compliance with the administrator's proxy voting policy" (OSFI, 2000, endnote 4, Appendix I, section I.6.6).*

Accordingly, trustees have a responsibility to provide directions in the SIPP and oversee the following four stages of voting proxies:

1. establishing guidelines,
2. assessing issues,
3. voting proxies, and
4. monitoring results.

Establishing guidelines

In the first stage, trustees are responsible for overseeing the development of proxy voting guidelines that provide direction on how proxies are to be voted. This involves defining criteria used to determine how to vote on issues relating to the governance, business affairs, and social and environmental practices of corporations. As with the SIPP, it is important that proxy voting guidelines are clear, and have sufficient scope and depth to allow them to be executed accurately and efficiently (Greifer, 2001). Trustees should also obtain expert advice on corporate governance and corporate social responsibility and then consult with the plan investment managers for plan implementation.

Trustees may also elect to have proxies voted in accordance with guidelines created by an investment manager or proxy voting service, but trustees should review the guidelines to ensure they reflect the interests of plan members. SHARE has developed an extensive set of generic proxy voting guidelines that pension trustees may consider when developing guidelines for their plan. In some cases, trustees elect to include authorization for shareholder activism as part of the SIPP provision dealing with proxy voting.

Proxy voting criteria are usually spelled out in a plan's proxy voting guidelines. Proxy voting guidelines can be included as part of the SIPP (in the text or as an appendix), but are more often contained in a separate document. In the later case, proxy voting guidelines should be incorporated by reference in the SIPP as part of the plan's investment policy.

Assessing issues

Most issues will be covered in a plan's proxy voting guidelines. However, guidelines are not comprehensive. Where the guidelines provide no guidance on how to vote on a particular issue, the SIPP should provide a process for assessing the issue, including consulting with the trustees or the body of trustees responsible (e.g., the investment committee or proxy voting committee if such exists).

In some instances, plans do not develop guidelines, but rather refer shareholder proposals to a designated body (e.g., the Board, committee, or an individual) to decide how the proxy will be voted (see Appendix D). If such a procedure is followed by a plan, it should be laid out in the plan SIPP.

Voting proxies

Proxies can be voted by the plan's investment manager, a proxy voting service, the plan administrator, the Investment Committee, the Board of Trustees, plan custodians, or any combination of the above. The voting of proxies may be retained by the trustees or delegated to any other party mentioned above. In practice, except for large pension plans (e.g., Ontario Teachers' Pension Plan), the physical exercise of voting proxies is usually delegated to investment managers or a proxy voting service. In such cases, the SIPP should include the right of trustees to vote proxies directly where the trustees deem it necessary to do so (see Appendix D).

Suggested model wording for proxy voting provision

Proxy voting is a fiduciary duty and an integral component of the investment process. Proxy votes are valuable plan assets and federal guidelines recommend that the authority to vote proxies be delegated or retained, and voted in the best interests of plan members.

The Board of Trustees shall be responsible for developing proxy voting criteria and approving proxy voting guidelines. The Board of Trustees shall review these guidelines on an annual basis and reserves the right to provide additional proxy voting direction to its investment managers and/or proxy voting service at any time.

[Investment managers/proxy voting service] shall be responsible for the timely voting of all proxies consistent with the proxy voting guidelines, or in the absence of guidelines on a particular issue, in the best interests of plan members. [Investment managers/proxy voting service] are prohibited from abstaining from voting proxies unless so directed by the trustees. Where the guidelines do not address a proxy issue, the [investment manager/proxy voting service] shall consult with the [Board of Trustees/Investment Committee/ other designated body] to determine how to vote on that issue. The final decision for such proxies will be based upon the merits of each case in accordance with the best interests of plan members.

The Board of Trustees reserves the right to direct or override the voting decisions of the investment manager/proxy voting service if it believes such action is in the best interest of the plan members.

The Board of Trustees reserves the right to exercise the voting of proxies directly in specific situations.

Investment Managers/proxy voting service shall maintain complete and accurate voting records indicating how shares were voted and the reasons for any deviations from voting instructions outlined in the proxy voting guidelines. The Trustees will have access to these records.

Investment managers/proxy voting service shall provide a proxy voting report to the Board of Trustees within 30 days from the end of each quarter, except where an extension is obtained in writing from the plan administrator. The report shall allow trustees to determine how all proxies were voted, outline changes in proxy voting policies adopted by the Board of Trustees over the past quarter, and any instances where proxies were not voted in accordance with the plan's proxy voting guidelines or the best interests of plan members.

Where investment managers are responsible for voting proxies for the plan, some SIPPs require that the Board of Trustees or Investment Committee be notified in advance of an intention to vote against a management proposal or an "unusual item" (see Appendix D).

With respect to pooled funds, pension plans generally cannot direct the voting of proxies. However, larger pension plans may be able to negotiate an arrangement that allows the voting of an amount of the pooled fund's proxies proportionate to the plan's stake in the fund. Plans that are unable to make such an arrangement should advise their investment managers of their voting preferences and request a report on how the pooled fund's shares are voted.

Finally, SIPPs should include a provision addressing conflicting interests between managers and particular investments. Where a manager voting proxies has a direct or indirect material interest in any matter in which the manager exercises a right to vote on behalf of the plan, the SIPP should require the matter to be referred to the plan administrator (see Statement of Investment Policies and Goals of the Steelworkers Members' Pension Benefit Plan (June 5, 2000) in Appendix D).

Monitoring results

In practice, trustees are often not aware if or how plan proxies have been voted. This is troubling in light of a recent survey conducted by SHARE (2001b) that demonstrated significant differences in how investment managers voted proxies under their discretion (i.e., where trustees had not directed their investment manager on how to vote the proxies). Without regular monitoring, trustees cannot be sure that proxies are being voted in accordance with the best interests of their plan members. One study has indicated that in the absence of proxy voting guidelines, proxies are often voted according to corporate management's recommendations, which do not necessarily reflect the interests of plan members (Zanglein, 1998, p.51-52).

The SIPP should require that the party responsible for voting proxies keep records and report to the board of trustees (or investment committee) on a regular basis, and that trustees must monitor the voting of proxies by reviewing proxy voting reports received from their investment manager(s) (see Appendix D). OSFI Guidelines recommend that "the administrator should receive a report showing how proxies were voted, and affirming compliance with the administrator's proxy voting policy" (OSFI, 2000, endnote 4, Appendix I, page I.11). This report should be received on a quarterly basis. Any deviations in voting, including votes not in accordance with proxy voting guidelines and on unusual items, should be noted in the report from the investment manager or proxy voting service, and discussed with the trustees. If reports are not clear or require explanation, trustees should seek clarification from their invest-ment manager(s) or proxy voting service. Failure to monitor voting prac-tices could constitute a breach of trustees' duties to plan members (OSFI, 2000, endnote 4, Appendix I, section I.6.6).

RECOMMENDATION

SIPPs should contain, at a minimum, provisions detailing:

- what proxy voting guidelines, if any, will be followed when voting proxies;
- who is responsible for developing proxy voting guidelines, and re-viewing and voting proxies;
- what procedure should be followed where guidelines do not pro-vide voting direction on a particular issue;
- that those responsible for voting proxies adhere to the guidelines;
- that trustees retain the right to vote proxies themselves on a case-by-case basis at their discretion;
- that complete and accurate voting records be maintained;
- that proxy voting reports be provided to all trustees on a regular (quarterly) basis; and
- that where the agent authorized by the trustees to vote plan proxies has a conflict of interest with regard to a particular vote, the agent will notify the trustees and seek direction.

Key questions for trustees in developing a SIPP:

- Who has been assigned to develop proxy voting guidelines?
- What process exists to consult plan members about the proxy vot-ing guidelines?
- How often are guidelines reviewed?
- In the absence of guidelines, or where guidelines don't cover the issue in question, who decides how to vote proxies and based on what criteria?

- Who is responsible and best situated to vote proxies in the long-term best interests of plan members?
- Does the SIPP require that proxies be voted in accordance with proxy voting guidelines?
- Do the trustees have the discretion to vote or direct the voting of proxies themselves?
- Does the SIPP require regular (quarterly) proxy voting reports to the board of trustees?
- Does the SIPP include a compliance check for proxy voting? Does the SIPP require proxy voting reports to detail when proxies are not voted in accordance with proxy voting guidelines?

Investment screening

Investment screening is the process of applying financial or non-financial criteria to the selection of investments. The Social Investment Organization estimates that social or environmental screens are applied to approximately $40 billion of pension assets in Canada (SIO, 2000).

Where a plan elects to use investment screens, trustees are responsible for developing social and environmental criteria used to establish the screens. Trustees have the option of developing a set of custom screening criteria that are applied to all or a portion of the plan's segregated portfolio. Alternatively, pension plans may invest in screened pooled funds. Such funds apply a set of generally accepted screens to a recognized index of companies. In either case, criteria should be measurable and applied equally to all companies under consideration. Examples of measurable criteria include general principles detailed in international agreements such as the Universal Declaration of Human Rights and the International Labour Organization's Declaration on Fundamental Principles and Rights at Work.

The application of investment screens is compatible with the fiduciary duties of trustees, provided they are applied in a prudent and impartial manner, authorized in the SIPP, and communicated to plan members (Yaron, 2001). While the exact legal interpretation of the duties of trustees in this area remains unclear in Canada, other countries, including Britain, Germany and Australia, have adopted pension regulations that acknowledge investment screening as an acceptable pension investment practice.[6]

As with proxy voting, the SIPP should contain a requirement that trustees review screening criteria and their impact on investment performance on a regular basis. The SIPP should also include an escape clause to allow trustees to deviate where application of the screening criteria is not in the best interests of plan members (see section on escape clauses below). SIPPs should also clearly state that the plan portfolio must maintain adequate diversification, and reasonable returns across the entire portfolio that satisfy the plan's financial objectives.

Pension trustees may take a variety of approaches to authorizing investment screening in the SIPP. In some cases, general provisions are included permitting the trustees to take financial and non-financial considerations into account when making investment-related decisions (see Appendix E). These general provisions allow trustees to look at issues on a case-by-case basis rather than providing specific screening criteria. This type of general authority can be helpful where trustees do not feel comfortable screening out an entire sector or all companies engaged in a specific activity. However, experience has demonstrated that such provi-

What is investment screening?

Investment screening is a process whereby positive or negative criteria are identified for selecting or rejecting investments. Exclusionary screens prohibit investments in certain enterprises such as the production or sale of alcohol, tobacco or military arms, or the use of poor labour practices.

Qualitative screens, including positive screening and the "best-of-class" approach, recognize that corporations that adopt economic, social and environmental policies tend to perform better over the long-term. Positive screening encourages investment in companies that meet certain social or environmental standards (e.g. the International Labour Organization's *Declaration of Fundamental Principles and Rights at Work*) or engage in environmentally sustainable practices.

The "best-of-class" approach evaluates companies against standards of best practice in their particular industry. For example, an environmental screen would grade within the mining industry for the best company within that sector. This allows investors to invest in all sectors of the economy and keep their investment portfolio adequately diversified. Both qualitative approaches encourage companies to improve their performance in a specific area to meet the benchmark for inclusion in the group of sector companies that are included in plan portfolios.

sions sometimes do not provide sufficient direction to plan administrators and investment managers, resulting in confusion that requires later intervention and clarification by plan trustees.

Pension plans that apply screening criteria should specify them in the SIPP or in an accompanying document that is incorporated into the SIPP. In many cases, SIPPs include investment screens for entire sectors, such as tobacco and nuclear production (see Appendix E). Such absolute screens are easily interpreted by investment managers and plan members, but trustees must be very cautious about their impact on portfolio diversification and investment risk.

Alternatively, SIPPs may apply a set of qualitative screens or refer to a set of qualitative screens to be applied to investments (see sidebar discussion of "qualitative screens").

Regardless of which approach(es) is (are) taken, trustees have a duty to ensure that the plan's portfolio remains adequately diversified, that overall performance is not substantially diminished, and that acceptable levels of risk are maintained.

Qualitative screens

The OPSEU Staff Pension Plan applies a qualitative labour screen of approximately 25 criteria to Canadian companies developed in part by surveying members support to ensure they reflect the interests of plan beneficiaries. Variables that are considered include the level of unionization, labour practices, diversity issues and community relations. Companies in the TSE 300 are reviewed periodically and are given positive or negative points based on the criteria. This review produces a list of ineligible and borderline companies. The list is then reviewed by the Board of Trustees to determine whether they should be placed on the list of ineligible companies. Once a company is determined to be ineligible, it is sent a letter, with copies to any unions representing workers at the company, advising that it has been placed on an ineligible list pending receipt of new information. The SIPP authorizes this process in the following simple manner:

"Investments in Canadian and non-Canadian equities will be made in compliance with ethical criteria, as established periodically by the Board and communicated to the Manager. Equities issued by corporations which do not satisfy the minimum standards adopted by the Board will be ineligible for inclusion in the Fund."

RECOMMENDATION

SIPPs should contain a provision authorizing trustees to develop, implement, and review investment screens for all or part of the plan's investment portfolio. The investment screening provision in a SIPP should detail:

- which types of screens and specific screening criteria will be applied;
- how often the screens will be reviewed by the board of trustees;
- how to address cumulative effects of multiple screens;
- how and to what extent plan members will be consulted about screening criteria;
- that professional advice will be obtained when developing and evaluating screening criteria;
- what benchmarks and procedures will be applied in testing performance; and

Suggested model wording for investment screening provision

The application of investment screens is permissible provided it is done in a prudent manner and in the best interests of plan members.

Investments will be made in compliance with financial, corporate governance, social and environmental criteria established periodically by the Board of Trustees in accordance with prudent investment practices. Trustees shall consult with the appropriate investment professionals in the development and application of screening criteria to ensure that acceptable levels of diversification, returns and risk are maintained, and that the screening criteria do not negatively impact the rate of return. Trustees will also consult with plan members to identify the interests of plan members.

Performance of screened investments should be, where possible, measured against equivalent non-screened benchmarks for the particular investment class to ensure that long-term performance is comparable to non-screened investments.

The Board of Trustees shall review the screening criteria and the plan's objectives annually to ensure that they represent the best interests of plan members.

The Board of Trustees may, at its discretion, deviate from the use of any or all screens where it is deemed that their application would have an undue effect on plan diversification or the performance of the portfolio as a whole.

- how trustees can deviate from investment screens where it is deemed to be in the best interests of plan members.

Key questions for trustees to consider

- What process will the plan use to choose screening criteria?
- How will plan members be consulted about the criteria?
- What type of screens are most appropriate for the plan?
- Do the screening criteria chosen allow for maintaining adequate diversification and return targets?
- What outside assistance (e.g., corporate research firms, investment professionals) will be obtained in the design and implementation of the screen(s)?
- Will the SIPP include a general statement authorizing the use of investment screens or list specific screens?
- If the SIPP only includes a general authorizing statement, where will the specific screening criteria be detailed?
- To what portion of the plan's portfolio will the screens be applied?
- What benchmarks will be used to assess the performance of screened investments?
- How often will the screen(s) be reviewed?
- Does the SIPP permit trustees to deviate from the screening criteria?
- What are the costs and benefits associated with the application of the criteria to the extent that they may be predetermined?

Economically targeted investment[7]

Economically targeted investment (ETI) involves "pension asset allocations [that] obtain both market-grade returns and economic or social benefits by addressing perceived financing gaps and under-investment" (Falconer, 1999; CalPERs, 2000). The intention of such investments is to support job creation and community development, along with obtaining a reasonable rate of return for the pension fund through investments in such ventures as mortgage trusts, affordable housing, commercial building, regional development, small business, emerging technology sectors, real estate, and local community investment (Carmichael, 2000, p.161-162).

There is a relatively higher degree of risk associated with ETIs and trustees must keep in mind their fiduciary duties, particularly conflicts of interest, when considering such investments. Canadian pension regulators have not provided any instruction about the legality of ETIs. However, the U.S. Department of Labor issued an official definition of ETI in the 1990s clarifying that investments can be made with the intent of providing collateral economic benefits, provided the "investment has a risk-adjusted, market-grade return that is equal or superior to a comparable investment of comparable risk and otherwise supports a plan's fiduciary imperatives" (CLBC, 2001). In other words, returns on such investments must be commensurate with similar types of investments with similar risk profiles. This approach appears to be consistent with the fiduciary duties of Canadian pension trustees.

The OSFI Guidelines suggest that ETIs are acceptable investments within a well-diversified portfolio. The OSFI Guidelines affirm that the prudent person portfolio approach, generally accepted by most institutional investors, "recognizes that risks that would be unsupportable for an individual investment may be suitable for a well-diversified portfolio" (OSFI, 2000, p.2).

As stated, there is a relatively high degree of risk associated with such investments, especially given the limited access to private capital markets in Canada. In order to minimize such risks, funds generally pool assets allocated to ETI with those of other pension plans through an independently managed investment vehicle. Creative organizational strategies have been developed in other countries to overcome perceived barriers associated with ETI, including long-term loans, mezzanine financ-

Economically targeted investment

The California Public Employees' Retirement System's (CalPER's) ETI investment policy defines ETI as "an investment which has collateral intent to assist in the improvement of both national and regional economies, and the economic well-being of the State of California, its localities and residents. Economic stimulation includes job creation, development, and savings' business creation' increases or improvement in the stock of affordable housing; and improvement of the infrastructure." (California Public Employees' Retirement System Statement of Investment Policy for Economically Targeted Investment Program (February 14, 2000). See Appendix J.

ing, and other varieties of debt and quasi-debt financing (Falconer, 1999; CLBC, 2001). Trustees should also be wary of investment proposals that are presented to them as ETIs, but are not.

There are few examples of SIPPs in Canada that specifically include a provision dealing with ETI. One example is the Pension Plan for Employees of the Public Service Alliance of Canada, which recently decided to allocate a specific sum for debt instruments (e.g., mortgages) to support more affordable housing in Ottawa and the Outaouais. The practice is more common in the United States, where access to private capital markets and the number of investment products available to institutional

Suggested model wording for economically targeted investment provision

The Board of Trustees is authorized to consider investments that assist in the growth and well-being of the nation, the Province and its localities on condition that such investments provide competitive risk-adjusted rates of return and are consistent with the Board's fiduciary obligations and approved investment policies and guidelines. The emphasis will be on the promotion of long-term sustainable economic, industrial and business growth, job creation and affordable housing.

The Board of Trustees will follow plan policies and procedures to assess such investments and to ensure they are made in a prudent manner and in the best interests of plan members. Trustees shall consult with the appropriate investment professionals in the selection of such investments to ensure that acceptable levels of diversification, returns and risk are maintained, and that the screening criteria do not negatively impact the rate of return.

It is recognized that investments made for the sole benefit of the Plan's beneficiaries may also generate collateral benefits. However, the interests of plan members must always be the primary concern of the Board of Trustees.

All such investments must comply with pertinent federal or provincial pension investment guidelines, the plan's asset allocation guidelines and overall risk/return profile for investments. ETIs shall be priced at market prices and shall be subject to the applicable performance measurements for like investments.

The Board of Trustees shall consult with investment advisors and plan beneficiaries when considering ETIs to ensure they are being made in the best interests of plan members and consistent with the plan's investment objectives.

investors is greater. For example, CalPERS has developed a separate investment policy specifically for ETIs. The Statement of Investment Policy for Economically Targeted Investment Program defines ETI and sets outs CalPERS' strategic objectives regarding ETI (see sidebar and Appendix F for a copy of the entire policy and samples of other ETI provisions) (CalPERS, 2000).

RECOMMENDATION

Where pension trustees decide to consider ETIs as part of the pension plan's investment strategy, the SIPP should:
- indicate the types of investments of interest to plan members; the SIPP may provide general authority for trustees to invest in ETIs or specific authorization for each type of investment, such as venture capital, private placements, mortgages, and real estate;
- detail the percentage of assets to be allocated to such investments and the plans overall risk/return profile;
- authorize such investments in the context of a prudent investment strategy that conforms to the terms of the SIPP, maintains adequate diversification and a reasonable rate of return within accepted levels of risk;
- include a provision restating the fiduciary duties of trustees, including reference to avoiding conflicts of interest;
- require investment decisions to be made by the board of trustees or representative committee on a case-by-case basis given the wide variety of ETIs;
- specify the approvals required in order to make such investments;
- require trustees to obtain expert legal and investment advice in considering ETIs;
- provide a mechanism for independent arms-length valuation of such investments; federal pension regulations require that SIPPs outline "the method of, and basis for, the valuation of investments that are not regularly traded at a public exchange" (PBSA, 1985, s.7.1(1)(g));
- assess performance of such investments against comparative benchmarks, where available; and
- indicate the degree to which beneficiaries should be consulted regarding such investments.

Key questions for trustees to consider

- What ETI options exist among the plan's authorized investments?
- What types of investments will be authorized?
- How much of the plan's assets will be invested in ETIs? Does the SIPP require ETIs to meet comparative risk-adjusted rates of return and plan asset allocation targets?
- Does the SIPP authorize investment in ETIs and include a requirement that ETIs be made consistent with the fiduciary duties of trustees?
- How will potential conflicts of interests be addressed?
- What process will be used in selecting and reviewing ETIs? What approvals are required before investing in an ETI?
- How will such investments be valued?
- How will such investments be assessed and monitored in relation to other plan investments? What benchmark will be used to assess performance?
- How and to what extent will plan members be consulted in the selection of kinds of investments?
- What intermediary investment vehicles (e.g., pooled funds) are available?
- What are the administrative costs associated with such investments?
- What weight, if any, will be given to collateral benefits?

Selection and review of investment managers

Most SIPPs include provisions for the review of investment managers. Guidelines for selection of investment managers are usually detailed in a separate policy, which should be incorporated by reference into the SIPP along with other documents pertaining to investment managers, such as investment manager mandates. OSFI Guidelines recommend that a SIPP "document how investment managers will be chosen, compensated and replaced in a manner that encourages compliance to the policy's goals and procedures" (OSFI, 2000, p.2).

Trustee involvement in the selection and evaluation of investment managers is essential and should be articulated in the SIPP. In the context of jointly trusteed pension plans, if responsibility for selecting and evaluating managers is left to an investment committee, the committee should have representation from both the union and management appointed trustees. In all cases, the SIPP should require that the board of trustees as a whole have the final say on the selection and review of investment managers. A suggested list of questions for trustees to ask during selection and review of investment managers is included in Appendix H.

Investment managers are responsible for executing the investment objectives detailed in the SIPP on a day-to-day basis. Clear performance criteria in the SIPP, including requirements regarding shareholder activism, proxy voting, investment screening, and ETI where applicable, will promote greater compliance by investment managers, and assist trustees in reviewing their performance. Trustees should actively participate in discussions with investment managers to ensure they understand the various practices, support their use, and are capable of implementing them.

RECOMMENDATION

The SIPP and/or related investment documents should provide a clear set of criteria and process for selecting and reviewing investment managers. Instructions and targets should be detailed, including reference to shareholder activism, proxy voting, investment screens, and economically targeted investments where desired.

SIPPs should include, at a minimum, the following elements regarding investment managers:

- a general provision on the selection of managers that points to a separate policy for manager selection;
- a compliance report on a semi-annual or annual basis;
- a requirement to report on investment performance on a quarterly basis, including risk and return;
- a general provision mandating the annual review of manager performance to determine compliance with SIPP objectives; this general provision should also refer to a separate policy outlining the evaluation process and criteria;
- a requirement that investment managers meet with the trustees or the plan's investment committee at least semi-annually to discuss investment strategy and past performance; and
- a termination provision (in some cases included in the service contract instead).

Model wording for selection and review of investment managers provision

The Plan may utilize investment managers to implement its investment programs. Each manager shall operate under a set of guidelines specific to the strategic role its portfolio fulfills in the overall investment structure and any other applicable investment related policies. Compliance with these guidelines is mandatory.

Selection

The [Board of Trustees/Investment Committee] is responsible for overseeing the process of selecting investment managers. In all cases, the Board of Trustees will have an opportunity to review recommendations and make the final decision in selecting managers. The criteria used for selecting an investment manager are set out in the Investment Manager Selection and Review Guidelines and will be consistent with the investment and risk philosophy set out in the Statement of Investment Policies and Procedures.

Monitoring

Trustees have an ongoing and constant obligation to monitor the plan's Investment Managers. In addition, the [Board of Trustees/Investment Committee] will meet with Investment Managers semi-annually but not less frequently than annually. Special attention will be paid to evaluating performance against mandatory guidelines and stated objectives.

Reporting

All Managers will provide quarterly performance reports using a standard reporting format specified by the Board. In addition, Managers are encouraged to provide their standard performance information in a different format in addition to the required report. It is anticipated that most Managers will meet with the [Board of Trustees/Investment Committee] semi-annually (but not less frequently than annually) to review past performance and discuss investment strategy and the economic outlook for the future. In addition, investment managers are required to report any significant changes or deviations from plan guidelines within five business days of occurrence.

Review

The [Board of Trustees/Investment Committee] will conduct an evaluation of each investment manager on an annual basis. The criteria used for reviewing investment managers are set out in the Investment Manager Selection and Review Guidelines and will be consistent with the investment and risk philosophy set out in the Statement of Investment Policies and Procedures. The Board of Trustees may have under contract a professional pension investment consultant qualified to provide the Board with investment advice. The investment consultant's relationship with the Board shall be fiduciary in nature.

Termination

The Trustees reserve the right to terminate the services of an investment manager at any time. Reasons for considering the termination of the services of an investment manager include, but are not limited to, the following factors:

- Performance results which are below the stated performance benchmarks;
- Changes in the overall structure of the Plan's assets such that the investment Manager's services are no longer required;
- Change in personnel, firm structure or investment philosophy which might adversely affect the potential return and/or risk level of the portfolio; and/or
- Failure to adhere to investment-related policies and guidelines.

Questions for trustees to consider

- Do provisions in the SIPP regarding the selection and review of investment managers include consideration of their ability to support shareholder activism, proxy voting, investment screening, and economically targeted investing?
- Should the SIPP detail guidelines for selecting and evaluating investment managers, or refer to separate guidelines?
- Does the SIPP support active involvement by all trustees in the selection and evaluation of investment managers?
- Does the SIPP include clear criteria for evaluating investment manager performance include clear, measurable targets in the areas of shareholder activism, proxy voting, investment screening and ETI, or refer to another document which addresses these practices?
- Are investment managers required to provide quarterly performance reports?
- Does the SIPP require investment managers to meet with the body responsible for direct oversight of investment policy (board of trustees or the investment committee) on a regular basis? Semi-annually? Annually?
- Are investment managers required to be evaluated on an annual basis?

Benchmarks

SIPPs specify the rate of return that is expected of the plan's investment portfolio in relation to a benchmark portfolio return for each asset class. The benchmark portfolio will be specified in the SIPP and generally consists of standard industry indexes such as the S&P 500 Index in the United States for equities, the Scotia Capital Markets Universe Bond Index for bonds, and the Russell Canada Property Total Return Index™ for real estate. Investment managers are usually assessed against a corresponding indexed benchmark that they must meet or outperform. The whole fund's performance may be measured against a mixture of benchmarks matching the fund's asset allocation.

There are also an increasing number of screened indexes that are gaining recognition as credible benchmarks. Indices such as the Jantzi Social Index (Canada), the Domini Social Index (U.S.), the New York Sustainability Index (U.S.), and FTSE4GOOD (UK) are all indexes that track a screened portfolio of investments.

In assessing the performance of a plan's screened portfolio, trustees must use care to use a screened index that is comparable to other standard indexes in its class and that contains a similar basket of investments to the plan's screened portfolio. It is advisable to track performance against both a screened and non-screened index, where possible.

While a number of standard benchmark indexes exist for equities, bonds, and real estate investment, benchmarks for economically targeted investments are rarer and depend on the type of investment and its respective sector. Currently, there is no universally recognized standard for financial performance of private capital market investments (Falconer, 1999, pp.74-76). However, pension plans have adapted common bond and stock indexes to private benchmarking and more precise benchmarking, and performance measurement methods for ETI are being considered. The important thing is that the benchmark chosen for a particular ETI should be relevant to the ETI investment itself.

RECOMMENDATION

Trustees must ensure that the SIPP uses relevant benchmarks as a basis for assessing investment and investment manager performance. Given the wide variation in investment strategies, it is not possible to provide model wording for the use of benchmarks

Question for trustees to consider
- Does the SIPP identify appropriate benchmarks for evaluating screened and economically targeted investments?

Escape clause

Trustees should always have the flexibility to deviate from investment policies and strategies in order to deal with changes brought about by market forces or plan requirements. Trustees have the ultimate fiduciary responsibility to ensure that investment decisions are made in the best interests of plan members, which may require different approaches where a policy is having an adverse affect on financial returns or is otherwise not in the best interests of plan beneficiaries. For example, trustees may need to deviate from a particular asset allocation strategy or the use of a particular screen where the policy significantly impacts the portfolio, or where the plan needs to generate short-term liquidity in order to handle unforeseen liabilities.

Decisions to deviate from plan policy must be made with appropriate knowledge and advice. This requires that SIPPs be reviewed at least annually to ensure that the investment policy continues to meet the objectives of the plan. Similarly, there should be procedures to regularly monitor investments and investment practices, and to assess the risk/return profile along with procedures for adjusting the portfolio if trustees are not comfortable with the risk profile. Investment manager mandates should also require them to notify trustees if the investment practice appears to be imprudent or restricts performance.

Model wording for an escape clause

The Board of Trustees may direct an Investment Manager to deviate from the investment guidelines with respect to a portion of the Fund if they have determined it to be imprudent to continue to follow such guidelines. Such direction shall be given in writing.

The Board of Trustees shall reassess this policy at least annually. However, if at any time a manager feels that the objectives cannot be met, or that the guidelines or restrictions are imprudent, or that the policy restricts performance, the Board of Trustees should be notified in writing.

RECOMMENDATION

SIPPs should include a provision that permits the board of trustees to deviate from the plan's investment policies where such variation is in the best interests of plan members.

Process issues

This section discusses a number of issues that commonly arise in the process of developing, implementing, and reviewing investment policies. The focus, as in the previous section, is on process issues that trustees may encounter when considering investment practices such as shareholder activism, proxy voting, investment screening, and economically targeted investing.

Trustees have the responsibility to oversee the development, implementation, and review of the SIPP. Accordingly, the process elements of the SIPP should provide for strong trustee involvement. The SIPP should detail the nature and degree of trustee involvement so that their role and the role of other parties is clearly understood by all those involved in managing plan investments.

Consultation with plan beneficiaries

Trustees have a fiduciary duty to invest plan assets in the best interests of plan members and with an even-hand towards all plan beneficiaries. (For more information about trustee fiduciary duties and their application to shareholder activism, proxy voting, investment screening, and ETI, see Yaron, 2001.) In order to determine the best interests of plan members and to avoid allegations of trustee conflict of interest, trustees should consult with plan members. Consulting with members in establishing the parameters of investment practices has multiple benefits by engaging members in the management of their pension plan, addressing plan member concerns, and providing member input to trustees. Trustees must ultimately make plan investment policy decisions independently, but demonstrating beneficiary support for a plan's investment policy and practices assists trustees in demonstrating that such practices are in the best interests of plan members.

It is therefore important that trustees develop two-way communication processes to provide information to and obtain information from plan beneficiaries. The consultation process should be outlined in the SIPP. At a minimum, it should detail how often, how much, and in what manner information will be provided.

In the past, pension plans have facilitated communication with plan members on fundamental investment issues by:

- providing information to them about progress of initiatives, including financial performance results, on a regular basis through newsletters, annual mailings, and reports; in the case of investment screens, this could include information about socially responsible investing, its impact on financial returns, and a review of the process that the plan followed in investigating such initiatives; and
- surveying member support for an initiative.

Consultation is a particularly important part of the investment process in the context of investment screening criteria. Trustees are often confronted with the argument that they cannot incorporate investment screening criteria into a SIPP because it is impossible to demonstrate that the criteria reflect the "best interests" of all plan members. According to this argument, assessing the interests of plan members is not possible because plan members have various interests, and the only common interest of all beneficiaries is their financial interest. Without consulting plan members, trustees have accepted this presumption.

While surveys are subject to bias and cannot be used as absolute indicators, recent polls call into question this presumption and suggest that financial interests cannot automatically be assumed to be the sole common best interest of all beneficiaries or that plan members want to maximize their financial interests at all costs. A 2001 Vector Survey commissioned for the Canadian Democracy and Corporate Accountability Commission found that 51% of those surveyed (including plan members and beneficiaries) wanted a pension fund that invested in companies with a good record of social responsibility even if it resulted in somewhat lower benefits for themselves (CDCAC, 2001). Similarly, a national opinion poll conducted in Britain for the Ethical Investment Research Service (EIRIS), a provider of screening services, in September 1997, found that 73% of 700 adults surveyed wanted ethically-screened pensions; 44% stated that their pension plan should include an ethical policy if that could be done without any reduction in financial return; and a further 29% felt that their pension plan should adopt ethical policies even if this led to reduced returns (Sparkes, 2000).

Furthermore, the law does not require that there be unanimous support from all beneficiaries (Yaron, 2001). While the duty of loyalty is sometimes defined to require that trustees make decisions in the best interest of each and every individual beneficiary, in practice the test that courts have applied is whether trustees have made a reasonable effort to ascertain the views of beneficiaries collectively before making an investment policy decision (Yaron, 2001). It is important that trustees consult with plan members to identify their interests, but unanimity is not required. (See, for example, the University Funds Investment Policy (University of Toronto) cited in Appendix I.)

Conflict of interest and standard of care

Pension trustees have a fiduciary duty to treat all plan beneficiaries, present and future, with an even hand. Accordingly, people entrusted with managing assets on behalf of others must always be aware of potential conflicts of interest. Pension trustees have a fiduciary duty to set aside their personal interests and act in the interests of plan beneficiaries. Similarly, investment managers and other professionals retained by a pension plan must execute their responsibilities in a manner that is consistent with the best interests of their clients.

SIPPs should include provisions that require pension trustees and investment managers to disclose any potential conflicts of interest (see Appendix G). In the case of pension trustees, this generally takes the form of a restatement of the pension trustee's duty of loyalty to act in the best interests of plan beneficiaries. In the case of investment managers, a provision generally states that an investment manager must disclose any potential conflicts of interest, such as where an investment manager is not dealing at non-arm's-length with securities (e.g., trading plan assets through an inside brokerage firm).

All-or-nothing approach

Trustees often feel overwhelmed by the belief that they must implement all of these investment practices at once, including developing and implementing screens, diversifying the plan's portfolio to include economically targeted investments, voting all plan proxies, and engaging corporations in dialogue on issues of corporate governance and corporate social responsibility. Trustees are reluctant to engage in these areas because of concerns regarding lack of experience, extra work, unsure outcomes, time demands and associated costs (Falconer, 1999).

In reality, trustee engagement in shareholder activism, proxy voting, investment screening, and economically targeted investing can be an evolutionary process. Trustees should take time to familiarize themselves with these practices and consider them in relation to the specific characteristics of their own plan. An incremental approach allows trustees and members to educate themselves about the particular investment practice, properly consider the appropriateness of each investment practice before incorporating it into the plan's investment strategy, and monitor the results of each step over time. Some changes can be made easily and with virtually no increased risk to the plan (e.g., hiring a proxy voting service), whereas others require more information before making a decision. Therefore, trustees may consider implementing some of the simpler practices first and adding others over time.

Following a two-year investigative process, the Joint Pension Advisory Committee of the Pension Plan for Employees of the Public Service Alliance of Canada recently decided to take such an incremental approach to these practices. They started by devoting a percentage (10%) of the current market value of the plan to screened and economically targeted investments, while ensuring that the plan's overall asset mix was not inappropriately changed. Rather than develop their own screen, they will invest in an established screened fund. They also instructed their investment managers to advise plan trustees when proxies were either voted against a management recommendation, or against the recommendation of a proxy voting service. Future steps will include participating in shareholder actions and supporting shareholder proposals filed by other investors where they are determined to be in the best interests of plan members. None of these steps is expected to result in significant financial or administrative costs to the plan.

Some recommended first steps with nominal time or resource requirements include:

- amending the SIPP to give trustees discretion in directing the voting of proxies;
- hiring a proxy voting service to assist in the development of proxy voting guidelines or to vote proxies in accordance with guidelines provided by plan trustees;
- voting proxies in support of specific shareholder proposals that are determined by the trustees to be in the best interest of plan members;
- establishing one or two screens with a high level of member support to apply to a segment of the plan's portfolio; and
- investing a portion of plan assets in a screened segregated or pooled fund.

Trustee education and training

All trustees require current and comprehensive knowledge about investment principles and plan governance in order to make prudent investment decisions. Trustees have the right and responsibility to obtain the education they need at the plan's expense in order to engage in a meaningful way with other trustees and investment professionals about matters pertaining to plan investment policy. Any person can be a trustee, not just "experts," provided they are committed to obtaining the education and training required to oversee the affairs of the pension plan responsibly. Training expenses should be borne by the pension plan as a necessary cost of effective and efficient governance.

Trustees should receive sufficient education necessary to "de-mystify pension fund governance and investment and allow pension trustees to make prudent decisions" (Carmichael, 2000, p.302). One trustee estimates that, in the absence of an education program, it took her approximately two years, relying on the knowledge of trustees who had been on the Board longer and her own education work to "get up to speed."

In addition to supporting trustee training, there are other ways in which pension plans can support the professional development of trustees. One approach is to have experienced trustees support new trustees in a mentorship arrangement. Trustees may also consider incorporating an extensive glossary of terms into the SIPP to make the document more accessible to trustees who may be less familiar with investment language.

Trustees should avail themselves of educational programs to meet their educational needs. There are a growing number of trustee education programs available in Canada provided by unions, independent organizations, and investment professionals. For example, Carleton University's Centre for the Study of Training, Investment and Economic Restructuring (CSTIER) and the University of Toronto's Ontario Institute for the Study of Education (OISE) in conjunction with SHARE, is currently developing a series of national trustee education programs.

Duty to question everything

Trustees may seek advice from professional investment advisors, including actuaries, consultants, and lawyers, as well as unions and other pension-related organizations, to assist in setting responsible investment policy. In doing so, it is the responsibility of pension trustees to actively engage their advisors in the development, implementation, and review of investment policy by asking questions about things they do not understand.

Trustees have the right and obligation to seek clarification from their professional advisors on any investment-related matter. In setting plan investment policy, investment professionals are often not questioned about the information they provide or the assumptions on which their advice is based, because trustees feel intimidated or presume that they should know the answers already. As a result, much investment-related advice is simply adopted without the requisite level of scrutiny and consideration required of prudent trustees.

Professional advisors are retained by the plan to serve the needs of trustees. Where there is confusion or uncertainty, trustees have a duty to ask questions and should not feel shy or intimidated when doing so. Trustees should also be aware of any potential conflicts of interests on the part of those providing responses to questions (see section entitled "Conflicts of Interest").

Plan investment committees

Although all trustees are responsible for plan investment policy decisions, in practice the investment committee of many plans usually has primary responsibility for development of the SIPP. Some plan investment committees are structured so that trustees have little or no involvement in developing investment policy recommendations. Investment committees may be composed of staff and financial professionals who are not trustees, others have a minority of trustees, and still others are composed of trustees assisted by finance industry professionals. As a result, trustees who are not part of the investment committee may have little input into the SIPP's development. In some instances, the board of trustees adopts investment committee recommendations with little or no scrutiny.

Whether a committee or the board as a whole develops investment policy, trustees should ensure that they are adequately represented within that body and have meaningful involvement in the investment policy development process. This may require restructuring the composition of the investment committee and amending procedures to ensure adequate review and input from trustees at all stages. In one instance, a board of trustees decided that investment-related decisions were so important that it expanded its investment committee from two trustees to include the entire board. Whichever arrangement is chosen by the trustees, trustee involvement should be balanced against the need for efficient and effective plan governance.

The SIPP or some other plan governance document should define the relationships and accountability of those involved in developing investment policy. The roles and responsibilities of the board, investment committee, pension advisory committees, investment managers, custodian, actuary, and consultants should be delineated. While smaller pension plans tend to include all this information in the SIPP, larger plans may choose to develop a separate governance document, as well as individual investment manager mandates. The Pension Investment Association of Canada and the Association of Canadian Pension Management recommend this approach.

Trustee communication

Trustees often have difficulty explaining the relevance and benefits of shareholder activism, proxy voting, investment screening, and economically targeted investing to their investment advisors and co-trustees. Their audiences may have misperceptions about these practices and automatically dismiss them because, in their view, they do not deal directly with the financial performance of plan investments.

Trustees should be clear about how they describe these practices in order to distinguish them from terms such as "ethical investing" or "socially responsible investing." Neither term adequately reflects the scope of these four investment-related practices, which together seek to support long-term returns and reduce investment risk by investing plan assets in companies that operate within a framework of sound corporate governance, social and environmental practices.

Before advancing these practices for inclusion in a plan's SIPP, trustees should set clear definitions of each term to avoid any confusion or misunderstanding. Trustees should also avail themselves of the latest performance data and research on each practice.

Administrative costs

Pension plans interested in incorporating shareholder activism, proxy voting, investment screening, or economical targeted investing into their SIPP are often told that the administrative costs of following such practices are prohibitive. Those interested in incorporating these practices into their SIPP will be concerned with ensuring that the associated administrative costs are reasonable.

In order to uphold their fiduciary duties, pension trustees must expend a certain amount of time and resources to evaluate investment practices, investment performance, and to update the SIPP. For example, trustees have a fiduciary duty to ensure that proxies are voted in a responsible manner. Reasonable expenditures in this area are therefore required.

In other instances, such as investment screening, costs must be weighed against the anticipated long-term benefits to plan beneficiaries. Accordingly, trustees should review all information regarding the administrative and financial costs and benefits associated with implementing and monitoring a desired practice. In some instances, trustees may elect to defer certain actions until more cost-effective mechanisms are in place (see section entitled "All-or-Nothing Approach"). In other cases, certain practices may have no or minimal additional costs, or a pension plan may already be paying for comparable services. For example, investment managers vote proxies on behalf of their clients according to the manager's guidelines. Requesting that the investment manager vote proxies in accordance with a pension plan's proxy voting guidelines may be cost-neutral, depending on their comprehensiveness and clarity. Again, trustees should review whether more than minimal costs may be required in the development and interpretation of the guidelines.

Trustees may also manage and minimize costs in a number of ways. Plans can share materials that they have developed with other plans or develop policies and procedures in cooperation with other plans. Trustees can use precedents from other plans as a basis for developing policies, although trustees must never simply adopt another plan's policies or procedures. Many large American and Canadian plans provide their investment policies on the Internet or upon request (see Appendix I).[8]

Finally, in an increasingly competitive environment, some services may already be offered as part of the existing service package or at little additional cost. By obtaining current information, trustees may find that a particular service is available at a reasonable or no additional cost to the plan.

Trustees should bear in mind the following when considering the issue of costs:

- The OSFI Guidelines recommend that trustees consider the transaction and custodial fees in developing a plan's investment policy.
- American courts have stated that trustees may incur "minimal" costs in implementing practices such as transfer costs associated with switching investments from a non-screened to a screened portfolio.[9]
- Legal requirements and prudent plan management require trustees to incur costs in order to carry out certain practices (e.g., development and application of proxy voting guidelines). Such costs are not "add-ons" but rather a non-discretionary cost associated with prudent plan governance.

Conclusion

It bears repeating: trustees have the ultimate responsibility for the plan's investment policy. Accordingly, they must be actively involved in the development and review of the SIPP, which details the framework of the pension plan's investment strategy. Along with setting out the plan's objectives and strategies, the SIPP acts as a guide for trustees, plan staff, and third party agents, and can provide some protection to plan trustees, provided it is developed and executed in a prudent manner.

Increasingly, pension plans are considering the incorporation of shareholder activism, proxy voting, investment screening, and economically targeted investments as part of a comprehensive and prudent investment strategy. In principle, these practices are permitted, and, in the case of proxy voting, are required as part of a pension plan's prudent investment strategy. This chapter has hopefully demonstrated how to construct a SIPP in a prudent manner to include these practices and to ensure that trustees have the requisite involvement in their oversight. The appendices that follow provide a variety of additional materials that can assist trustees further in the development of a SIPP.

Appendix A: Statutory provisions

Section 7.1 of the federal *Pension Benefits Standards Regulations* require that every SIPP include provisions addressing:
a. the categories of investment and loans;
b. the investment portfolio's diversification;
c. the asset mix and expected rates of return for various asset classes;
d. the liquidity of investments;
e. the lending of cash and securities;
f. the retention or delegation of the voting rights attached to investments; and
g. the method for valuing investments that are not regularly traded at a public exchange; and related party transactions.

The federal regulations have been adopted by all provinces except Prince Edward Island and Quebec.

The OSFI Guidelines recommend that trustees consider the following general factors in developing the plan SIPP:
h. the plan's existing investments;
i. the rate of future contributions;
j. the amount and structure of current and future liabilities (pension benefits, member services and plan administration);
k. how these liabilities and contemplated investments would respond to plausible economic events;
l. the plan's financial situation;
m. its risk tolerance;
n. the plan's maturity;
o. the estimated cash flow requirements; and
p. the financial risks the plan sponsor may face in funding the plan. (OSFI, 2000, p.1.2-1.3)

The OSFI Guidelines also recommend that SIPPs address the following additional risks and issues:
q. pledging and borrowing assets;
r. the level of foreign investment;
s. the percentage of actively and passively managed investments, taking into consideration the effects of management fees; and
t. transaction costs and custodial fees.

Appendix B: Fiduciary checklist for pension trustees

The following is a brief checklist for trustees when considering incorporating shareholder activism, proxy voting, investment screening, or ETI into their plan's investment policy. This is not a comprehensive list of all issues that trustees must consider when setting investment policy and does not constitute legal advice. Trustees are advised to seek independent advice regarding their plan before making investment decisions.

Incorporating Documents

- Do the plan's governing documents or trust agreement restrict trustees from engaging in shareholder activism, proxy voting, screening and ETI?

Statement of Investment Policy and Procedures

- Does the plan have a separate SIPP?
- Does the SIPP explicitly authorize trustees to engage in shareholder activism, proxy voting, investment screening and/or ETI?
- Are the investment criteria in the SIPP consistent with the mission and/or purpose of the plan as stated in the incorporating documents/ trust agreement?
- Have appropriate diversification levels been maintained in accordance with any statutory or common law requirements?
- Are there provisions in the SIPP specifying a required rate of return on investments that limits the ability to apply other investment criteria in any way?
- Has discretion been reserved for trustees to deviate from the SIPP where it is deemed to be in the best interests of plan beneficiaries?

Investment Review Process

- Have the incorporating documents and investment policy been reviewed to determine who is responsible for making investment decisions?
- Are there procedures in place for the implementation and annual review of the SIPP?
- Have methods for developing and reviewing investment criteria been approved by the board of trustees?

Expert Advice

- Has ongoing, current, and comprehensive expert legal and financial advice been obtained in the process of developing the investment policy?
- Has the plan obtained several opinions with regards to SIPP provisions dealing with shareholder activism, proxy voting, investment screening, or ETI?

Trustee Independence

- Have all decisions been made in an independent fashion in accordance with the SIPP rather than simply adopting recommendations of experts or fund managers?
- Have all steps taken in authorizing investment decisions been documented?

Member Communications

- Is there a process for receiving input from beneficiaries about investment policies and specific investment decisions?
- Is there a process in place to survey plan members/beneficiaries about their interests so that trustees can speak with confidence about their "best interests"?

Investment Performance

- Does the plan have evaluation procedures in place to ensure that all screened and economically targeted investments are commensurate with long-term rates of return of non-screened and traditional investments with similar risk characteristics?

Investment Managers

- Does the SIPP have guidelines and procedures or refer to separate documents addressing the selection and review of investment managers?
- Do selection and review criteria include the requirement that investment managers have an understanding of shareholder activism, proxy voting, investment screening, and ETI, where applicable?
- Do the review criteria assess the ability of the investment manager(s) to meet the requirements imposed in the SIPP regarding such practices?

Proxy Voting

- Does the plan/trust have proxy voting guidelines? If they are separate from the SIPP, are they incorporated into the SIPP by reference?
- Do the proxy voting guidelines authorize trustees to instruct fund managers on how to vote proxies or to delegate that function to a proxy voting service or other party responsible for voting proxies?
- Does the SIPP require those responsible for voting proxies to adhere to the pension plan's proxy voting guidelines and provide a regular (quarterly) record of all proxy votes to the trustees?
- Does the SIPP require investment managers to consult with the trustees or investment committee where proxy voting guidelines do not cover the issue in question?

Appendix C: Examples of general provisions

The following are excerpts from the investment policies of pension plans that provide general direction on the incorporation of social and environmental criteria into pension plan investment policy and practices.

Excerpt from the Code of Prudent Investment Policy 2000 for the Dutch plan "Stichting Pensioenfonds ABP" (ABP) on Social Responsibility

The aim of ABP's investment policy is to obtain a maximum return for the (former) participants in the pension fund, within the risk parameters established by the Governing Board. ABP requires from all those involved in its investment process an undivided dedication to this investment objective.

In light of this objective, ABP will resist all investment compulsion and investment restrictions which have a negative effect on an optimal investment return. There is no room for socially initiated investments or for economically targeted investments, if such investments do not meet the return requirements formulated by the ABP.

ABP is conscious of the social role it fulfills as a large investor. This role compels ABP to exercise great care in its actions. ABP is prepared at all times to account for the consequences of its investment practice for society, the environment, employees, and human rights.

Naturally, ABP will not become involved in any investment transaction which would, for instance, contravene international law. Moreover, ABP will avoid an investment:

- if illegal or morally reprehensible behaviour is thereby promoted;
- if the investment—were it to be made—is directly related to a violation of human rights and fundamental freedoms; if it is likely there will be such a relationship and if ABP is aware of this, ABP will refrain from the investment;

ABP will promote that criteria for a social, ethical and environmental nature will be integrated in its investment process. In this context, one or more experimental investment portfolios may be created whereby investments are selected, managed and divested on the basis of special concern for these criteria. Of course, this leaves the goal of ABP's investment policy unaffected.

Excerpt from the British Columbia Public Service Pension Plan's Investment Policies and Procedures (January 2000)

Introduction

The Public Service Pension Plan (the Plan) exists to provide its members with retirement income and related benefits. Empirical studies have shown that investments provide up to 80% of the funding of a pension plan. Therefore, the fiduciaries have a moral and legal obligation to maximize the return on investments on behalf of the Plan's current and future beneficiaries.

Good social management is part of good business practices. Companies which implement and maintain high ethical standards are expected to be the best performing and most profitable companies in the Canadian and world economies.

Given the above, the Plan wishes to use its influence to actively encourage socially responsible behaviour and ethical conduct in companies in which it chooses to be a shareholder.

Ethical Performance Criteria

The following criteria have been identified by the stakeholders as being important in terms of encouraging ethical behaviour in the Plan's Canadian and world equity investments:

1. Environment: Companies should comply with all environmental regulations. It is recognized that implementing new procedures or pollution controls can be a lengthy process. However, failure to address such problems can pose future costs and liabilities to the company. Preferably, the company will have long-term plans for environmental protection and an environmental policy.

2. Labour Relations: Companies should have a track record of progressive labour relations. This should include high standards of employee health and safety, equitable hiring and promotional practices, and promote non-discriminatory workplace behaviour.

3. Human Rights: Companies should not have business dealings with countries where human rights, according to United Nations standards, are violated.

4. Products: Companies should not have as their primary activity the production of armaments.

5. Code of Ethics: Companies should have a Code of Ethics with respect to appropriate business practices. This should include such issues as conflict of interest, obeying the letter and spirit of the law, and corporate objectives. A formal training program should be in place to ensure understanding and compliance by all employees.

Ethical Evaluation Process

The Plan will implement its ethical investment objectives by the use of one or more of the following practices:

- Voting proxies;
- communicating ethical objectives to company management and/or boards;
- communicating ethical objectives to other large institutional shareholders to generate support;
- sponsoring shareholder resolutions; and,
- should the foregoing actions fail to achieve the desired change, the stock may be sold (provided an alternative equally desirable investment, from a financial return and risk point of view, is available).

Shares held by index funds are to be excluded from this process if, in the view of the investment manager, the sale would have an adverse impact on the index fund performance.

The goal of this process is to influence corporate behaviour and change their practices when they do not meet the standards outlined in this statement. This, in turn, will make them better corporate citizens and more profitable organizations.

The effectiveness of these measures will be monitored. A corporation that is not responsive will result in the Plan withdrawing its support for the Board of Directors.

Conclusion

At all times, this policy will be conducted within the framework of fiduciary responsibility. It will therefore be implemented in a manner which does not interfere with the efficient investment of the Fund's assets to achieve investment return objectives, which are in the best interest of the Plan's current and future beneficiaries.

This policy will be reviewed annually with all external fund managers.

Appendix D: Examples of proxy voting provisions

The following are examples of proxy voting provisions from the SIPPs of various pension plans.

Ontario Municipal Employees' Retirement System (OMERS)

4.1 The Senior Vice-President, Investments is responsible for voting all proxies related to securities owned by OMERS; however, where appropriate, this responsibility may be delegated to a Vice-President, Portfolio Manager, or external agent designated by the Senior Vice-President, Investments.

4.2 In all cases, such voting will be done using the best interests of OMERS as the sole criterion.

4.3 OMERS has issued Proxy Voting Guidelines which include general statements of OMERS policy on various aspects of corporate governance and specific recommendations for voting on individual issues. OMERS approach is to take into account the quality of a company's overall governance in deciding to vote for or against a specific proposal.

OMERS makes this publication available to all companies in which it invests, and to all other interested parties in Canada and elsewhere.

If an item of specific concern arises, OMERS initial step is to examine the applicability of the relevant proxy voting guideline. OMERS may then elect to write to an individual company informing the company of the fund's concern. The fund may subsequently request a meeting with the Chief Executive Officer of the company or the Chair of the Board of Directors. The fund may also request a meeting with other members of the Board of Directors, specifically the Chair of the Corporate Governance Committee. If the company is in general agreement with OMERS principle of governance and is receptive to concerns of the fund, OMERS will take this into consideration in voting for any specific proposal. If, however, there is little evidence of agreement or willingness to change, it should be expected that OMERS would vote in favour of proposals in keeping with OMERS specific guidelines. Finally, OMERS will consider introducing specific shareholder proposals itself.

OPSEU Pension Trust

At the time of publishing these guidelines, OPTrust hired an outside firm to research and vote our proxies. The voting fiduciary is expected to vote OPTrust proxies according to the guidelines in this booklet. Resolutions or shareholder proposals should be closely examined to ensure that voting criteria and guidelines are consistently met. OPTrust will conduct random spot-checks to ensure that this voting process is followed.

For resolutions or shareholder proposals that are not covered in this booklet, the voting fiduciary is to provide OPTrust's Chief Investment Officer with background information and analysis of the issue in question. If the Chief Investment Officer deems the issue to be outside the scope of the guidelines, OPTrust's proxy voting subcommittee—composed of one union-appointed and one government-appointed trustee—will examine the item and decide how it should be voted.

Canadian Labour Congress Staff Pension Plan

The Committee has delegated voting rights acquired through the investments held by the Fund to the custodian of the securities, to be exercised in accordance with the Investment Manager's instructions. The Investment Manager is expected to exercise all voting rights related to investments held by the Fund in the interests of the Plan's members. On a quarterly basis, the Investment Manager shall report their voting activities to the Committee.

CLC reserves the right to take back voting rights of assets held in segregated portfolios for specific situations. Further, the Investment Managers should advise the Committee regarding their voting intentions for any unusual items.

Steelworkers Members' Pension Plan (excerpt)

In the event the manager or its agents has any material interest, whether direct or indirect in any matter in which the manager exercises a right to vote, prior to exercising any such right, the manager shall bring this matter to the attention of the administrator, who shall inform the Chair of the Board of Trustees. The Chair is entrusted with either (a) instructing the manager on how to exercise the right to vote; (b) referring the matter to another money manager which does not have such an interest for decision; or (c) referring such matter to a committee of the Board of Trustees to determine. The Chair or committee may request the manager to exercise the voting rights in accordance with the manager's discretion should they be satisfied the interest of the manager is not such as to impair or colour the decision of the manager, or alternatively, may instruct the manager how to exercise the voting rights after seeking such counsel as the Chair or committee may deem appropriate.

Pension Plan "A"

The Board has directed that the individual investment managers will be responsible for voting proxies in the best interest of plan members. Each investment counsellor is responsible for maintaining records of how each proxy is voted. A written report of proxy voting will be provided to the Board within 30 days from the end of each quarter. A detailed explanation will be given for each instance where the proxy is voted against management.

Pension Plan "B"

Proxy voting is an integral component of the investment process. The Board shall establish an overall policy of voting proxies. The Investment Staff shall be responsible for the timely voting of all proxies in a consistent manner with the proxy voting policy. Investment managers shall vote proxies consistent with their respective policy and in the best economic interests of the System. The staff shall periodically provide a proxy voting status report to the Board.

Pension Plan "C"

Stock proxies are voted in accordance with the following procedures:

The proxy servicer receives and reviews all proxy statements. The proxy servicer will vote all proxies in accordance with the Board's Proxy Voting Policy, except those where a specific concern has been raised by a Board Member, advisor, consultant, or Staff member.

The proxy servicer may also vote any proxy involving other issues essentially the same as those on which the Board's Proxy Voting Policy is well defined.

With regard to proxies requiring special attention under the Board's Proxy Voting Policy, as well as special issues not covered or anticipated by the Proxy Voting Policy, proxies and all pertinent reference material shall be sent to the Chief Investment Officer, who will evaluate the issues with respect to the intent of the Proxy Voting Policy. On issues not covered by the Proxy Voting Policy, controversial, high-profile, and contested change of control issues, the Chief Investment Officer will communicate with the Board's Proxy Committee to determine how such proxies will be voted. Each member of the Proxy Committee will register his/her choices with the Chief Investment Officer as to how the proxies should be voted. The Chief Investment Officer will then direct the proxy voting servicer to vote the proxies in accordance with the wishes of the majority of the Proxy Committee members voting.

The Chief Investment Officer shall regularly report to the Board the types of issues that are being considered or that have been voted by the Chief Investment Officer and the Proxy Committee.

The Chief Investment Officer shall cause to be maintained by the proxy voting servicer, a file of all proxy votes and issue annually a summary report to the Board. This report, along with all individual actions, shall be available for public inspection.

Appendix E: Examples of investment screening provisions

The following are examples of investment screening provisions from the SIPPs of various pension plans.

Exclusionary screens

United Methodist Church of America Board of Pensions' and Health Benefits' Investment Policy

J. Investments shall not knowingly be made in securities in which the corporate entity has a significant interest in distilled spirits, wine or other fermented juices, tobacco, gambling, pornography or firearms.

Investments shall not knowingly be made in securities in which a core business of the corporate entity—

- manufactures cigarettes, cigars, chewing tobacco, smokeless tobacco, or in a company in which 10% or more of gross revenues are derived from supplying key component elements to the tobacco industry (cigarette papers, flavourings, adhesives) or the sale and marketing of tobacco-related products;
- produces alcoholic beverages (beer, wine, distilled liquor);
- or in a company in which 10% or more of gross revenues are derived from supplying key elements for alcohol production or from the sale, distribution or marketing of alcoholic beverages;
- owns or manages casinos, racetracks, off-track betting parlours; or in a company that derives 10% or more of gross revenues from the production of goods and services related to the gaming or lottery industries;
- derives 10% or more of gross revenues from the production, distribution, or sale of products or services that are interpreted to be pornographic, meet the legal criteria for obscenity or legal definition of "harmful to minors.

Investments will not be made in corporations in which 10% or more of gross revenues are derived from the manufacture, sale or distribution of antipersonnel weapons such as land mines, "assault-type" automatic and semiautomatic weapons, firearms and ammunition provided for commercial and private markets. Restrictions are waived on percentages of revenue derived from the manufacture, sale or distribution of firearms and ammunitions provided for legitimate military or law enforcement organizations.

The General Board of Pension and Health Benefits will make no further investment in non-voting equity securities of companies whose ratio of Department of Defense contracts (or contracts with the comparable agency or department of any foreign government) related to the production and distribution of conventional military armaments or weapons-related systems to gross revenues is higher than 5%.

The General Board of Pension and Health Benefits will make no further investment in voting or equity securities with voting rights or fixed income securities of companies whose ratio of Department of Defense contracts (or contracts with the comparable agency or department of any foreign government) related to the production and distribution of conventional military armaments or weapons related systems to gross revenues is higher than 10%.

The General Board of Pension and Health Benefits will make no purchase of any security of a company whose identifiable ratio of nuclear weapons contract awards to gross revenues is higher than 3%. The measurement of any nuclear weapons contract award will be based on the most current information available to General Board of Pension and Health Benefits from the Department of Defense and other research sources.

The General Board of Pension and Health Benefits will give consideration to the divestment of the securities of any company which remains in violation of the Board's DOD or nuclear weapons guidelines for three consecutive years.

Qualitative screens

United Methodist Church of America Board of Pensions' and Health Benefits' Investment Policy

It is expected that Investment Managers will invest by consideration of financial issues rather than by non-economic criteria. However, once investments of seemingly equal value and potential have been determined to be available, preference is to be given to companies that:

8. do not employ anti-union policies;

9. promote occupational health and safety; and

10. provide equal employment and opportunity regardless of race, creed, colour, national origin or gender.

In accordance with these general tenants, these special considerations are not designed to exclude investment in any one industry or company.

The Trustees may direct their investment managers from time to time to make investments only in investments which the Trustees consider ethically appropriate. The Trustees shall, in giving such direction, take into consideration (i) the return on investments, (ii) the security of such investments, and (iii) the ethical nature of the investments.

The United Methodist Church of America Board of Pensions' and Health Benefits' Investment Policy directs its trustees as follows:

The General Board of Pension and Health Benefits shall make an effort to invest in institutions, companies, corporations or funds which are making or which are expected to make a positive contribution toward the realization of the Social Principles of The United Methodist Church.

To the extent that investments are consistent with the trust imposed upon the Board, investments in those industries, companies, corporations and funds deemed likely to make positive social, moral and economic impact on society shall be sought, which are expected to fulfill one or more of the following:

1. Nurture climates in which human communities are maintained and strengthened for the good of every person.

2. Support the concepts of family and equal opportunity of life, health and sustenance of persons.

3. Provide opportunities for persons with handicapping conditions, and for all persons irrespective of sex, age or race.

4. Support the rights and opportunities of children, youth and the aging.

Appendix F: Examples of economically targeted investment provisions

The following are examples of economically targeted investment provisions from the SIPPs of various pension plans.

CalPERS Statement of Investment Objectives and Policy for the Economically Targeted Investment Program (February 2000)

Strategic Objectives

The primary objective of Economically Targeted Investments (ETI's) is to provide competitive risk-adjusted rates of return, while still promoting growth and development of the national and regional economies. ETIs will provide collateral economic benefits to targeted geographic areas, groups of people, or sectors of the economy while providing pension funds with prudent investments.

Furthermore, prudent investment in ETIs is to create jobs, housing, and improve the general infrastructure, and serves the broad interests of the beneficiaries of the System. By strengthening the State's economy and the well-being of employers, ETIs help promote the continued maintenance of employer contributions to the California Public Employees' Retirement System (CalPERS).

The Board will consider the secondary objective of promoting economic growth and well-being in the state of California and its localities when not in conflict with the Board's duties of loyalty, care, skill, prudence, diligence, and diversification. The emphasis will be on the promotion of long-term sustainable economic, industry and business growth, job creation and affordable housing.

All ETI investments shall be consistent with Board's fiduciary obligations and approved investment policies and guidelines.

Purpose

For purposes of this policy, an ETI shall be defined as an investment which has collateral intent to assist in the improvement of both national and regional economies, and the economic well-being of the state of California (the state), its localities and residents. Economic stimulation includes job creation, development and savings, business creation, increases or improvement in the stock of affordable housing, and improvement of the infrastructure.

General

A consistent and methodical means of evaluating all ETI opportunities is of paramount importance. ETIs are not uniform in structure, method or objective. Consequently, a policy to evaluate risk, return and liquidity characteristics must be established to assure that these investments are comparable on a risk/return basis with more traditional opportunities and are consistent with the financial requirements of CalPERS.

The lack of homogeneity of these instruments, likewise, makes ETIs difficult to market on a large-scale basis. Each ETI must be separately evaluated based on its unique structure and potential in accordance with CalPERS investment criteria and this ETI policy. This will ensure that all CalPERS responsibilities and investment requirements are being addressed in the evaluation and investment process.

The existence of this ETI policy shall not be construed as a mandate to invest in ETIs, but rather should be viewed as an additional set of suggested parameters within which to consider such investments.

Investment Approach and Parameters

The Board's constitutional duties, as defined and clarified by the recent amendments to California Constitution Article XVI, Section 17, take precedence over any other considerations. Any other considerations will be entertained only when not in conflict with any of these duties. It is recognized that investments made for the sole benefit of the System's beneficiaries may also generate collateral benefits.

CalPERS will only consider ETIs which, when judged solely on the basis of economic value, would be financially comparable to alternatively available investments. Comparability will be judged on a risk-adjusted basis, with CalPERS willing to accept no less in return and incur no additional risk or cost.

The collateral benefits shall not be considered part of the return to CalPERS nor shall any improvement to the State's economy be considered part of risk reduction. The decision to make the ETI and consideration of its broader benefits may only occur after the investment is deemed acceptable to the fund exclusively on its economic investment merits.

Any benefit an ETI may confer on other interests (the "targets") is not the responsibility or with the ability or control of CalPERS, but only of those who manage or are otherwise responsible for the target enterprise. This will be made expressly clear to third parties and CalPERS beneficiaries.

For allocation purposes, ETIs will be included with similar investments that are free of economically targeted elements, and the combined assets will be subject to the Board's asset allocation guidelines, ranges and targets. Investments shall not be made so as to alter the overall risk/ return profile of CalPERS investments, which derives from CalPERS liability profile and funding level.

ETIs shall not materially alter CalPERS' approved allocation policies. Particular attention should be paid to the California representation in the CalPERS' portfolio. CalPERS' exposure to the State's economy, inclusive of investment in ETIs, at a minimum, shall generally be in line with California's representation in the eligible investment universe and consistent with the Board's fiduciary obligations.

ETIs must at all times conform to the laws, requirements, policies and procedures governing CalPERS.

ETIs shall receive the proper level of due diligence consistent with the type of investment product and portfolio classification. This due diligence, to be conducted by staff, designated outside consultants or advisors, shall at a minimum address:

- legal sufficiency;
- identification of any potential conflicts of interest;
- investment sufficiency—the standard for investment sufficiency shall be consistent with existing internal policies and practices of due diligence analysis for each specific asset type.

CalPERS may invest in ETIs so long as the Board has determined and can demonstrate that the investments properly discharge the Board's duties under the provisions of California Constitution, Article XVI, Section 17—namely, the duties of loyalty, care, skill, prudence, diligence, and diversification—and are consistent with the California Government Code statutes applicable to CalPERs (Cal. Gov't Code secs. 20000 et seq.). Consequently, all other economic objectives must necessarily be secondary to—and not impair—those duties imposed by the California Constitution and the CalPERS statutes.

Pursuant to the above criteria, consideration will be given in order of preference to those investments which may benefit:

- current and retired members of the California Public Employees' Retirement System;
- residents of the State of California;
- enterprises that operate for the benefit, support, and the employment of residents of the State of California; and
- enterprises that address the economic and social need of the United States residents with unique major representation in the State of California.

ETIs, whether in a stand-alone portfolio or incorporated with like investments which have no economically-targeted orientation, shall be priced at least at market prices and shall be subject to the applicable performance measurements.

Indiana Public Employees' Retirement Fund
Restatement of Investment Policy

The Board shall investigate alternative investment vehicles. Alternative investment vehicles may include, but are not limited to, venture capital, real estate, and private placements. Some may improve the Indiana regional economy. The Board may consider investing in these assets if, and only if, the vehicles meet all standards for prudent investments. These investments must satisfy all standards of diligence, skill, and risk-adjusted market return that apply to all other pension investments.

[Note: The following provisions from OMERS and PSPP deal with all non-marketable securities, not just ETI.]

Ontario Municipal Employees Retirement System
Valuing Investments Not Regularly Traded

5.1   Non-traded investments will be compared with a reasonable market proxy when one is available.

5.2   When a reasonable market proxy is unavailable, the investment is held at book value unless:

a. a subsequent (third party) financing has occurred; or

b. there has been a significant permanent financial or operating change in the company, in which case the value will be adjusted accordingly; or

c. the securities subsequently become public traded, in which case market values will be used.

5.3 In situations where none of the aforementioned valuations are applicable (i.e., venture capital, private placements, and real estate), a third party accredited appraiser or a valuation committee, made up of investment specialists and management, shall appraise the investment to current market values, using generally accepted valuation criteria.

5.4 Valuations of non-traded investments shall be reviewed periodically by the Audit sub-committee of the OMERS Board.

Public Service Pension Plan's Investment Policies and Procedures (January 2000)

10. The Method of, and the Basis for, the Valuation of Investments that are not Regularly Traded at a Public Exchange

It is expected that during the period covered by this Statement all investments will be either regularly traded at a public exchange or will be subject to the valuation provisions set out in a pooled fund or mutual fund trust indenture.

Investments which are not regularly traded at a public exchange, shall be valued as follows:

(a) Equities and Bonds: Average of bid and ask prices from two major investment dealers, at least once every calendar quarter.

(b) Mortgages: Unless in arrears, the outstanding principal +/- the premium/discount resulting from the difference between face rate and the currently available rate for a mortgage of similar quality and term, determined at least once every calendar quarter.

(c) Real Estate: A certified written appraisal from a qualified independent appraiser at least annually.

Appendix G: Conflict of interest

The following are examples of conflict of interest and disclosure provisions from the SIPPs of various pension plans.

College of Applied Arts & Technology (CAAT) Pension Plan

These guidelines apply to:
  d. the Board;
  e. the Investment Managers;
  f. the Custodian(s)/Trustee(s); and
  g. any employee or agent retained by the Board or by a person listed in (a) to (c) to provide services to the Plan or the Fund.

Conflict of Interest

Any person listed above must disclose any direct or indirect material association or material interest or involvement in aspects related to his or her role with regard to the Fund's investments that would result in any potential or actual conflict of interest.

Without limiting the generality of the foregoing, this would include material benefit from any asset held in the Fund, or any significant holdings, or the membership of the boards of any corporations, or any actual or proposed contracts.

Related Party Transactions

Any person listed above may enter into a related party transaction if:
  h. the transaction is required for the operation of the Plan and the terms and conditions are not less favourable to the Plan than market terms and conditions; or
  i. the securities of the related party are acquired at a public exchange.

Procedure on Disclosure

The person involved in the conflict must disclose the nature and extent of the conflict to the Board in writing, or request to have it entered in the minutes of a meeting of the Board upon first becoming aware of the conflict. The disclosure must be made orally if knowledge of the conflict arises in the course of a discussion at a meeting of the Board.

If the party does not have voting power on decisions affecting the Plan, the party may elect not to participate in the activities related to the issue in conflict, or the party's activities may continue with the approval of the Board.

If the party disclosing the conflict does have voting power, the Board may continue with respect to the issue in conflict only with the unanimous approval of the other members of the Board. In this situation, the party in conflict may elect not to participate with respect to the issue in conflict, but the party must not participate without the unanimous approval of the other members of the Board. The notification made by the party in conflict shall be considered a continuing disclosure on that issue, subject to any future notification by the party, for the purpose of the obligations outlined by the guidelines.

OPSEU (Ontario Public Service Employees Union) Pension Trust

These guidelines apply to:

j. any member of the Board;

k. the Manager;

l. the Custodian;

m.the Pension Consultant;

n. any employee or agent retained by those listed above to provide services to the Fund.

Conflict of Interest

All persons listed above must exercise the care, diligence and skill in their administrative and/or investment capacities that the ordinary prudent person would exercise in dealing with the property of another person. All persons listed above shall use all the relevant knowledge and skill that they possess in the administration and investment of the Fund.

All persons listed above shall at all times act in the best interests of the beneficiaries of the Fund and shall not knowingly permit their personal interests to conflict with their duty to act in the best interests of the beneficiaries of the Fund.

Without limiting the generality of the foregoing, any situation involving receipt of any benefit from any asset held in the Fund, or any significant holdings, or the membership on the Board of Directors of other corporations, or any actual or proposed contract, shall be considered a conflict of interest.

In order to avoid a potential conflict of interest situation, the Manager shall not knowingly, without prior written consent of the Board, make any investments in securities of his company or any affiliated companies.

Disclosure Requirements

All persons listed above shall fully disclose the particulars of any actual or potential conflicts of interest with respect to the Fund immediately upon becoming aware of the conflict. Without limiting the generality of the foregoing, such person shall disclose in writing to the Co-Chairs of the Board of Trustees the nature of his/her interest in any investment or transaction to be made or entered into by the Fund or on behalf of the Fund, forthwith after becoming aware that the investment or transaction is proposed for or has been entered into by the Fund or after such person becomes interested in the investment or transaction, as the case may be.

The Co-Chairs of the Board of Trustees shall arrange a meeting of the Board to discuss and resolve the outstanding conflict of interest situation as soon as reasonably possible. The person in conflict shall not participate in any discussion on the subject of the conflict nor participate in any vote on the matter, except insofar as the Board may call upon that person to provide a statement regarding the conflict of interest. All such proceedings shall be recorded in the minutes of the Board of Trustees meeting during which the conflict is discussed.

The Co-Chairs of the Board of Trustees shall advise the person with the conflict of interest forthwith of its remedial decision. That person shall act in accordance with the decision of the Board of Trustees subject to his/her right to seek the consent of the beneficiaries of the Fund.

Appendix H: Questions for selection and review of investment managers

The following questions are provided to *supplement* standard questions asked of investment managers in their selection and evaluation. They deal only with the issues of investment screening, ETIs, proxy voting, and shareholder activism.

General

- Are you willing to work as an agent pursuant to the *Pension Investment Standards Act*?
- Is your investment style compatible with the active trustee oversight and the inclusion of shareholder activism, proxy voting, investment screens and ETI?
- Are you able to comply (or to what extent have you complied) with the plan SIPP?
- Are you able to meet (or to what extent have you been able to meet) the plan's performance targets as identified in the SIPP?
- Are you willing to attend (or have you attended) no fewer than one Investment Committee meeting per year in addition to regular reporting requirements?
- Have you had experience working with clients who are interested in shareholder activism, proxy voting, screening, or economically targeted investment?
- How many staff do you have that are experienced with these investment practices?
- How many staff work in these areas within your firm?
- What research services do you (your company) use to help determine which stocks/bonds to buy? Would you change services or add services that use a socially responsible view to your research? If yes, what impact would this have on your (company's) decisions?
- How do you keep up to date on shareholder activism, proxy voting, investment screening, and ETI?
- What is your historical performance record with respect to screened investments?
- What have been the changes (significant) to the portfolio holdings since the last report, and why?
- Are you aware of any community action, environmental group initiative, labour dispute/boycott involving any of our holdings? If so,

what are they? Do you think this will have an impact on the value of our holdings? What, if anything, have you done to get management to deal with the issue?

- Does your company have socially progressive internal policies and practices? Can we see them?

Proxy Voting

- What is your (company's) policy with regard to evaluating and voting proxies? Do you always vote with management?
- Do you use a proxy voting service?
- Do you provide quarterly proxy voting reports?
- Have you ever or will you ever put a proposal to a shareholder meeting?
- Are you prepared to vote our shares differently if we so direct, either by following our proxy voting guidelines or on a case-by-case basis?
- How do you receive shareholder proposals?
- How does your firm handle those proposals and are you prepared to take direction and/or joint initiatives of the various socially responsible proposals put by other shareholders?

Screening

- Do you offer screened products?
- Are you willing and able to find appropriate screened investments or develop them if desired?
- Are you willing to work with the pension plan's screening criteria?
- How do you select benchmarks for screened portfolios that satisfy the fiduciary duty of prudence?

Economically-Targeted Investments

- Have you invested in "private placement infrastructure bonds"? If so, what is the project being financed? Is it an infrastructure bond or other bond that privatizes public sector services? If so, what do you think of this initiative? Are you aware of contradictory views? Why do you think a public sector pension plan should support privatization of public sector services (the plan's own membership)?

The above list includes questions from the CUPE publication "Pension Talk" - Bringing Union Values to Pension Investing, Vol. 1, Number 4: Questions For Your Money Manager(s).

Appendix I: SIPPS available on-line

The law requires that a SIPP must be provided to trustees and pension plan members upon request. The following SIPPs were available on-line as of April 2002. SHARE makes no representations as to the terms of the policies listed below.

California Public Employees Retirement System (CalPERS)
www.calpers.ca.gov/invest/policies/toc.htm

Canada Pension Plan
www.cppib.ca

Greater Manchester Pension Fund
www.gmpf.org.uk/invest/sip2001/default.htm

Manitoba Civil Service Superannuation Board's Statement of Investment Policies and Goals
www.cssb.mb.ca/sipg.pdf

McGill University Pension Plan
www.is.mcgill.ca/pensions/investments/Statement/stmt.HTM

McMaster University Contributory Pension Plan for Salaried Employees
www.mcmaster.ca/bms/policy/invest.htm

Missouri State Employees Retirement System (MOSERS)
http://www.mosers.org/html/investmentsinvest.html

Newfoundland and Labrador Teachers' Association Pooled Investment Fund
www.nlta.nf.ca/HTML_Files/html_pages/publications/handbook/invest.html

Ontario Municipal Employees Retirement System (OMERS)
www.omers.com

Ontario Teachers' Pension Plan
www.otpp.com/web/website.nsf/web/InvestmentStrategy

Pension Fund Master Trust Investment Policy (University of Toronto)
www.utoronto.ca/govcncl/pap/policies/pensionfund.pdf

Pension Plan for Academic Employees of the University of New
Brunswick
www.unb.ca/pension/content/unbipnov2000.pdf

Tyne and Wear Pension Fund (UK)
www.s-tyneside-mbc.gov.uk/Pensions/FundInvestmentPolicies.htm

State of Connecticut Retirement Plans and Trust Funds
www.state.ct.us/ott/pensiondocs/IPS010402-
Feb%2015%20draft2__.pdf

University Fund's Investment Policy (University of Toronto)
www.utoronto.ca/govcncl/pap/policies/investpolicy.pdf

University of Northern British Columbia Pension Plan Statement of
Investment Policies
www.unbc.ca/policy/pdf/bene-p4.pdf

University of Toronto Employees' Pension Plan of the Ontario Institute for Studies in Education (OISE)
www.finance.utoronto.ca/policies/oise.htm

University of Toronto Pension Fund
www.finance.utoronto.ca/policies/pension.htm

Notes

[1] This document is provided as a guide to assist pension trustees in developing their plan investment policies and procedures. It is not to be taken as legal advice. Pension trustees are strongly advised to seek independent legal and financial advice in developing their plan investment policies.

[2] Some jurisdictions refer to the investment policy statement as a Statement of Investment Policies and Guidelines (SIP&G). For the purposes of this document, reference to a SIPP includes all forms of investment policies created by statute.

[3] Persons acting as "trustees" are different for different types of plans. Pension legislation uses the term "administrator" to cover board of trustees, an employer, or a person appointed administrator of a plan by the Superintendent of Pensions or the Minister. In all cases, we use the term "trustee" to refer to the person(s) with ultimate responsibility for the plan's administration.

[4] The authors wish to express their gratitude to the many individuals and organizations that contributed to the development of this model document, especially our committee of reviewers including Darcie Beggs (Senior Research Officer, Pension and Benefits Specialist, Canadian Union of Public Employees (CUPE)), Clive Curtis (Senior Vice President, Morrison Williams Investment Management Ltd), Alf Ducharme (Ernst & Young Investment Advisors), Heather Gavin (Central Services Administrator, Ontario Public Service Employees Union (OPSEU)), Gary Goddard (Plan Administrator, Pension Plan for Employees of the Public Service Alliance of Canada), Michael Mazzuca (Partner, Koskie Minsky, Barristers & Solicitors), Harry Satanove (Satanove & Flood Consulting Ltd.), Karen R. Shoffner (Executive Vice-President, Castellum Capital Management Inc.), Brent Sutton (Vice President, Phillips, Hager & North Investment Management Ltd.), and Tony C.L. Williams (National Practice Leader, Asset Management Consulting, Buck Consultants).

[5] See for example *Pension Benefits Standards Regulations 1985*, SOR/87-19, s.7.1(1)(f); *Pension Benefits Regulations*, R.R.O 1990, Reg. 909, amended to Reg. 680/00, s.78(2).

[6] For Britain's regulation see *The Occupational Pension Schemes (Investment, and Assignment, Forfeiture, Bankruptcy etc.) Amendment Regulations 1999*, S.I. 1999, No. 1849 (29 June 1999). This is especially significant because the regulations contradict the earlier 1984 British case of *Cowan v. Scargill*, which has been interpreted in Canada to severely limit

application of social and environmental screens. The Financial Services Commission of Ontario issued a memorandum in February 1993 stating that the application of investment screens is not imprudent provided that it is permitted by the plan's SIPP and communicated to plan beneficiaries. This statement has since been rendered "obsolete" with the Province's adoption of the federal investment guidelines for pension plans under Schedule III of the *Pension Benefits Standards Act*, although the opinion has not been contradicted.

[7] For the purposes of this paper, ETI includes investments in small businesses, emerging technology sectors, housing and real estate, and local economic development and community economic development.

[8] The Council of Institutional Investors in the United States has compiled a three-volume set of SIPPs available to all pension plans.

[9] *Board of Trustees* v. *City of Baltimore*, 562 A.2d 720 (Md. 1989).

Canadian Centre for Policy Alternatives

Why some pension funds and labour-sponsored investment funds engage in social investment

An organizational analysis[1]

by Jack Quarter and Isla Carmichael

THE OBJECTIVE OF THIS CHAPTER IS TO UNDERSTAND WHY pension funds and labour-sponsored investment funds that engage in social investment are likely to do so. In other words, what are the dynamics that lead such funds in the direction of social investment and thus depart from the norm for pension funds and labour-sponsored investment funds in general?

This chapter builds upon an earlier study that attempted to understand the extent of social investment among union-based pension funds in Canada, as well as labour-sponsored investment funds, and also to understand the factors that affect social investment strategies among such funds in Canada (Quarter, Carmichael, Sousa & Elgie, 2001). For that study, a national sample of pension funds with assets of at least $50 million was drawn, using the *Canadian Pension Fund Investment Directory* (Toronto: Maclean Hunter), which lists 504 pension funds of that size. All of the funds were contacted and 189 (37.5%) agreed to participate. The sample also consisted of 10 labour-sponsored investment funds, half of that group in Canada.

The data indicate that pension funds in Canada have minimal social investment. The following eight items were used to address this issue:

- Does your fund have formal screens of ethical criteria for its investments?
- Has your fund withdrawn investments or boycotted particular investments (for example, tobacco companies) for social reasons?
- Has your fund invested in particular corporations because, in addition to their business performance, they also represent social values that you would like to support?
- Has your fund invested in other funds that emphasize social criteria (for example, ethical or environmental mutual funds)?
- Does your fund submit shareholder proposals?
- Has your fund invested in community economic development?
- Has your fund invested in regional economic development?
- Has your fund invested in affordable housing?

The range in the degree of agreement was from a high of 11.1% for the item on provincial/regional economic development to a low of 2.6% for the item, investing in other funds that emphasize social criteria. In other words, the responses to all items reflected a consistently low degree of social investment. Of the 189 pension funds in the sample, 130 (69%) responded negatively to all eight items on the Social Investment Index, and another 35 (18.5%) responded positively to only one. In other words, 87.3% of the sample either had no social investment or were in agreement with only one of the items on the Index. Considering that the fund managers who completed the survey might have sensed that the researchers viewed social investment as socially desirable, the mean of only 0.53 is remarkably low. At the opposite pole, only one fund responded positively to five of the eight items, and three others responded positively to four of the eight items.

While the degree of social investment was strikingly low for pension funds, it was somewhat higher for labour-sponsored investment funds. The data indicate that on average they responded positively to three of the eight social investment categories. When explored further, the data indicate that the difference between pension funds and labour-sponsored investment funds on the Social Investment Index is due largely to labour-sponsored investment funds that have genuine union sponsorship. That group had a mean of 4.6 on the Social Investment Index as opposed to 1.4 for the rent-a-union funds (those in which labour associations serve as a front for management groups).[2]

In other words, the scores on the Social Investment Index can be arranged on a continuum: pension funds, 0.53; rent-a-union labour-sponsored investment funds, 1.40; and genuine labour-sponsored investment funds, 4.60.

A second objective of this earlier study was to understand the factors that affected social investment strategies among such funds in Canada. In part, this appears due to the fund's mandate: whether the fund is for pension investment or whether it is a labour-sponsored investment fund, with its associated mandate to serve as risk capital for small- and medium-sized businesses. However, since genuine labour-sponsored investment funds are more likely to engage in social investment than the rent-a-union-funds, it appears that it is not simply the mandate of a fund but the attitude of the fund's sponsors (that is, unions) that is a critical factor in social investment.

There is some other evidence that union involvement is facilitative of social investment. (For example, for pension funds there is a positive correlation between union representation on the board and the Social Investment Index; a similar relationship exists for union representation on the investment committee.) However, we could not jump to the conclusion that union involvement, per se, is critical to social investment. If that were the case, we would have expected more social investment in general among these funds, given that all had a union membership. Moreover, we would have obtained a strong correlation between the percentage of a pension fund's members that are unionized and the degree of social investment, but that did not materialize.[3]

Nevertheless, it appears that it is not unions, per se, but having a supportive framework that influences whether or not an organization engages in social investment. For example, the question—"Did any of the sponsoring organizations take the lead in encouraging a social investment strategy?"—correlated positively with the Social Investment Index. Similarly, the attitude to social investment among the trustees/directors, senior management, and sponsoring organizations correlated positively with social investment, as was training of the fund's trustees/directors—not specifically for social investment, but training more generally.

It was probably not coincidental that, among pension funds engaged in at least some form of social investment, they were disproportionately located in Quebec, which seems to have a more supportive environment for this type of work. Both the major fund for public pensions, the Caisse de dépôt et placement du Québec, and the major labour-sponsored investment fund, Fonds de solidarité des travailleurs du Québec, have a mandate that ties them to provincial economic development and to the development of local communities within the province.

The mandate of the fund might be viewed as part of the supportive framework. Labour-sponsored investment funds have a mandate that appears more supportive of social investment than the mandate of pension funds. Among pension funds, one of the factors that correlated negatively with the Social Investment Index was conflict with fiduciary responsibility—a concern for pension fund managers. When compared to labour-sponsored investment funds, pension funds had significantly higher scores on conflict with fiduciary responsibility, concern about reduced rate of return, investment too high risk, and inadequate government incentives. These findings seem to support the view that the mandate for labour-sponsored investment funds is more supportive of social investment than that for pension funds.

In addition to looking at the factors that are related to social investment among the entire sample, the earlier research attempted to determine whether the small group of funds that had relatively high social investment scores had any distinct characteristics in relation to the overall data set. To make the group meaningful, only funds with a score of 4 or higher on the 8-point Social Investment Index were included. This group was limited to only seven funds: four pension and three genuine labour-sponsored investment funds. When profiled against the overall data set, there did not appear to be a distinct pattern to the characteristics of these seven funds. The only striking difference was a much higher score on the Attitude towards Social Investment item, indicating that the leadership and sponsors of those funds were more positive in their orientation.

The earlier study does not address in detail the dynamics of the seven funds that have high scores on the Social Investment Index. As noted above, with the exception of the strikingly high score on the attitude to social investment by the leadership of these organizations, their profile was similar to that of the other funds. This current study takes off where the earlier work finished by exploring in depth the dynamics of the pension funds and labour-sponsored investment funds that have some commitment to social investment. This investigation consists of two parts: first, a study of Concert Properties in British Columbia undertaken by Carmichael (2000), and, second, a study of five additional cases—three pension funds and two labour-sponsored investment funds that had a score of at least 4 in the earlier study described above (Quarter et al., 2001).

Concert

Concert, a real estate development company, is a classic example of economically targeted investment, one of the primary forms of social investment. Arguably, Concert is the outstanding example in Canada and one of the most outstanding internationally.

In the early 1990s, 26 pension funds in British Columbia pooled a small proportion of their funds—$30 million—and created a real estate development company to provide affordable rental housing. The recipients of these jobs, predominantly in the construction trades, pay into the pension funds that were investing in Concert. The project was initiated by the then president of the Telecommunication Workers of Canada, Bill Clark, and supported by the other unions. Union labour only worked for the development company. Concert Properties is now the largest developer of rental housing in Western Canada, with an asset base of $607,800. The company gains a good rate of return for its investors and works closely with local communities in its development projects.

To complement the work of Concert, a mortgage trust was created—Mortgage Fund One—that provides a portion of the financing for each project. Typically, Mortgage Fund One finances from 30% to 50% of each Concert project, the remainder coming from conventional sources such as banks. Mortgage Fund One's own statement of purpose makes it clear that it is not simply to provide financing for real estate development in British Columbia, but development "constructed by contractors whose employees are represented by approved unions under a collective agreement" (Mortgage Fund One, 1999).

Mortgage Fund One now has 45 investments with an approximate value of $353 million. Thirteen union pension plans in British Columbia invest in Mortgage Fund One, with the Telecommunication Workers making 57.4% of the investment and the Carpentry Workers nearly 10%. From 1993 to 1999, the rate of return ranged from 7.69 to 10.02.

In a typical development, Concert provides 20% to 25% of the equity. Of the remaining financing, two-thirds comes from the banks and one-third from Mortgage One (Carmichael, 2000). In total, 4.9 million hours of work have been created through Concert.

In her analysis of Concert, Carmichael (2000) argues that at least three factors account for its rise: leadership, support and expertise, and education. We shall discuss each of these in turn and then subsequently discuss to what extent these factors fit with the other cases that were studied.

Leadership

In Carmichael's research, union leadership was critical to the social investment strategy pursued through Concert. From the time that the plan for Concert was discussed with the British Columbia Federation of Labour, the key leaders have remained in place and others have joined. Initially, there was a lack of models to follow and skepticism about the plan within union circles, but it was possible to override these doubts because all of the leaders of Concert were well placed within the union movement.

Bill Clark, the president of the Telecommunication Workers and a trustee of that union's pension plan, exerted an almost visionary role in moving Concert forward. Another key player was Wayne Stone, the administrator of the Carpenters' Pension Plan.

Because Clark had a leadership role in both the union and the pension fund, he was well positioned to gain the necessary support from within his group. His potential influence was enhanced by the size of the Telecommunication Workers' pension fund at approximately $1.8 billion of assets. By using only a small percent of the assets, the Telecommunication Workers could still have a substantial stake in Concert and Mortgage Fund One and play a valuable role as the anchor fund.

For the Carpentry Workers' Fund, Stone lacked some of these advantages. The fund was relatively small at $200 million, and his role was strictly with the pension. However, there were mechanisms for sharing information between the union and pension fund, such as reports and resolutions at annual conventions and fairly constant contact. The trustees of the Carpentry Workers' pension fund, who worked closely with

Stone, were leaders of the union locals within their organization (Quarter, 1995).

Where there is little or no relationship between labour trustees and their union—and this is not an unusual circumstance (Carmichael, 1998)—it can be problematic for either the leaders of the union or the trustees to encourage social investment strategies for the fund. The union leadership is not party to the decision-making circle of the fund, and, without the union's support, the pension trustees are unlikely to take risks.

Clark attributed much of the success of Concert to the ability of the main players to build a new organization without political obstacles from their unions. For union trustees with the desire to innovate, it is very difficult without the support and resources of their union. In the survey by Carmichael (1998), trustees complained that they lacked this support and therefore have to rely on fund managers, thereby perpetuating the hegemonic approaches to investment. Ironically, the key players in creating Concert and Mortgage Fund One received no formal training from either their union or its pension fund.

An important feature of the leadership of Concert and Mortgage Fund One is that the Telecommunication Workers' Pension Plan served as an anchor with more than half of the investment. With 26 pension plans involved, having the anchor fund was a stabilizing force.

Support and expertise

Support and expertise can be subdivided into political and technical types of support, the latter more appropriately labelled as expertise. While leadership of strategically placed union officials was critical in getting Concert off the ground, without ongoing support from the broader movement it would have been very difficult for Concert to proceed. The trade union movement, particularly in British Columbia, played a critical role in policy development and general support of Concert, providing legitimacy to the work of a relatively small group of trade unionists that took the lead.

In British Columbia, the provincial Federation of Labour has shown positive, enduring, and informed support for Concert; its former president, Ken Georgetti (currently President of the Canadian Laobur Congress), sits on Concert's board of directors. Support from the Federation of Labour was not always there. Bill Clark nominated Ken Georgetti for president of the Federation, and he won in a hotly contested election resulting in the upset of the incumbent, Art Kube. This support has provided an important link to other trade unions as potential shareholders in Concert, and also solidified the support needed to ensure the long-term viability of the investment vehicles.

It is important to note that, for Concert to succeed, union trustees have had to win the support of employer trustees sharing their pension boards, an important exercise in alliance building. While the idea of Concert and Mortgage Fund One came from trade unionists, it was critical that they have the respect and support of their employer trustees.

Because of the dynamics normally associated with joint trusteeship, the relationship between employer and union trustees tends to be less combative than the adversarial process of collective bargaining. Joint trusteeship arrangements for pension funds tend to avoid decisions made by one side only, and instead attempt to make compromises that result in consensus (Carmichael, 1996). The process is not unlike other labour-management committee structures negotiated in collective agreements.

An important type of support was the technical expertise that was critical to Concert's effectiveness. Even unions with joint trusteeship of their pension plan face steep learning curves in participating effectively in plan administration and investment, as these forms of expertise are alien to the union experience. Since the dominant view of financial industry opposes social investment, it is difficult for union pension trustees to obtain fund management support for alternative investment strategies. A survey by the Canadian Labour and Business Centre underlines this point (Falconer, 1999).

To address this problem, Concert and Mortgage Fund One involved people with the necessary expertise: Bruce Rollick, an actuary, and David Podmore and Jack Poole, who are real estate developers, yet who were also union sympathetic and willing to work within the social investment mandate of those organizations. In Quebec, the Confédération des syndicats nationaux (CSN) faced a similar problem when, in 1987, it set up its own consulting group to assist union locals who wanted to organize worker cooperatives and also various forms of employee ownership (Quarter, 1995). However, through its networks, it was able to find a partner in a large Montreal accounting firm, who in turn brought in others with training in business planning and financial analysis, but who shared the union's mandate. For both Concert and the CSN, good referral networks were important in accessing the right types of expertise.

Although unions often are lacking in the expertise needed for social investment strategies, in Canada there is a growing cadre of expertise in labour-sponsored investment funds that can be shared with pension trustees. In the U.S., the Heartland Project, under the leadership of Leo Gerard, President of the United Steelworkers of America, involves a group of union pension trustees, international researchers and experts working on innovative, 'high-road' investment strategies for pension funds (Fung, Hebb & Rogers, 2001).

Education

While Concert and Mortgage Fund One hired experts who had the knowledge for technical decisions about investment and planning, the labour trustees involved in this project relied largely on their own training; that is, informal learning to get themselves up to speed for their role. However, those involved in this process have mentioned the steep learning curve to catch up with investment professionals, and the tendency to depend on fund managers for advice.

This inability to accesss knowledge about social investment strategies is exacerbated by existing training for pension trustees, which is provided primarily by the financial industry through the Institute for Fiduciary Education, an American educational institution that is corporate and anti-worker in its focus. Relying on this one institution reinforces hegemonic approaches to pension fund education and training.

Gradually, valuable resources on pension fund governance and investment are emerging for practitioners in Canada, but there is no institutional base for co-ordinating this work and for transforming it into an educational program that rivals that of the Institute for Fiduciary Education, but with a social investment focus. Rather, there is a loose-knit group of researchers, educators, and practitioners across the country. Select trustees find their way to some of these sources and gain the knowledge that they require, but it is very informal at this point.

Five additional case studies

In analyzing these five additional case studies, we have attempted to determine whether the factors that seemed critical to Concert's success were equally applicable, and if not, what factors were of importance. The sample consisted of three pension funds and two labour-sponsored investment funds, all of which scored relatively high on social investment in the survey referred to in the first part of this chapter and also reported in the study (Quarter et al., 2001). The pension funds were[4]:

The **United Church of Canada Pension Plan** was started in 1925; by 1998 it had 4,041 active members, 3,448 retired members, and $843 million of assets. The plan applies an array of social screens for "sin" stocks related to alcohol, tobacco, gambling, and armaments. It does this directly and also through investment in other funds (for example, the Domini 400 Social Index). This plan has also boycotted and even withdrawn from investments related to South Africa under apartheid.

The fund's members are also engaged in shareholder action strategies through participation in the Task Force on Churches and Social Responsibility, which the church took a leading role in creating. Its Corporate Responsibility Guidelines state:

> *In managing the Funds, the Investment Committee shall attempt to be consistent with stated church policies in regard to corporate social responsibility. In the belief that good social management is consistent with, and a part of, good business management, corporate social responsibility will be one of the normal tests in assessing corporations as eligible investments* (United Church of Canada, 1989, p. 1).

Ontario Northland Transportation Pension Plan, representing the employees of Ontario Northland Transportation (telecommunications, railroad, bus and marine transportation), has been operating since 1950. By 1998 it had 1,192 active members and 1,288 retired members in a small plan of $391 million. The fund's primary social investment is the development of communities in Northern Ontario, the region in which its members live. The fund's Statement of Investment Policies is very conventional: "The sole focus of the fund's investment policies and goals is to maximize the earned return without exceeding a reasonable level of risk."

However, within that constraint, the pension plan's treasurer, John Hayne, states that, in making its investments, the plan is mindful of community and regional development in Northern Ontario. It goes out of its way to purchase bond issues by Northern Ontario communities, with about 8.6% of its entire portfolio in such holdings. To illustrate this point, he indicates that, when he received a call from the mayor of Hurst asking the fund to purchase its million dollar bond issue, "we said, 'Yeah, we'll take it. Whereas if I got a call from Cornwall, where we don't service, I probably wouldn't be as willing to partake."

Montreal Urban Community Transit Commission Pension Fund, representing bus drivers, subway operators, maintenance workers and office staff, was started in 1956. By 1998 it had 7,200 employed members and 3,400 who were retired, and had assets of $2.2 billion. This fund has engaged in a variety of social investment strategies. It has a written policy about avoiding investments in armaments industries and child labour. Under apartheid in South Africa, it dropped Rothman's as one of its investments. The fund is an active participant in shareholder action strategies, exercising its proxy votes regularly.

Claude Dalphond, the director of the fund for 30 years until his recent retirement, emphasizes that, when the fund is concerned about a particular issue, "we deliver a message to the chairman or CEO with my card attached." This fund is also active in community and regional economic development by investing in "municipal bond issues of the municipalities in and around Montreal" and Government of Quebec bond issues. He argues that such investments have broader benefits.

Crocus Investment Fund is a labour-sponsored investment fund whose sponsoring organization is the Manitoba Federation of Labour. Crocus went to market in 1993, two years following its incorporation. In 1998, it had 22,500 investors and assets of $165.9 million. The Manitoba Federation Of Labour's interest in Crocus was inspired by the Solidarity Fund in Quebec, and was initiated by a resolution at its 1983 convention (Manitoba Federation of Labour, 1983). Crocus engages in a variety of social investment strategies. It applies social screens to its prospective investments for such criteria as workplace health and safety, environmental compliance, commitment to participatory management and employment equity (Crocus Investment Fund, 2002). This policy is written into the fund's enabling legislation, called "The Manitoba Employee Ownership Fund Corporation Act" (assented July 26, 1991). The name of the Act emphasizes another objective of the fund: to encourage "employee ownership in Manitoba businesses."

Crocus also invests in other funds that emphasize social criteria and also sits on the board of directors of its investments to ensure that acceptable policies are being enforced. As a labour-sponsored investment fund, Crocus is obliged to channel its investment into Manitoba, thereby making it an active participant in community and regional economic development. Again, this role is stated in the enabling legislation and in Crocus's Mission Statement, which the fund uses to promote its activities.

Working Opportunity Fund is a labour-sponsored investment fund whose sponsoring members are the British Columbia Federation of Labour and six B.C. unions. It has been operating since 1992, and in 1998 it had 34,000 members and assets of $167 million. The Working Opportunity Fund takes an active role in social investment strategies. Companies applying for funding are required to complete an Ethics Review that covers a number of exclusionary social screens such as tobacco, nuclear power, and military (Working Opportunity Fund, 2002). The review also screens for environmental compliance, employee relations (for example, health and safety, work stoppages, company benefits, and attitude to unionization), community relations, employment equity, and human rights.

The Working Opportunity Fund is actively engaged in community economic development, not only through its mandate requiring that it invest in British Columbia, but also through the creation of small pools of capital around the province that are managed directly by the local community. The Working Opportunity Fund helped to create the Shareholder Association for Research and Education (SHARE), and supports its efforts at shareholder action strategies (for example, the child labour campaign against Hudson's Bay and Sears).

Critical factors in social investment

Each of these cases is different. The pension funds are constrained by fiduciary trust rules that to a degree colour their investment policies; the labour-sponsored investment funds are pools of risk capital, but do have to attract investors who are concerned about their rate of return. This section is organized around each of the factors that Carmichael (2000) argues were critical to Concert's success: leadership, support and expertise, and education. We shall look at these five additional case studies within the context of each of these factors, and then turn to a more general discussion as to whether additional factors are needed to account for why some pension funds and labour-sponsored investment funds engage in social investment.

Leadership

For each of these funds, there was at least one leader in a pivotal role who encouraged and sustained social investment, as manifested in the fund's activities. For the Working Opportunity Fund, David Levi (the CEO since the fund's inception) had a prior history in social investment, as the founder of the Ethical Growth Fund (Canada's first socially screened fund) when he was the chairman of the VanCity Credit Union. Ken Newman, the current chairman of the Working Opportunity Fund and the Western Director of the United Steelworkers of America, acknowledges the importance of Levi's background: "His [Levi's] social thinking was also an important element when we decided to make David the CEO."

In fact, the elaborate set of screens applied to prospective investments by Working Opportunity Fund is heavily influenced by the Ethical Growth Fund. Yet, for the Working Opportunity Fund, it would be too simplistic to attribute the initial leadership to Levi alone, a point that he makes also: "The labour movement was very heavily involved in the startup of the fund." The sponsoring organizations, as mentioned, were the British Columbia Federation of Labour and six major unions in that province. The first chairman of the fund was Ken Georgetti, then the president of the B.C. Federation of Labour and currently President of the Canadian Labour Congress. Therefore, while Levi was a key player in shaping the social direction of the fund, he was selected by the British Columbia labour movement because it wanted the Working Opportunity Fund to engage in social investment and it appreciated his track record in that regard.

For Crocus, there is a similar pattern to the Working Opportunity Fund. Crocus, as noted, also took a strong social investment direction, but one of its unique features was the emphasis on employee ownership and worker cooperatives. The enabling legislation, titled "The Manitoba Employee Ownership Fund Corporation Act," highlights this emphasis. This direction wasn't coincidental; a key player in the fund since its feasibility analysis prior to its founding is the current executive director, Sherman Kreiner, who was a Philadelphia-based social activist and the executive director of PACE, with a mission to "develop and maintain employee-owned businesses in the mid-Atlantic region" (Manitoba Federation of Labour, 1990).

Rob Hilliard, the president of the Manitoba Federation of Labour and the chairman of Crocus since its inception, acknowledges Kreiner's influence: "Sherman's influence was considerable. And he was very much inspired by the worker co-op system in Mondragon [the Basque region of Spain] and in many ways looked around for some opportunities to do something like that."

Kreiner's initial involvement with Crocus was through a federal grant arranged by the Canadian Cooperative Association and involving a Toronto-based group, the Worker Ownership Development Foundation, whose mission was to encourage democratic forms of employee ownership. Kreiner was hired through that grant, and the feasibility analysis for Crocus (not yet named as such) came from that grant (Manitoba Federation of Labour, 1990).

However, like the Working Opportunity Fund, it would be too simplistic to focus on Kreiner only in discussing the leadership of Crocus. Prior to Kreiner's involvement, the Manitoba Federation of Labour passed a resolution that "the Manitoba Federation Of Labour investigate the possibility of implementing a Solidarity Fund in Manitoba that is similar to the Quebec Federation of Labour program" (Manitoba Federation of Labour, 1983, p. 1). The initial resolution of September, 1983, did not give the fund a direction, that coming from Kreiner. However, the leadership of the Manitoba Federation of Labour did embrace that direction and did go after Kreiner as the executive director of Crocus. From the beginning, the then president of the Manitoba Federation Of Labour, Susan Hart-Kulbaba, was behind Crocus, as were other key leaders within the federation. She and other leaders of the federation were able to win the support of the membership for Crocus and the direction that was proposed by Kreiner.

Unlike Working Opportunity Fund and Crocus, which are labour-sponsored investment funds and whose set-up is guided by the requirements of that program, the next three cases are pension funds and have come about for different reasons. The Montreal Urban Transit Commission Pension Plan was under the leadership of one man, Claude Dalphond, for 30 years. Although he worked with a board of trustees and a investment committee, both he and his successor at the helm, Claude Kettie, make it clear that the social investment direction of the fund came from Monsieur Dalphond. Dalphond acknowledges that many years earlier a union leader (now retired), whose members were part of the fund, had pushed a social direction for the fund's investments. However, as the current leader, Claude Kettie, indicates, it was "Mr. Dalphond who was instrumental in this [social investment]".

For the Ontario Northland Transportation Pension Plan, John Hayne, the director, works closely with his investment committee and advisors, but within the fund's policy goal to "maximize the earned return without exceeding a reasonable level of risk," it is he who uses his discretion to invest heavily in bond issues in Northern Ontario, where the fund's members reside. Hayne agrees that he operates with a lot of latitude. Through his social networks, he is contacted by mayors in Northern Ontario, who ask: "Would you like the issue? And we've said, 'Yes, we'll take it.' …It is not a formal kind of thing. Like Monsieur Dalphond, as manager of the fund, he has the discretion, as long as he operates within the fiduciary requirements.

The United Church of Canada Pension Plan has had a different pattern than the four aforementioned funds. For the plans of the Ontario Northland Transportation Commission and the Montreal Urban Transit Commission, senior management initiated the direction and has operated with a relatively free hand. For the labour-sponsored investment funds, Working Opportunity Fund and Crocus, the initial leadership came from the sponsoring labour federations, but within that context, the particular pathways towards social investment came from the director of the fund. If placed on a continuum, the United Church of Canada Pension Plan would fall more closely toward the labour-sponsored investment funds, but it differs in that its plan members have pushed strongly the social investment direction. The fund's leaders have responded to that pressure and have shaped it.

The members of the plan are the employees of the church, including its clerics, and generally they are people with strong convictions about investments in alcohol and tobacco, and more recently, against gambling and armaments. According to Steve Adams, who is the church's General Secretary of Finance, and in that role responsible for its investments, including the pension plan: "The Church, because of its Methodist roots, has a long-standing prohibition against holding any funds that are invested in the alcohol and tobacco sectors. More recent to that, the Church has taken some strong stands against gambling and the military armament industries."

Moreover, the pressure to uphold these traditions comes from the grassroots: "We get people who write letters that say they're are upset this has happened with XYZ corporation; do we hold funds [in it], and if we do, why?" Operating within that context, he and his predecessor, Bill Davis, made investments that avoid companies in those sectors and to invest in socially screened mutual funds, such as the Domini 400 Index.

Davis (1959-1991) took an active role in shaping the pension plan's pathway within the overall direction demanded by the Church: "When Consumers Gas merged with Hiram Walker, we simply got out...Lockheed was a major player in the airlines industry and a good percentage of its income came from armaments; it just was never considered."

In addition to applying social screens, Davis led the pension plan's involvement in shareholder action strategies, initially in response to apartheid in South Africa and the fascist coup in Chile in 1973. He was an active participant in the formation of the Task Force on the Churches and Corporate Responsibility in 1975, through which churches initiated actions against corporations involved in South Africa, Chile, and more recently, harming the Aboriginal way of life and the environment (Task Force on the Churches and Corporate Responsibility, 2002). In March, 1989, the United Church of Canada's Investment Committee issued Corporate Responsibility Guidelines that have continue to shape its investment practices (United Church of Canada, 1989).

Therefore, for all five plans, leadership has played a crucial role in shaping the direction of investment policies and practices. For the United Church, it could be argued that the grassroots pressures are so strong that the leaders operate with limited degrees of freedom. It would be difficult to imagine a leader who did not embrace social investment surviving as head of the United Church of Canada's Pension Plan.

In contrast, for the Ontario Northland Transportation and Montreal Urban Transit Commission Pension Plans, there is no particular grassroots pressure and no formal policy for social investment. Therefore, with a change of leadership, that direction could be at risk. For Crocus and Working Opportunity Fund, the directors have worked closely with the sponsoring organizations to shape a social investment direction that has become institutionalized. Unlike the United Church, this direction is institutionalized at the level of the leadership, not at the grassroots of the sponsoring unions.

Support and expertise

For all of these investment vehicles, the leadership required ongoing political support and assistance from technical experts in order to sustain their policies. For Working Opportunity Fund, the political support was embedded in the board of directors, consisting largely of the labour leaders in British Columbia. Of the 15 board members, eight are labour leaders in British Columbia, from such organizations as the British Columbia Federation of Labour, the B.C. Government and Service Employees Union, and CUPE (Working Opportunity Fund, 2001). In addition, the board also consists of representatives from the business community, and senior management and the investors elect two others. The unions represented on the board were the sponsors of the fund, hired Levi as the CEO, and also worked with him to give the fund its direction. Therefore, the fund has been embedded in a labour context from its inception; even though participants on the board change, from an organizational perspective, the system of support has remained relatively constant.

A fund of this scale, however, requires a management team with appropriate expertise. Each investment proposal is subjected to "due diligence;" that is, a detailed analysis. Since these investments are not in publicly listed companies, it takes extensive research to compile the necessary information for taking an investment decision. In addition to Levi, there are eight senior vice-presidents of investment, each with specialized knowledge and training, a controller who is an accountant, and a counsel who is a lawyer (Working Opportunity Fund, 2001). In addition, there is a nine-person advisory committee of experienced business people who provide the board with feedback on investment proposals.

Ken Newman, the current chair of the board, emphasizes the important role of the advisory committee when the board is taking a decision about an investment proposal: "We listen to the presentation and then we ask for their recommendation. Then we excuse those individuals who have given the presentation and survey the Board to see if they approve. If they approve, it goes to the Investment Committee of the Board." Emphasizing the importance of the Advisory Committee's role, Newman adds: "We have never had a situation where the Advisory Committee said, 'No, it's not a good investment,' and then it came to us [the Board]. It has always been consensus."

Like Working Opportunity Fund, Crocus Investment Fund is embedded in a supportive labour environment that originally sponsored the fund. The chair of the board, Rob Hilliard, is the president of the Manitoba Federation of Labour. Five major affiliates of the Manitoba Federation of Labour also have representatives on the board. In addition, there is a representative of the government, two representatives of the individual shareholders, and one other of the institutional shareholders. That is the collective political support framework in which the fund functions. Sherman Kreiner, the executive director, states: "Each evaluation of an investment is done by the board, each is approved by the board."

As with Working Opportunity Fund, there is a separation between the board's role and that of senior management. This same separation between the board representing the members and the investment advisors exists for the pension plans. For the Montreal Urban Community Transit Commission Pension Plan, there is a 15-person board of trustees who can vote, with seven from the labour side (primarily representatives of the unions) and eight representing the employer. Five of this group constitute the Investment Committee. There are seven professional staff, each a specialist on a particular portfolio.

Unlike a labour-sponsored investment fund, pension funds generally make equity investments in publicly traded companies with evaluative information in the public domain. They also use an external brokerage house for advice. However, the dynamic is similar: the professional staff bring the proposals forward to the board for approval. Monsieur Dalphond is quite candid about this: "I was management and … it's management that comes with the proposition." He adds, facetiously, "I didn't have to break any arms. The environment was totally supportive."

As a pension plan, Ontario Northland Transportation is relatively small with about $390 million of assets. There is a board of nine members and an Investment Committee of three. John Hayne, the fund's manager, reports to the Audit and Finance Committee of the Commission, which oversees the fund. Hayne operates within the fund's Statement of Investment Policies, based on standard fiduciary criterion: "The sole focus of the fund's investment policies and goals is to maximize the earned return without exceeding a reasonable level of risk...No non-investment-related criteria should be considered." However, as noted, within that constraint, he, with the approval of his overseers, makes it a policy to give preference to bond issues from Northern Ontario municipalities. The term "social investment" is never used, but to a degree it enters into the practice.

Whereas social investment depends upon executive discretion for the pension plans of Ontario Northlands and Montreal Urban Transit, for the United Church of Canada the pressure is from the grassroots, with management wrestling with the practical implications of that pressure. For management, the investment decisions have to be based on more than principles. Steve Adams, the United Church's Chief Officer of Finance, is the chief trustee of the pension plan and is an accountant by training. Adams emphasizes that the 14 members of the Investment Committee "all have expertise in various specialties. Some of them are equity specialists; some are fixed-income specialists; or they have retired from similar positions where they have managed funds. They are investment professionals in one shape or form...Right now, the people who are on the Investment Committee, or on the trustees, all have backgrounds in either pensions, investments, or accounting."

While the internal dynamics of the United Church pension plan are similar to the other funds that were studied—that is, experts making a recommendation to a board of trustees—this plan is unique in that, on particular issues, management may experience pressure from the Church and its members. On the issue of withdrawing investments from South Africa under its apartheid regime and the more recent Talisman investment in Nigeria, there have been disputes between the management of the pension plan and the Church, with management eventually giving in to Church pressure. However, Adams indicates that, in general, management of the pension plan and the Church are on the same page. For the past four years, he states, he can't think of any disagreements with the Church.

Education

Of the five funds that were studied, none engaged in education of its membership with respect to social investment polices. The two labour-sponsored investment funds in the study conducted public education, but that might be viewed as a form of promotion for their shares. Crocus also set up a certificate program at the University of Manitoba to promote participatory management, as part of its social agenda of encouraging employee ownership.

Of the pension plans that were studied, the only one with an active membership with respect to investment issues was the United Church of Canada. However, the plan's leadership do not specifically conduct seminars about the investment policies. "We report to the members annually, but as far as education as to investments, I can't say that's happened." In defence, Steve Adams feels that it isn't necessary: "The people are involved in the Church; it's like a given."

Where education occurred, it was directed at lay members of the board of trustees, and in some cases, lay members of the investment committee. The pension plan of the Montreal Urban Transit Commission stands out in this regard. According to Monsieur Dalphond, the fund hired a consultant at $40,000 per year to work with the union members of the board. Moreover, he adds: "In order to make things easy, we decided why not bring your advisor to the meetings of the Investment Committee? It made them feel secure."

Crocus and Working Opportunity Fund do not go to such an extreme, but they do have an orientation for new members of the board. At the United Church, the members of the board typically bring expertise in investment. The plan is to expand the trustees to include Church members without business experience. Adams indicates that, if this plan proceeds, "there will be people who do need the education and we have talked to some consultants about developing a package for us."

Concluding observations

From these case studies, it appears that leadership is the critical factor in whether or not these funds adopt any social investment practices. Of the pension plans that were studied, only in the United Church was there grassroots pressure for social investment. In the other two pension funds, social investment occurred largely at the leave of the principal leader. Although the leaders were accountable to a board, as long as they met fiduciary responsibilities for the rate of return, they were given a relatively free hand.

At Northlands Transportation, John Hayne agrees that he has a lot of latitude as long as the rate of return is good: "We are essentially a 'buy and hold' kind of fund; we don't actively manage the bond fund." Hayne reports at least twice a year to an Audit Finance Committee. Although he is engaged in social investment with respect to his preference for bond issues from Northern Ontario communities, this practice does not create controversy. In fact, Mr. Hayne does not even view his practice as social investment. To him, it is simply good investment practice that is consistent with his fiduciary responsibilities. With a change of leadership, it is questionable whether the social investment practices would be sustained.

At the Montreal Urban Transit Commission, Claude Dalphond was conscious of engaging in social investment. Unlike the United Church, there was no grassroots pressure for this, nor was there any great resistance; in his words, "I didn't have to break any arms." Moreover, unlike Ontario Northlands, Monsieur Dalphond did formalize policies with respect to not investing in corporations engaged in child labour and armaments. He acknowledges that, for particular types of investments, such as Montreal bonds, "we're not looking for the maximum financial return, provided we get a decent return like 8%." He recognizes the collateral benefits of such investments for the members of the plan: "The employees' money would be put to work with normal return, but towards building parks, building streets, creating infrastructures in the places where they lived. So their own money is working for them."

Monsieur Dalphond's successor, Claude Kettie, worked with him for 13 years. He, too, defends the investment policies of the fund, noting proudly that the rate of return was 12% in 1999 and nearly 10% in 2000, when the economy was in decline. It is not clear that he will continue with the exact same practices as Monsieur Dalphond. Nevertheless, he defends those decisions, including the fund's heavy investment in Quebec bonds. Therefore, even though leadership is also an important aspect of the direction taken by this fund, the direction is partially institutionalized and operates with support.

For the two labour-sponsored investment funds, leadership also has been important in the specific paths that have been taken, but the leadership goes beyond the individuals who head the funds and involves the sponsoring unions and their leadership as well. The sponsoring unions were not experts in investment, and neither did they establish the social investment policies. However, they created a framework that was sympathetic—that is, fertile ground for the leaders (David Levi and Sherman Kreiner) to operate—and they sanctioned and supported the specific social investment policies that the leaders created. Therefore, more than at Ontario Northlands and Montreal Urban Transit, social investment at the Working Opportunity Fund and Crocus represented a collective effort. As such, even with a change of leadership, it is likely that the social investment policies would be sustained.

Of the funds that were studied, including Concert, the United Church of Canada is distinct because the pressure for social investment came from the membership. The leadership of the fund has responded to that pressure, but has also shaped the direction. Steve Adams's predecessor, Bill Davis, was an activist as Senior Financial Officer from 1959 to 1991. He took a leading role in formulating the fund's shareholder action strategy and its Corporate Responsibility Guidelines. Steve Adams has been less of an activist, but nevertheless has followed the same direction. But he laments the complexity surrounding decisions about social investment: "It was probably a lot easier in the 1960s, but now, with all the crossholdings, even good companies probably have a little operation that isn't the best from a labour relations standpoint, for example." Nevertheless, these complexities notwithstanding, it might be expected that, of all these funds, the United Church's social investment direction would be the most secure. Yet the size of the fund has caused the board of trustees to seek external management to invest it. Adams confesses: "It is just too big to do in-house." Assuming that happens, it remains to be seen whether social investment policies will be sustained.

Therefore, size might be viewed as a complicating factor in social investment. As the size of a fund increases, outside management becomes more likely. With that, the influence of the grassroots and the sponsoring organizations may be less important.

Notes

[1] The research for this paper was funded by a three-year grant from the Social Sciences and Humanities Research Council of Canada. An earlier publication related to this project appeared in *Industrial Relations*, 2001, Vol. 56(1): 92-114.

[2] This has occurred in Ontario where the Ontario Federation of Labour couldn't reach agreement on whether to proceed with a labour-sponsored investment fund, and the provincial government let the door open to any union who wished to do so. Some groups that came forward had a questionable status as a union (for example, the Canadian Football League Players Association).

[3] The result was approaching significance, but not significant, suggesting that even though there is some evidence that union involvement is facilitative of social investment, other factors are of importance. This weak relationship may be attributable in part to the relatively small variance both among the Social Investment Index (69 per cent had no social investment) and the percentage unionized (since all of the funds in the study had some unionized members).

[4] Interviews were conducted with the principals of each fund referred to in this section. Where quotes are not otherwise referenced, they are taken from these interviews.

CHAPTER 5

It's our jobs, it's our money: A case study of Concert

by Isla Carmichael

IN CANADA, THERE ARE FEW EXAMPLES OF ECONOMICALLY targeted investment by union pension funds (Quarter, Carmichael, Sousa and Elgie, 2001). Therefore, union trustees interested in economic development have no case studies to guide them; nor, for the most part, do they appear to be in contact with experts with experience and advice in this area (Falconer, 1998). Finally. they receive no training in social investment or in economically targeted investment (Carmichael, Thompson and Quarter, 2001). This case study provides a model of a Canadian ETI for trustees and—hopefully—some encouragement to union pension trustees to begin to undertake economic development initiatives in Canada.

This chapter also tentatively proposes ways of measuring the social/ economic or collateral value of investments. There are no generally accepted tools available for trustees to measure collateral value. Yet trustees, as well as members of plans, want—and in some cases demand— non-financial information on their pension funds' investment. Such measuring tools are necessary if collateral value may be *a* reason for selecting an investment, as trust law suggests (Carmichael, 2000; Lane, 1991; Scott, 1987; Waitzer, 1991; Yaron, 2001; Zanglein, 2001).

Furthermore, existing accounting methods can be accused of disguising the real story behind an investment through their reliance on a narrowly constructed model supposedly based on calculating financial rates of return to the exclusion of non-financial criteria. A financial model excludes, for example, such collateral damage affecting the value of an investment as poor management practice (Baker and Fung, 2000; Bruyn, 1987), projected costs of environmental damage (Rubenstein, 1989), long-term estimates of the cost of privatized water services (Ogden, 1995), damage to pension funds through loss of jobs or lower pay for beneficiaries (Carmichael, 2000; Hebb, 2000; Baker and Fung, 2000), and economic impoverishment of workers and communities through privatization (Canadian Union of Public Employees, 2002; Kelsey, 1995, Minns, 2001).

It also excludes collateral benefits such as increase in jobs in a community (Calabrese, 2000), increase in fund contributions (Barber, 1982; Carmichael, 2000; Ghilarducci 1994; Quarter, 1995), effective risk management plans (Rubenstein, 1989), increases in government revenue through income, sales, and property taxes (Ellmen, 1996; Jackson and Lamontagne, 1995; Moye, 1997; Quarter, 1995).

This chapter argues that public policy should be based on a view of a social/economic return on investment or collateral benefit that extends to contributors, beneficiaries, the broader community, and government (Barber and Ghilarducci, 1993; Carmichael, 2000; Deaton, 1989).

Concert Properties (formerly Greystone)

In the late 1980s, 26 pension funds in British Columbia pooled a small proportion of their funds—$30 million—and created a real estate development company to provide rental housing. This project was initiated by the then president of the Telecommunication Workers of Canada, Bill Clark, and supported by a number of other unions. The development company was to use union labour only. Concert Properties is now the largest developer of rental housing in Western Canada. Concert, guided by criteria including self-sustaining community development as well as rate of return, works jointly with communities on massive neighbourhood redevelopment projects. In the year 2000, Concert Properties had a $450 million asset base. The company reports returns of 7.51% on its residential income properties and 8.75% on its commercial/industrial properties (Concert, 2002).

In 1968, as the new president of the Telecommunications Workers Union (TWU), Bill Clark negotiated the right to bargain pensions, and then joint trusteeship of the pension fund. Bruce Rollick, a young actuary working for union/employer pension funds at the time, was sent on the road to visit every local to explain the importance of pensions, of collective control of this large pot of money, and of a collective agreement and a trust agreement to prevent abuse of these funds by the employer. Membership involvement was crucial to back up negotiations with the employer and support the union in its new role as trustee of the fund.

Bill Clark was astonished when he learned of the large amount of money in the pension fund. He considered pension money "just different wages," even though the money was in a pension fund rather than a pay-cheque. He was strongly influenced by Peter Drucker's 1976 book *The Unseen Revolution*. He reasoned that, if other pension funds were similar, there must be a lot of money leaving British Columbia "because Ontario, Quebec, New York and places like that were better investments for fund managers." When interviewed by a reporter from the *Vancouver Sun*, some years later, he said:

> *You can only drain a community so long and too late you realize it has a serious effect on employment and that has a serious effect on (payments into) pension funds (Casselton, 1988).*

Both Clark and Wayne Stone, then administrator of the British Columbia Carpentry Workers' Pension Plan, attested to the continuing loss in B.C. of unionized employment in the construction trades. The percentage of union work on construction sites had been decreasing for years as developers used more and more non-union labour. Clark estimates now that the building trade unions are still only getting about 27% of the commercial construction work in British Columbia, and even less of the residential construction.

Construction workers, on average, are the lowest paid group of workers in the goods-producing industries, as reported by BCStats (Government of British Columbia, 2000), with gross weekly wages in 1998 of $723. This works out to be $20.67 per hour based on a 35-hour work week. This figure is based on predominantly non-union labour but combines union and non-union wages. By comparison, an average Concert construction wage is $33 per hour. Both rates are gross, including benefits and vacation. Getting control of pension funds, then, was a way for union members to fight union-busting in the construction trades in B.C. and create well-paid construction jobs.

Pooling pension funds and Company "A"

Clark's goal was to pull together a group of pension funds, and create a new fund where "nobody [had] to put in more than they're comfortable with, but you still end up with a huge pool of equity funds". The pool of money would not be directly managed by the funds, but by experts hired by the funds, to invest according to the policies established by the trustees.

First attempts at creating a model were too "all-encompassing, too complex, and scared people off". One model proposed was a trust company, funded by a multiplicity of pension funds with a board of directors to deal with real estate, mortgage funds, venture capital, and other financial services. Driven by a desire to own some of the B.C. corporations that were being bought up by foreign interests, this direction sought to use pension money to start buying up the B.C. corporate sector. This model, called Company "A", is shown in Figure 1. The model was developed by Bill Clark, then President of Telecommunication Workers' Union, Bruce Rollick, the union's actuary, and others to provide economic development from pension fund investment in B.C.

As a result of resolutions pushing for pension funds to be used to rebuild the B.C. economy and provide jobs for union members, the group was instrumental in getting a policy paper produced by the B.C. Federation of Labour entitled *A New Look at British Columbia's Economic Future*. Company "A" was to use union labour to make pension funds accessible as capital in the B.C. economy in a broad base of sectors. Pension funds would commit a certain percentage of their assets to the pooled fund.

The model laid the groundwork for the pension fund investment vehicles that were to be created. It illustrated a basic shareholder structure for larger and smaller pension funds, reserving the directorship for the larger funds, which could invest more. Company "A" was to be the management company of a number of specialized investment vehicles, designed to provide capital to different sectors of the economy. At the time, Company "A" was considered ambitious but still was approved by a number of unions. However, it ultimately failed to get the support of employer pension trustees (Baldwin et al., 1991). As Bruce Rollick later pointed out, this strategy did not fly with the employer trustees, since it often involved investing in competitors.

Finally, the new group settled on real estate "because you can build it, you can see it, and you can sell it". There was also a familiarity with real estate. Some of the building trade unions were already investing in construction, but were doing it individually. However, this was to be different. The idea behind the earlier Company "A" proposal of pooling small amounts of money from a number of pension funds to spread the risk was retained, as was the concept of a management company and investment vehicle.

One of the earliest projects was 424 Drake on Pacific Point in Vancouver. This project was called a "precedent-setting first joint venture" by the *Vancouver Sun* (Casselton, 1988) and financed by 13 separate pension funds, with no more than 2% of assets from each fund. It was a plan to construct residential housing in two phases: condominium and rental. The idea was for the sales of the condominiums to finance the rental accommodation.

Bill Clark and others recruited the support of trustees of the pension funds for the plan. Some of the unions that committed funds were the Telecommunication Workers' Union, the retail food and pulp and paper unions, carpenters, floorlayers, shipbuilders, electrical workers, and piledrivers. In 1988, each phase of the Pacific Point project was worth more than $14 million, with the long-term expectation of 14-15% returns. First, the mortgage on the land would be paid off by rental returns; once the mortgage was paid off, these payments would revert directly to the pension funds. In the meantime, returns were projected at approximately 9%. At this point, there was no management company.

Pension funds, affordable housing and rates of return

While many pension funds were still moving their assets into the stock markets, Clark and Rollick were arguing that long-term investment of 30 or 40 years in real estate was a perfect strategy for pension funds. They suggested a limit of 10% of their assets. This investment strategy could be put to best use in the residential rental market, where long-term ownership over a long period could stabilize rents and provide a stock of affordable housing in the Vancouver region.

Developers were (and are) reluctant to build rental accommodation. Building housing for sale provides immediate returns. Building rental accommodation is a longer term investment with low returns in the short-run unless the project is well capitalized. To avoid investment in the longer-term rental accommodation, developers have often sold rental buildings to get the immediate return. This has the consequence of increasing rents, since the new owner will gear the rents to the new purchase price. Pension funds could provide the guarantee of long-term investment, stabilized ownership and affordable rents, if government had the land for development and the pension funds gathered enough capital to fund the project.

To this end, in 1988, under Clark's leadership, five pension plans put together a real estate and property management company called Westcan, with employer and union representatives of jointly trusteed plans as shareholders. Westcan employed six experts in real estate development and property management. At the time, Clark said enthusiastically to the *Vancouver Sun*:

> *If we're able to pull this together, we'd have available $300-400 million without anyone having to put up more than 10% of their assets. The potential is absolutely staggering* (Casselton, 1988, p. D12).

Clark noted recently that "we had money and land, but nobody knew how to do anything." The new management team, led by Jack Poole, now Chair of Concert, was critical. A team of experts would put into action what the pension fund trustees had in mind.

Affordable housing was the leading criterion for development. The pension funds guaranteed that, in any given year, rents would not go up more than inflation plus 1%. The City of Vancouver had unused land, and the partnership was ideal. Led by Mayor Gordon Campbell, the council was enthusiastic about this new cooperative venture (Casselton, 1988).

The City of Vancouver was particularly interested in this partnership since Vancouver had been losing its stock of rental housing through demolition and conversion to condominium development. From April 1986 to October 1988, the vacancy rate in West End Vancouver was under 1%. There was "little prospect" of rental housing being built *without* the combination of capital from pension funds, land from the city, and the expertise of the management team assembled by the funds. The city agreed to be a 25% financial partner and create a new company. The city was to lease the land under long-term leases to the new company, and the new company would build and manage the rental housing.

However, the provincial government, led at that time by the Social Credit party, was not a supporter of this new proposal, nor was it a supporter of labour. It turned down the joint venture proposed by the City of Vancouver and the group of pension funds to make a bid on the Expo lands in downtown Vancouver. But in 1990, when a new government was elected, led by the New Democratic Party under Mike Harcourt, the province was willing to be connected to this new company, popularly known as the Vancouver Land Corporation, but called VLC Properties. The province was prepared to contribute five-year mortgage subsidies under its rental supply program. Westcan was eclipsed by VLC.

Incorporated in May 1989, VLC Properties had a mandate to provide economically priced, multi-family rental and for-sale housing in B.C. at a reasonable rate of return to shareholders. It was a remarkable collaboration of business, labour and government. With an initial capitalization of $27.3 million, the company had as shareholders the province, the City of Vancouver, pension funds, and private interests. The pension funds owned 75% of VLC, with capital invested of $20.5 million.

The VLC's objectives were to provide quality, economically priced housing and job creation for skilled, unionized labour, with reasonable rates of returns (Greystone Properties Ltd, undated). The City provided the land on long-term leases, and the pension funds were to put up the capital and expertise to build and manage guaranteed rental housing. Pension funds would get their returns through rental income.

Table 3 illustrates the housing projects built on city-owned land by VLC, from 1990-1992. The table does not include later rental accommodation built by Concert on city-owned land. In total, 460 rental units were built with the land for a cost of approximately $35.5 million. It is important to note that no property taxes were paid by VLC, since the land remained under the ownership of the city. Over this short period, almost 400,000 hours of on-site labour was used in the construction. Pension funds, most of them shareholders, gained over $1 million in additional contributions to their funds.

Table 3 illustrates that pension funds, for an original investment in VLC of $20.5 million, created in returns a total of $12.7 million in work, contributions to the health and welfare plans, and additional contributions to the pension funds. These returns are for the four projects which

Table 3: Construction of rental housing projects by VLC with land leased by the City of Vancouver 1990-1992

Project	# of rental units	construction date	total project cost	construction hard costs[1]	total labour component[2]	hours of on-site labour[3]	contributions to benefits plans[4]	contributions to pension plans[5]
Parkside Village	52	Jan-August 1990	$ 4,050,000	$ 3,550,000	$1,597,500	48,409	$72,614	$137,482
Fraser Pointe 1	177	Jun 90-Sept 91	$13,850,000	$10,600,000	$4,770,000	144,545	$216,818	$410,509
Cassiar Court	48	Jan-Sept 91	$4350,000	$3,250,000	$1,462,500	44,318	$66,477	$125,864
Fraser Pointe 2	183	Apr 91-Jun 92	$13,200,000	$10,750,000	$4,837,500	146,591	$219,886	$416,318
Total	460		$35,450,000	$28,150,000	$12,667,500	383,863	$575.795	$1,090,173

Source: Extracted from 'Concert Properties from 1989 to 1999'; 'Summary of company activities, December, 1999' (Concert Properties, 1999).

Notes 1. Construction hard costs represent labour costs as well as construction materials purchased for the construction project.

2. The total labour component is the amount of hard costs spent on on-site labour (i.e. hard costs minus materials equals labour). This figure is the equivalent of gross pay, before deductions for taxes, vacation and benefits.

3. Hours of on-site labour is calculated on an average rate of pay of $33 per hour.

4. Contributions to benefit plans are calculated based on an average rate of $1.50 per hour deducted from pay for health and welfare.

5. Pension fund contributions are calculated based on an average rate of $2.84 per hour deducted from pay.

were to remain in VLC. Another way of expressing these gains is that, for every dollar of investment, 62 cents came back in returns in the form of work and contributions to health and welfare and pension funds. On increased pension fund contributions alone, pension funds made returns of 5.3% on their original investment[1].

The provision of rental housing capitalized by pension funds with land leased from the City of Vancouver has been extremely successful. In fact, David Podmore, the Chief Executive Officer of what was to be Concert—in an interview in 1999—reported that 80% of the rental housing built in Vancouver since 1989 was built by Concert. Moreover, VLC met its target of not increasing rents beyond inflation plus 1%.

However, the actual rate of return resulting from these investments was reduced because the pension funds did not provide 100% of the capital that was required to build the units. The company, therefore, had to have mortgage debts on the properties, at the high borrowing rates that existed in the early part of the 1990s. While the decision to mortgage was vehemently opposed by Clark, shareholders did not have the confidence to inject more pension fund capital into the company. Employer trustees were not prepared to invest a higher level of capitalization. Podmore described the lack of capitalization as generated by "a new initiative and a natural reluctance to go too far at the outset". Clark, however, has said that:

> we don't like paying any profits to the bank. But that has always been the feeling in my union. That it's nuts to build a beautiful property and then borrow from the bank (Interview with Bill Clark and David Podmore, April 1999, p. 7).

This experience, for Clark, formed the genesis of the concept of Mortgage Fund One, which will be described later in this chapter.

Structure of the company

When VLC Properties was originally structured, Podmore estimates that 29-30 pension plans were investors. There were also 20-22 private investors, including the City of Vancouver and the provincial government. Included in the private group were the Bank of Montreal, Toronto-Dominion Bank, several major property developers, and some business people in the community. He described the company as follows:

We really set three goals for the company and they were laid out in the offering. Obviously, the company was created with a social purpose, which was to address the housing needs at the time with the creation of rental housing. Secondly, [the company was] to generate a return on the invested pension capital over a long term. There was a deliberate emphasis to caution everyone that this was a very long-term investment, rather than an immediate return. And the third objective was to create employment, union-only employment. We're a union builder, we build on an all-union basis (Interview with David Podmore, April, 1999, p. 3).

VLC Properties was restructured in 1992. There were a number of reasons for the restructuring. First, Podmore, Clark and Rollick reasoned that a pension fund investment mechanism should not be taxable. A company of pension funds and others as shareholders could not qualify for tax exemption.

Further, the *Income Tax Act* only allowed for pension fund investment in real estate development if the company were established before 1978. The reason that this ruling came about is that during the 1970s a number of Ontario pension funds invested in real estate as active builders. Real estate development companies fought this competition by successfully lobbying the federal government to change the *Income Tax Act* to restrict pension funds to buying existing real estate only. Pension funds with companies registered before 1978 were exempt.

To guarantee fiduciary responsibility, the pension funds themselves needed a shield from the liabilities of real estate development. While they insisted that quality work was a natural outcome of union labour, civil suits were always a possibility. Given the proliferation of "leaky condo" suits in B.C., they could not put members' pension benefits at risk. A company that dated pre-1978, called Collingwood, was found and purchased from the Air Canada pension fund. The company, re-named Greystone, was registered as a pre-1978 company under section 149 (1) (o.2) of the *Income Tax Act.*

It was clear that more capital was needed and that the capital would come from pension funds rather than private investors. The company was to be restructured as a tax-exempt real estate development corporation, provided it was wholly owned by pension funds. This made it possible to raise capital from pension funds only. On restructuring, the company went from $27.3 to about $80 million. One later additional offering took the company to $128 million.

At this point in 1992, most of the land owned by the City of Vancouver had been developed. VLC Properties had completed four major buildings with the City of Vancouver on the leased land. To avoid tax penalties, these buildings (and their management) remained with VLC, which was re-named VLC Leaseholds and retained the same ownership structure. Shares were valued at $5.00, and shareholders were repaid $4.75 of their original share capital. They continued to hold shares valued at 25 cents, which in 1999 were worth approximately $1.60. The long-term mortgages went with the new company. Returns therefore have been "substantial" on the four buildings. Pension funds transferred the share capital returned to them into the new company at a dollar a share.

The new company had only pension funds as shareholders. The larger pension funds were represented on the Board of Directors and the Board also retains to the present day the President of the B.C. Federation of Labour as a member. If VLC was a remarkable alliance of business, labour and government, Greystone was an equally remarkable multi-sector collaboration across labour.

Pension fund investment

The new company, Greystone, was to exist in the form of two companies, Greystone Real Estate Corporation and Greystone Properties. This enabled the pension funds, through the company, to both own and develop land. The name, Greystone, was challenged in 1995 by Greystone Capital Management, an investment management company based in Saskatchewan. To overcome this problem, the new name—Concert—was formally adopted in 1999. The shareholders' major investment is in Concert Real Estate Corporation, effectively a holding company for equity and title of properties. Concert Properties Limited is a taxable corporation that exists to enable joint ventures with other groups besides the shareholder-pension funds.

Table 4 shows the percentage shares in both companies held by shareholders as of 1999. The shareholders are listed by sector. Clark has maintained that, for the model to work, there should be a large anchor pension fund to set the pattern for the other investor funds in terms of the proportion of funds it invests. His own fund, the Telecommunications Workers' Pension Plan (TWPP), is the anchor with investments of 40.78% of Concert Real Estate and 31.15% of Concert Properties. The

Table 4: Concert shareholders by sector (per cent)

Building trades	Concert Real Estate Corp.	Concert Properties Ltd.
Boilermakers' Pension Trust Fund	0.77	0.59
Bricklayers and Masons Pension Plan	0.30	0.23
Carpentry Workers Pension Plan of B.C.	3.54	2.70
Ceramic Tile Workers Pension Plan	0.14	0.10
Floorlayers' Industry Pension Plan	0.27	0.21
Gwil Industries	0.08	0.06
Heat and Frost Local Union 118 Pension Plan	0.46	0.36
Labourers Pension Plan of B.C.	0.39	0.30
Local 213 Electrical Workers' Pension Plan	3.10	2.37
Marine and Shipbuilders' Local 506 Pension Plan	0.15	0.12
Operating Engineers Pension Plan	2.32	1.77
Piledrivers, Divers, Bridge, Dock and Wharf Builders	0.23	0.18
Sheet Metal Workers (Local 280) Pension Plan	1.23	0.94
Shopworkers Industrial Union Local 1928 Pension Plan	0.17	0.13
Teamsters Canadian Pension Plan	3.61	2.75
Teamsters (Local 213) Pension Plan	3.06	2.34
The Plumbers Union Local 170 Pension Plan	1.13	0.87
Subtotal	**20.95**	**16.02**
Food Service		
Retail Wholesale Union Pension Plan and Trust Fund	2.73	2.09
United Food and Commercial Workers Union Pension Plan	11.25	8.59
Subtotal	**13.98**	**10.68**
Forestry		
Canadian Forest Products Ltd. Pension Master Trust Fund	4.89	3.74
Pulp and Paper Industry Pension Plan	11.06	8.45
The Trustees of The IWA Forest Industry Pension Plan	8.32	6.36
Subtotal	**24.27**	**18.55**
Telecommunications		
Telecommunications Workers Pension Plan	40.78	31.5
Subtotal	**40.78**	**31.15**
Other		
Concert Real Estate Corporation	0	23.62
Total	**100%**	**100%**

Source: Concert, 12/14/99

second largest shareholder is the United Food and Commercial Workers Union Pension Plan (11.25% of Concert Real Estate and 8.59% of Concert Properties), whose members do not derive on-site work from construction projects. The next three largest shareholders are pension plans with members in the forestry sector and constitute the largest sector excluding the anchor. The building trades pension plans constitute the largest number of investors in Concert, but none has investments exceeding 3.61%.

Pension fund asset allocation

Concert recommends that no more than 5% of plan assets should be invested in its shares. Table 5 shows share ownership as a percentage of fund assets for selected owners of Concert Real Estate Corporation[2]. Owners were selected based on the availability of data on their pension fund assets[3] The data was drawn from the Canadian Pension Fund Investment Directory (1999). It is important to note that none of the organizations allocates a large percentage of their pension funds to Concert. The Telecommunication Workers' Fund remains the anchor fund, with the largest percentage of assets in Concert at 2.3%. It is closely followed by the Teamsters Local 213 which has 2.1% of its assets in Concert.

There are data available for two of the three forestry funds, the Pulp and Paper Industry Pension Plan and the I.W.A. Forest Industry Pension Plan. Both have over $1 billion in assets. Yet their asset allocations in Concert are 0.9% and 0.5%, respectively. There are several reasons cited for a lower commitment of pension funds to Concert. First, employer trustees resisted these investment strategies. Union trustees in pension funds that are trusteed by the union only (particularly in the building trades) have far greater freedom than those union trustees in a jointly trusteed fund.

Second, some union trustees are reluctant to invest in Concert as their only real estate investment. Concert argues that pension funds should not invest more than 5% of their assets in real estate, and a maximum of 5% in mortgages (which count as fixed assets). Nevertheless, Concert maintains that its investments are low risk because of its reliance on the rental residential market and the security provided by its assets. Further, in order to increase its short-term returns, Concert did diversify by moving into housing sales (of condominium town-homes).

Table 5: Estimates of selected ownership in Concert Real Estate Corporation as a percentage of fund assets

Pension fund	Fund assets[1]	% Ownership in Concert Real Estate[2]	$ Outstanding share ownership in Concert[3]	Ownership as % of fund asset
Building trades sector				
Heat and Frost Local Union 118 Pension Plan	$51,500,000	.46%	$475,000	.9%
Teamsters Local 213 Pension Plan	$150,000,000	3.06%	$3,126,890	2.1%
Carpentry Workers Pension Plan of B.C.	$200,000,000	3.54%	$3,613,561	1.8%
Operating Engineers Pension Plan	$374,000,000	2.32%	$2,370,555	.6%
Food service				
Retail Wholesale Union Pension Plan	$209,000,000	2.73%	$2,791,666	1.3%
Forestry				
Pulp and Paper Industry Pension Plan	$1,250,000,000	11.06%	$11,301,599	.9%
IWA Forest Industry Pension Plan	$1,831,000,000	8.32%	$8,500,000	.5%
Anchor Pension Fund				
Telecommunication Workers Pension Plan	$1,791,000,000	40.78%	$41,658,896	2.3%

Notes 1. Drawn from the Canadian Pension Fund Directory (1999).
2. % ownership in Concert Real Estate Corporation taken from previous table.
3. Letter from David Podmore, dated January 14, 2000.
Source: Estimated from cited sources by author.

Third, as Clark had said earlier, a way to increase capitalization of Concert was to decrease borrowing from the banks and establish a financial institution owned by pension funds.

Mortgage Fund One (MFO)

Concert has been, in some ways, too successful. While the attempt to build a real estate development company based entirely on equity had not worked since Concert was under-capitalized, the company, as Podmore has said, has a far greater capacity than it was delivering. Overall, the model worked.

However, as Rollick noted, if the company was to own everything it built, it would need much more funding. So the idea was to manage both the equity and the debt. Mortgage Fund One was created and could not have existed without Concert. Clark called it a "politically integrated company" because, firstly, MFO was conceived to decrease the influence of private lenders who may, in the long run, have interests antithetical to Concert. Thus, MFO would stabilize the long-term interests of Concert. MFO was set up in 1992 and essentially enabled the growth of Concert from $27.3 to approximately $130 million.

Second, while MFO is independent of Concert, it exists to fund not less than 30% or more than 50% of total loans to Concert projects. Concert, for its part, receives approximately 33% of its financing from MFO and is working to increase borrowing to about 50% of long-term requirements. In the long run, MFO should be about three times the size of Concert (Interview with MFO, April, 1999). However, this does not mean that there will be no borrowing from banks. Both Concert and MFO assert that lending to and borrowing from conventional lenders (without being dependent on the banks) provides an additional test to ensure non-preferential treatment.

Third, the more Concert borrows, the more returns go back to MFO, and thus to pension fund shareholders, who compensate their lower short-term returns on Concert with their higher short-term returns on the mortgage fund. The MFO Financial Statements for 1998 describe it as an investment trust established under British Columbia law for the benefit of its unit-holders by trust agreement originally dated by September 30, 1992 (Price, Waterhouse, Coopers, 1998, p.1). It meets the conditions of a Unit Trust under the *Income Tax Act*, since all net income reverts to the unit holders. There is therefore no income tax paid (ibid, p.3). There is one class of units, and no limit on the number of units that can be issued. The work of the Trust is managed by ACM Advisors Ltd, created for the purpose, who are paid fixed fees for portfolio management services (ibid, p.3).

Pension funds investing in MFO achieve diversification in their fixed income portfolio by using the MFO investment as an alternative to bonds. ACM recommends that pension funds invest about 5% of their assets. The unit-holder or investor base is just slightly different from the Concert Properties shareholder group.

Union-built housing

The objective of MFO is to provide:

by way of investments in mortgages, interim and long-term financing to fund the development, re-development and construction of residential housing, office, retail, industrial and mixed-use buildings located in British Columbia all of which will be constructed by contractors whose employees are represented by approved unions under a collective agreement (MFO, 1999).

Table 6: Capitalization and investment growth of Mortgage Fund One 1992-1998 ($ millions)

Investors	Capital invested	Capital invested as a % of MFO	Investment growth	Market value 31 Dec. 1998
Telecommunications Workers Pension Plan	$45.0	57.4%	$18.8	$63.8
United Food and Commercial Workers	$6.0	7.7%	$1.0	$7.0
Pulp and Paper Industry Pension Plan	$3.0	3.8%	$1.8	$4.8
Carpentry Workers Pension Plan of B.C.	$7.6	9.7%	$1.8	$9.4
Others	$16.8	21.4%	$4.3	$21.1
Totals	$78.4	100%	$27.7	$106.1

Source: Derived from Business Plan Summary, 1999-2003, Mortgage Fund One, ACM Advisors Limited.

As of 1999, it had 14 investments with an approximate value of $91 million in term and interim construction loans, all in British Columbia. MFO insists that any project funded, however partially, must be 100% union built[4]. While all Concert projects are union-built, ACM staff report examples of projects of other developers that would not have been 100% union-built and therefore would have paid lower non-union wages without MFO's involvement. "Eight. One. Nine," a high-rise condominium tower in Vancouver, and The Grande, another tower in North Vancouver, are two examples. This condition is signed into the covenant the borrower has to sign. Building sites have also been inspected by MFO for potential violations of the condition of funding.

MFO's shareholders are very similar, but not identical to Concert. Again, the Telecommunication Workers' Pension Plan plays an anchor role (see Table 6). Since the average maturity of loans is approximately five years, by 1999 MFO had already established its track record of returns. These are shown in Table 7. Table 8 shows that MFO's management fees are lower than two other Canadian mortgage benchmarks. In addition, MFO's net annual yield exceeds those other benchmarks and therefore provides a higher return to the pension plan investors.

The Carpenters' — another perspective

The Carpenters' is the largest construction union in B.C. with over 9,000 members. Its pension fund was one of the first to work with the Telecommunication Workers Union on economic development in British Columbia. While its membership (and organizing policy) is not restricted to carpenters, this trade predominates. The Carpentry Workers' Pension Plan has been in existence for 30 years, and for much of that time Wayne Stone was the administrator. The Pension Plan (referred to as the Carpenters') is a Special Multi-Employer Plan under the *Income Tax*

Table 7: Rates of return of Mortgage Fund One						
	1993	1994	1995	1996	1997	1998
Rate of return	8.26%	8.11%	8.22%	10.02%	7.69%	8.40%
Source: Business plan summary, 1999 – 2003, Mortgage Fund One, acm advisors limited.						

Act, and all contributions are technically classed as employer contributions. However, all seven trustees are from the union side. It has about 14,000 members and its total assets, as of 1999, are $2 billion.

The Carpenters' has been involved in real estate since the late 1970s. Its original involvement was through cooperatives, buying the land and building for the cooperative. Wayne Stone views this period as the only time when the Carpenters' was able to provide social housing, through government funding. He has said:

> *With the wrap-up of social housing and the cooperative program, we started looking for other alternatives so that we could still provide good quality homes for people. We worked very closely with Bill Clark to set up VLC. That's been part of our history.*

Indeed, Wayne Stone and Bill Clark were the core union leaders working with Ken Georgetti at the B.C. Federation of Labour to set up first Westcan and then the VLC. The three were the first union champions of pension fund investment. In 1988, in response to a question from a *Vancouver Sun* reporter (Casselton, 1988) about a "marriage of convenience" between labour and capital, Stone said:

> *It's created some problems for us as individuals. We've overcome it from the point of view we've created employment and provided quality housing (p. D12).*

Stone goes on to say that, if Carpenters' pension money was with "money managers whose main concern is best possible returns, ethical guidelines [will likely be] violated through investment in armaments and

Table 8: Investment comparison 1993-1998

	Mortgage Fund One	Wyatt Pooled Mortgage Funds Survey	Scotia McLeod Mortgage Index
Cumulative yield	62.20%	58.20%	63.00%
Annual yield	8.4%	7.94%	8.48%
Management fee ratio	0.52%	0.61%	1.25%
Net annual yield	7.88%	7.33%	7.23%

Source: Business Plan Summary, 1999-2003, Mortgage Fund One, ACM Advisors Limited.

atomic power" (ibid., p. D12). Georgetti was more forthright at the time. He is reported as saying:

> *It's just the old tired attitude that if you believe in labour or social democracy, you have to be against capital and profits. We can use pension income to create jobs, union jobs, that pay a fair rate and get a fair return. We can make a profit...but...without exploiting people (ibid., D12).*

Carpenters continued its interest in real estate development by investing in Concert and, later, Mortgage Fund One. However, it also set up a real estate development company of its own, Western Housing Development Corporation. Through this company, it has done joint ventures with other development companies to build quality rental and affordable housing. While the returns on this wholly-owned subsidiary were exceptional, Revenue Canada determined that the company was not exempt under the *Income Tax Act*, and assessed the Carpenters' $4.5 million in back taxes. This matter has been resolved out of court with no back taxes payable by the Carpenters', but a guarantee that the company will be disbanded. Stone concludes that the only way pension funds can go into real estate development is through a model such as Concert.

Collateral benefits for the Carpenters'

The benefit of social investment for the Carpenters' is in the union jobs created for carpentry workers and the increased contributions in health and welfare and pension to the fund. Since 37% of Concert's trades are carpenters, and carpenters outnumber any other trade, it should be no surprise that the Carpenters' favours real estate and mortgages as investment. Table 9 shows the impact of nine years of Concert's construction activity on job creation and pension fund contributions for the Carpenters'.

There are several points to be made about the calculations. First, labour costs are usually estimated by Concert at about 45% of the construction value, the other 55% of which is materials. Second, Concert calculates its average on-site labour costs at $33 per hour (a gross figure which includes taxation, vacation, pension, and health and welfare payments). This should be compared to the average gross rate of pay of $20.67 per hour for a construction worker in B.C.. (The average carpenters' gross union wage—not used in this table—is actually $27.75 an hour).

Such is the impact of union wages. Third, a carpenter's contribution to the union's health and welfare plan is $1.195 per hour, as governed by the collective agreement. Finally, contributions to the pension fund are at the rate of $2.34 an hour, also governed by the collective agreement and having remained unchanged for a number of years.

Table 9 estimates that 4.9 million hours of work have been created by Concert projects, of which an estimated 1.8 million hours were for carpenters. This on-site work has an estimated value of $162 million, of which the total Carpenter benefit is estimated at $50.4 million. This does not include the 'soft' costs of professional or administrative services.

Hours of work and union rates

What is a fair way of calculating the hours of work—and hence the pay— of carpenters on Concert projects? Could they have found other work? Would the work have been union rate? Prevailing practice is to attribute all hours to investment projects, but this assumes that those jobs would

Table 9: Carpentry workers' construction activity in Concert 1990-1999

Project value (construction) completed by February, 2000	$360,000,000
Labour component ($360,000,000 x 45 per cent)	$162,000,000
Hours of on-site labour created ($162,000,000 divided by $33.00/hour)	4,910,000 hours
Hours of employment for carpenters (4,910,000 x 37 per cent)	1,817,000 hours
Contribution to carpenters health and welfare plan (1,817,000 hours @ $1.195/hour)	$2,171,000
Contribution to carpenters pension fund (1,817,000 hours @ $2.34/hour)	$4,252,000
Total carpenter benefit (wages, vacation, health and welfare, and pensions) [$21.62 x $1.12 + (1.195 + 2.34)] x 1,817,000 hours	$50,421,000
Carpenters' pay net of contributions	$43,998,000

Source: Concert Properties, November 12, 1999; Department of Finance.

not have existed otherwise. Pension trustees need more rational social accounting practices to account for the social/economic impact of their investment strategies.

What is agreed by those interviewed in Concert, Mortgage Fund One, and some of the unions involved is that the *union* work would not have been created. For example, carpenters may have found work—taking into account average unemployment rates of 7%—but it would have been for lower wages on non-union construction sites. Concert, then, can at least be credited with contributing to community wealth through providing higher (union) wage rates for its construction labour.

As well, Concert has been credited with providing 80% of rental housing in Vancouver since 1989. Therefore, on rental accommodation projects, it can be assumed that 80% of the work would not have been created without Concert and can be directly attributed to Concert. It can also be assumed that 10% of the remaining work would have been done by carpenters who would otherwise be unemployed and the other 10% by carpenters who otherwise would have had non-union work. This, at least, results in a slightly lower number of hours directly attributable to Concert *for a rental accommodation project*. Of course, this rule could not be applied to a housing sales project. The results are on Table 10 for 600 Drake Street, a rental housing project.

Table 10: Calculation of hours of work of carpenters directly attributable to Concert from the 600 Drake Street (rental accommodation) construction project

Hours of work for carpenters	47,931	
Carpenters' labour component		$1,330,085
80% of hours	38,345	
Value of 80% hours of work @ $27.75		$1,064,068
Remaining hours of work	9,586	
10% @ $27.75		$26,601
90% @ $7.08		$61,082
Total value of carpenters' work directly attributable to Concert		$1,151,751

Table 11: A social accounting statement of the Carpentry Workers Union Pension Fund investment in 600 Drake Street, a Concert project (construction period 1992-1993)

	Concert	Carpenters
1. Concert's total project cost	$14,350,000	
2. Total equity required by Concert (25% of cost)	$3,587,500	
3. Carpenters' equity in Concert (@ 3.54%)	$126,998	
4. Mortgage Fund One loan to Concert	$9,000,000	
5. Carpenters equity in Mortgage Fund One (@ 9.7%)	$873,000	
6. Total investment of carpenters	$999,998	
7. Total value of on-site employment (129,545 hrs @ $33 per hr)		$4,275,000
8. Carpenters on-site employment (37% of 129,545 hrs)		(47,931)
9. Contributions to the Carpentry Workers Pension Plan of B.C. (@ $2.34 per hr)		$112,159
10. Contributions to the carpentry workers health and welfare plan (@ $1.195 per hr)		$57,278
11. Pay to carpenters, net of contributions		$1,160,648
12. Estimate of on-site employment directly attributable to Concert		$1,151,751
13. Return on investment to Mortgage Fund One (@ 8.26%)		$72,110
14. Total return to carpentry workers (add lines 9, 10, 11, 13.)		$1,402,195
15. Return to carpenters net of investments (subtract line 6 from line 14)		$402,197
16. Per cent gain to carpenters (line 15 divided by line 6, times 100)		40.22%
17. Net per cent gain to carpenters in work directly attributable to Concert as against investment (lines 12 minus (lines 9 plus 10) as a % of line 6)		98.2%
18. Total returns to carpenters pension fund (add lines 9 and 13)		$184,269
19. Per cent return to carpentry workers pension fund based on investment (line 18 divided by line 6 times 100)		18.4%

Sources: Data derived from: Concert Properties: Savona, November 12, 1999; Letter from David Podmore dated January 17, 2000; Business Plan Summary 1999-2003, Mortgage Fund One, ACM Advisors Ltd.; B.C. Stats: unemployment rates, labour average rates of pay.

Union-built rental accommodation

From all of Concert's construction activity between 1990 and 1999, the Carpentry Workers' Pension Fund is estimated to have received contributions of $4.25 million as a direct result of the work created by Concert. This increase in contributions flows directly from the adherence to union labour on construction sites, since the pension plan is a creation of the Carpentry Workers' Union. It is unlikely that the pension plan would have received this increase in contributions had it not been for Concert projects and its ability to capitalize on a gap in the market by building and managing rental accommodation.

The union also benefits directly through increased union dues, although this has not been shown. In fact, the union benefits to the extent that the pension fund benefits through an increase in its revenue base. However, the union's benefit is not the goal of the investment.

An example of pension fund gains is shown in Table 11. This table illustrates the impact of one Concert project on the Carpenters' Pension Plan. The project, 600 Drake Street, was controversial when it was being built in 1992-3 because it aimed to provide housing for low-income people. The land was provided by the City. Its design is contemporary, and it is a high-rise of 192 small apartments, a mix of studio, junior one-bedroom, and one-bedroom apartments. Since the accommodation is affordable, residents of 600 Drake may be on welfare or unemployment insurance. It is likely the closest a private developer has come to providing social housing in Vancouver.

The project, 600 Drake Street, was one of the first Mortgage Fund One projects. MFO provided a 20-year term mortgage for 63% of the total cost of the project. For the purpose of the table, it is assumed that Concert financed 25% of the total cost of the project, which it normally does. (The remaining $1.76 million would be provided by other investors, likely the banks.) Carpenters' equity in Concert is in Table 5 and in MFO is in Table 6.

Concert and community

The final question is the extent to which Concert's work has benefited the larger community. Table 12 provides another social accounting of Concert's work from 1989, since Concert's inception, to 1999. It sum-

Table 12: A social account of on-site employment directly attributable to Concert from 1989-1999 (both rental and sales)

Total hours of work	3,922,527 hours
Total labour component (@ $33 per hour)	$129,443,400
Value of work on rental accommodation projects to be attributed to Concert[1]	
Total hours of work on rental accommodation projects	1,528,799 hours
80% of hours	1,223,039.2 hours
80% hours of work @ $33	$40,360,293
Remaining hours of work	
10% @ $33	$1,009,007
90% @ $12.33 (@$33 minus $20.67)[2]	$3,393,017
Subtotal	$44,762,316
Value of work on housing sales projects to be attributed to Concert	
Total hours of work on housing sales projects	2,393,728 hours
10% of hours	239,373 hours
10% hours of work @ $33	$7,899,302
90% of hours	2,154,355 hours
90% of hours @ $12.33	$26,563,199
Subtotal	$34,462,501
Total labour value directly attributable to Concert	**$79,224,817**
Total hours to be directly attributed to Concert (@ $33/hour)	**2,400,752 hours**

Note 1. Included in this list of 'rental accommodation' are the Collingwood Neighbourhood House, several parks, a baseball diamond and a health centre. All, with the exception of the health centre, are on land owned by the city and leased to Concert. The health centre is on land owned by Concert and leased to the Vancouver/Richmond Regional Health Board.

Note 2. The average construction rate of pay for British Columbia is $20.67 (B.C. Stats, 2000).

marizes the total number of hours of on-site employment and the value of that work that can be directly attributed to Concert. It is important to note that this is an account of on-site labour only. This work includes bricklaying, cement masonry, carpentry, electrical, glazing, iron work, engineering, painting, plastering, plumbing, roofing, and carpentry. It is therefore a conservative account, since there is also professional and administrative work to support the on-site labour. The total cost of Concert projects was $498,585,000, almost half a billion dollars.

Table 12 shows that, of a total labour value (or component) of $129.4 million, only $79.2 million should be directly attributed to Concert, largely based on the proportion of hours spent on rental construction, as opposed to housing sales construction. This represents 2,400,752 hours of work, 61% of the actual labour component.

What impact does this work have on the community? Input-output models and their multipliers present a simplified way of accounting for economic interdependence[5]. They have been used in many studies of economic impact (Jackson and Lamontagne, 1995; Ontario Arts Council, 1997). In this case, they allow for an estimation of the indirect and induced effects of Concert's projects and the work it has created. Multipliers are acknowledged to be somewhat crude and mechanistic, but useful. Therefore, for example, multipliers were not used to estimate the direct effect of Concert's production in creating jobs in this study. Nevertheless, they are useful as estimates *in the absence of* information such as:

- the value added to capital by the Concert projects that have been built;
- the impact of the value added on spending in B.C.;
- the impact on the suppliers of construction materials and services in the B.C. community in relation to their own economic growth and spending;
- how many jobs have been created indirectly by suppliers or more distantly by commercial ventures benefiting from Concert projects;
- how much spending has been created (or induced) by Concert, as a consequence of its production;
- how much spending is lost to other provinces; and
- how much is paid for employment, property and business taxes.

Table 13 uses multipliers against Concert's total project costs for its 10 years of existence to attempt to provide estimates in response to these questions. It illustrates that, over a period of 10 years, the indirect and induced effects alone of Concert outweigh the total project costs. Even though the multipliers chosen for employment effects are the more conservative in that they take account of social safety nets in the absence of employment, indirect and induced employment increases the direct effect of Concert's estimated labour component by 71%.

Using multipliers, the social accounting shows that Concert's impact on indirect and induced employment created 5,529,524 hours of work, more than doubling its direct, attributable on-site employment. Furthermore, its value added or contribution to productivity (in the community) through its indirect and induced effects is $508,556,700, just over its total project cost for the 10 years.

Table 13: Indirect and induced effects based on total project costs of Concert of $498,585,000, from 1989-1999[1]

	Indirect	Induced	Total
Output	(.55) $274,221,750	(.15) $74,787,750	$349,009,500
GDP – value added	(.23) $114,674,550	(.09) $44,872,650	$159,547,200
Subtotal	$388,896,300	$119,660,400	$508,556,700
Employment			
(person years)	(4.4) 2191.2	(1.7) 847	3038.2
(person weeks)			157,986
(person hours)			5,529,524

Taxation[2]	Direct/indirect	Induced	Total
Federal	(.14) $69,801,900	(.01) $4,985,850	$74,787,750
Provincial	(.11) $54,844,350	(.01) $4,985,850	$59,830,200
Municipal	(.02) $9,971,700	(.00)	$9,971,700
Total			$144,589,650

Note 1. Multipliers are shown in brackets and are taken from the multiplier tables, item 154: Residential Construction (B.C. Ministry of Finance, 1996).
Note 2. Taxation collected on direct, indirect and induced employment and businesses.

Finally, the taxation revenues for all levels of government generated through Concert's productivity total $144,589,650, which amounts to 29% of the total project cost. How does this compare with taxes forgone by government through tax exemption of contributions and returns on investment? Table 14 estimates taxes forgone by (the federal) government for both Concert and Mortgage Fund One.

Calculations are based on methods used by the Department of Finance of the federal government[6]. On the basis that tax revenue on investment and contributions is forgone by the federal government, this level of government more than recoups its investment through direct, indirect, and induced returns in the form of personal and business taxes. Forgone tax revenues on pension fund investment returns in Concert and Mortgage Fund One over 10 years are estimated at $66 million.

Table 14: Foregone tax revenues for Concert and Mortgage Fund One 1989-1999 on total project costs of $498,585,000

Concert	
Equity (@25%)	$124,646,250
Foregone taxes on[1]	
Investment	$31,161,563
Returns (@ 6.1%)[2]	$1,900,855
Total	$33,062,418
Mortgage Fund One	
Equity (33% of financing)	$123,399,788
Foregone taxes on:	
Investment	$30,849,947
Returns (@7.07%)[3]	$2,181,091
Total	$33,031,038
Total foregone taxes for Concert and Mortgage Fund One	**$66,093,456**

Notes   1. As estimated by the Department of Finance.
2. As estimated by the Department of Finance, in the absence of information on rates of return.
3. Average rate of return—see Table 6.

Therefore, the federal government had a net gain of $8.7 million on its investment. However, all levels of government benefited in the amount of $144.5 million. For all levels of government, it is clear that the work of Concert and Mortgage Fund One yields opportunities for tax revenue that far outweigh government subsidization of pension funds. Clearly, the benefits of Concert extend beyond the interests of construction workers and their pension funds.

In Canada, there are few examples of pension fund investment in economically targeted investment. This case study of Concert has provided a model of a Canadian ETI for trustees. It has told a story of trade unionists and their friends who, in spite of numerous legal and practical obstacles, have built a real estate development company that is a leader in affordable housing in Canada. From an investment perspective, it has shown the structure of VLC, the two Concert companies, as well as its sister investment vehicle, Mortgage Fund One.

This chapter has also pointed the way for trustees and trade unions in assessing the collateral value of investment vehicles to their members and the general community. There are no generally accepted measuring tools available for trustees at the moment for this purpose. Yet there are generally accepted measurement tools commonly used in soci-economic analysis. Research in the area of social accounting needs to continue to support the social investment initiatives of trade unions and their trustees.

Notes

[1] This calculation does not include dividends returned to pension funds during these periods of construction, and it also assumes that the work would not have been available otherwise to construction workers. It is also important to note that the gains are made in unionized work for a broad group of construction unions, not all of whose pension funds invest in Concert.

[2] It is important to note that this table does not show the total investments of each pension fund in both Concert companies. Nor does it show investments in VLC. The percentage figure therefore does not reflect the full investment in Concert and its related companies. Nor does it reveal the total real estate asset class for the pension fund.

[3] Data drawn from the Canadian Pension Fund Investment Directory

[4] Since this research was undertaken, MFO has extended its operations into Ontario.

[5] Multipliers drawn from the Input-Output model of the Analysis and Evaluation Branch of the Ministry of Finance of the Government of B.C. (designed with the assistance of Statistics Canada). Base year— 1990.

[6] The Department of Finance calculates foregone revenue on pension fund asset returns by multiplying the total pension fund assets in Canada (as re--ported by Statistics Canada) by the reported interest rate on 10 year government bonds (6.1percent in 1997). This sum is multiplied by an 'average tax rate' (Interview with Ian Pomeroy, January 6, 2000).

CHAPTER 6

Collaboration between labor, academics and community activists to advance labor/capital strategies

The origins of the Heartland Network

by Tom Croft and Tessa Hebb

PENSION FUND CAPITAL NOW UNDERPINS ALL THE MAJOR financial markets in the world (Davis 2001, Monks 2001, Clark 2000). Last valued globally at $10 trillion dollars (Anand 2000), this capital represents the deferred wages of today's workers. Despite this fact, pension fund capital is seldom employed in the long-term interests of workers themselves (Fung 2001). That reality was the driving force behind a coalition of trade unionists, academics, political representatives, community activists, and charitable foundations drawn from both the U.S. and Canada, dedicated to advancing a capital strategy for labour. The Heartland Labour/Capital Project, now known as the Heartland Network, is a model of capacity building within both trade union and academic spheres. It helped forge a capital agenda for labour, and its story is worth examining.

In the fall of 1995, United Steelworkers of America Secretary-Treasurer Leo Gerard and Steel Valley Authority Director Tom Croft called together an informal group of representatives from trade unions, industrial retention organizations, academia, think tanks, and investment firms to examine the dynamics behind continuing job losses in key American industries. Gerard found others equally concerned that the current operation of financial markets undermined the very workers whose savings they deploy.

While corporate profits soared in the 1990s, most working families saw their real wages fall. Despite the economic expansion of the mid-1990s, mass layoffs and downsizing had become permanent features of the economic landscape, eroding union jobs and destabilizing the economy. In addition, a growing capital gap, caused partly by financial industry restructuring, was hobbling investment in the small and medium-sized firms that employed significant numbers of industrial union members (Heartland 1996). Given the billions of dollars flowing from pension funds into risky ventures in emerging markets, Gerard wanted to understand why it was so difficult to identify financing for investment in a solid U.S. company, generating a good rate of return.

Gerard, long a powerful force in the Canadian trade union movement, had newly arrived in Pittsburgh in 1995 to take on his new role as Secretary-Treasurer of the United Steelworkers of America. His involvement with the Canadian branch of the Steelworkers in key capital projects such as the restructuring and employee ownership buyout of Algoma Steel in 1993 and the creation of the labour-sponsored investment fund First Ontario, convinced him of the importance of a capital strategy for labour on both sides of the border. Gerard called a meeting in Pittsburgh with other key individuals he felt shared his concern.

The group Gerard brought together called itself the 'grievance committee,' and the grievance was simple: financial markets were destroying jobs through the mis-investment of workers' own pension funds, and it had to stop. The construct of the 'grievance committee' allowed each participant to leave their official capacity at the door, and represent only themselves while participating in this initiative. It proved to be a useful structure and one that helped speed the advancement of the capital strategies agenda.

The Heartland Project began to promote an aggressive agenda to push capital strategies, both inside and outside the labor movement. The idea was to raise awareness with labor's pension fund trustees that there were investment options beyond those currently being offered (Ghilarducci 1992, Fung 2001), and to put money managers on alert that the trade union movement was looking more closely at the manner in which they handled its members' retirement savings.

During the fall of 1995, the AFL-CIO was itself undergoing a major change in direction. John Sweeney from the Service Employees Union and Richard Trumka from the United MineWorkers challenged the 'official' slate and won the Presidency and Secretary-Treasurer of the AFL-CIO. Among several key items in their "New Voice" leadership, they identified capital strategies as an area of future growth for the trade union movement. With support and engagement from both the Steelworkers and the AFL-CIO, the Heartland Project gained significant momentum and political weight from which to draw together a larger coalition of interests.

In addition to senior labour leaders and academics, the Heartland Project pulled together a network of progressive regional economic democracy groups that had been fighting to save jobs, create worker ownership, and revitalize industrial communities. It organized a number of working committees to research labour capital issues, and prepared for its first national conference held in Pittsburgh in 1996. The Heartland group wanted to replicate the success and experience of the labour-sponsored investment funds (LSIFs) in Canada (Falconer 1995), arguably North America's most progressive investment and development program. To facilitate this cross-border adaptation of the best of labour's capital strategies, the Heartland Project asked several leaders of the Canadian LSIFs to join its Working Group.

In less than a year, the Heartland Working Group grew from a small gathering of committed individuals to a large, successful national conference. Academic and union researchers participating in the Heartland Working Group agreed to write short papers to help shape discussion and debate at the conference (Heartland 1996), and in June of 1996 the first Heartland Conference was held in Pittsburgh. It proved to be a significant milestone in building a broad coalition to advance labour's capital strategy agenda. In addition to Gerard's leadership and participation, AFL-CIO Secretary-Treasurer Rich Trumka delivered the keynote address signalling the political weight the AFL-CIO was prepared to put into the Heartland initiative.

Gerard and Trumka, having both been raised in coal-mining labour communities, found great common ground in the issues, and together they began to fashion a more aggressive and long-range strategy for organized labour. With deep roots in Western Pennsylvania's UMW local unions, Trumka's ascendancy in the labour federation's leadership was in no small part due to the industrial union coalition (including USWA) which backed him. Trumka set the stage for the emergence of a new international labour-capital movement, with a riveting call-to-arms, during his Heartland Forum keynote address: "There is no more important challenge for the labour movement today than to stop the use of our own money from cutting our own throats!"

As a result of this successful conference, the Heartland Working Group continued to meet and plan its next strategic move to advance a capital strategy for labour. While part of the success of the initial project had been its informal 'ad hoc' nature allowing flexibility and quick movement, the project had now reached a point where it either secured formal outside funding and a corresponding formal structure or disbanded, handing the initiative over to the newly conceived AFL-CIO Center for Working Capital.

While the Center for Working Capital offered the best long-term base for this initiative, the Center was still in early development, and the Working Group had concerns that the momentum behind Heartland could be lost if not acted on immediately. As a result, the Heartland project sought and secured significant financial support from the Ford and Rockefeller and Mott Foundations, as well as McKay and Veatch Unitarian Funds. With external financial support, the Heartland Working Group continued to be a major pressure point in forging a capital strategy for labour.

By early 1997, the Heartland Working Group organized itself into three task forces to manage a number of initiatives, leading to a second successful national Heartland Labour Capital Conference held in 1999. The first group was the Research Task Force bringing together leading economists, pension and investment experts, labour and pension lawyers, and other academics. The second was the Regional Network Task Force focusing on the creation of a network of regional funds for investment in small and medium-sized firms across America. The third task force took on communication, with the realization that, in order to advance this agenda, expert communication tools would be required. Each task force played an integral part in preparing the work for the subsequent national conference held in 1999 and is examined in greater detail later in the chapter.

Following the second Heartland Conference in 1999, the Heartland Project transformed itself into the Heartland Network. Today, the union partners of the Heartland Network are seed-financing, through their pension trusts, a number of new "Heartland" funds in the U.S. The first, with five Taft-Hartley pension investors committed to a goal of $75 million, will invest in worker-friendly industries, a critical need in the current economic restructuring period. Overall, some $3 billion has been invested by Taft-Hartley pension funds in more worker-friendly investment funds (Calabrese 2001). Innovative regional funds are under development in several cities. All this has garnered considerable national media attention and stories.

The underlying policy impacts of the Heartland Network, and the Heartland Project before it, have been far-reaching. Heartland has been directly responsible for helping to mobilize labour Taft-Hartley pension funds to invest in small, private businesses for the first time. The advisors to Taft-Hartley funds have become more vocal in advocating a 5% investment goal for pension portfolios (from under 1%), a timely development given the need to diversify investment strategies since the large falloff in the stock market.

Consistent with Leo Gerard's long-held position against the mis-investment of workers' savings in speculative, overseas sweatshops, the California Public Employees' Retirement Fund (CalPERs) passed in 2000 new "emerging markets" rules requiring labour standards. The New York City pension system (NYCERS) and other public pension funds also adopted this policy. And the largest public pension funds, led by CalPERs, are making major new commitments to worker-friendly private capital and ETI initiatives. While state pension funds have been more active in investing in venture capital, these programs have historically been more focused on technology start-ups.

Public pension funds (with $2 trillion in assets), and Taft Hartley funds (with $370 billion in assets) represent over one-third of all pension assets in the U.S., which total over $7 trillion (Zanglein 2001). Pension funds are a large part of the institutional holdings that own 45% of all corporate stock in America (Davis 2001); similar and larger percentages dominate in other countries. Well-known writers from Peter Drucker in *The Unseen Revolution* to Randy Barber and Jeremy Rifkin in *The North Shall Rise Again*, along with labour-friendly scholars and analysts, have, for two-and-a- half decades, predicted the eventual power of pension funds (Ghilarducci 1992, Clark 2000, Hawley 2000, Davis 2001, Monks 2001), or sought to persuade labour to realize the potential for worker-owners to dramatically influence the behaviour of capital markets.

This shift in the labour community to become stronger stewards of its retirement assets has come at a critical time, within the gravitational pull of the progressive new role of the labour movement in the U.S. There have been major conflicts around unfettered globalism, the growing power of multinational corporations, and resultant crises in the economy and with trade problems (Strange, Sassen, Sen). The economy has become unstable as the new century moves into its first decade. At this writing, a global recession and the likelihood of a long, slow recovery threaten the livelihoods of millions of working families around the globe. The worker-owners of the world's pension funds, and their allies, have an unprecedented potential role to play in the economic recovery and stabilization of the world's economy, thereby promoting the profile of labour and the democratization of capital on a scale heretofore unimaginable.

To the extent that the Heartland Network played a role in the evolution of organized labour's new activism around this sizeable capital source, a chronology and analysis of that effort is worthwhile at this time. This chapter will focus on the collaboration that occurred between organized labour, regional economic democracy groups, and progressive academia in order to move this agenda forward. As Leo Gerard, now President of the Steelworkers, said in his foreword to the book *Working Capital: The Power of Labor's Pensions*, (Fung 2001) "Power never shifts without a struggle." Through the collaborative work of the Heartland Project, we hope to equip those who confront the orthodoxy of financial markets and help define an important agenda for labour.

Building the case

Labour's capital is an enormous asset for the nation, and potentially a powerful force for improving our economic performance and the distribution of opportunity and reward. But labour has historically lacked a capital strategy. The original Heartland Working Group participants felt that mobilizing capital owned by workers toward responsible investment offered a new way for labour to improve the situation of workers.

Unions and community groups had developed innovative economic development, industrial retention and alternative ownership initiatives in the 1980s and 1990s to counter the onslaught of plant closures, corporate restructuring and downsizing. But, over time, even the most sophisticated efforts have been overmatched by the relentless pressures of global trade and economic dislocation. Time and again, firms with decent markets, efficient factories, successful managers, productive workers and respectable earnings, fell prey to downsizing and disinvestment. In many situations, the critical factor was lack of capital.

The United Steelworkers of America has long been concerned with capital market issues and alternative ownership strategies, including ESOPs (employee stock ownership plans) (Quarter 1995), and progressive corporate governance programs. It assisted several thousand members in the buyouts of dozens of industrial companies and plants, and won union seats on the boards of directors of the largest steel companies. The USWA's strategies for addressing corporate restructuring, starting in the 1980s, became a model for other unions in North America.

The Steel Valley Authority (SVA), a unique labour-affiliated regional development organization in Western Pennsylvania, was chartered as a governmental body in the mid-1980s, after campaigns by steel and electrical local unions fighting the de-industrialization of the Mon Valley. The SVA has utilized innovative strategies, such as its eminent domain powers[1], in an effort to save essential workplaces and jobs. Its primary mission is to retain and revitalize the manufacturing jobs base of the Pittsburgh region.

Meanwhile, Trumka, through his Secretary-Treasurers' group, a pension committee composed of affiliate leaders, and the Department of Corporate Affairs began to create the infrastructure in the AFL-CIO to engage affiliates directly around workers' capital issues. The Office of Worker Investment and the Center for Working Capital, two AFL-CIO-initiated programs, began to mobilize shareholder campaigns, and instituted a new trustee education certificate program with the National Labour College of the George Meany Center for Labour Studies. Other AFL-CIO projects included the web site *www.paywatch.org* designed to monitor excessive executive compensation practices.

Linkages between the Heartland Working Group and the AFL-CIO were established through Leo Gerard's participation with Trumka's Secretary-Treasurers' group, complemented by paticipation in the Working Group by key influencial staff of the AFL-CIO such as Ron Blackwell, Director of AFL-CIO Corporate Affairs, and Bill Patterson, Director of

AFL-CIO Worker Investment, interacting with the Heartland Working Group.

Joined by a number of up-and-coming and relatively young leaders in their respective fields, the Heartland Working Group initiated a number of research papers at the beginning of 1996 that would ultimately be presented at a forum that spring. The Heartland Group began to explain that the daily lives of Americans and their communities are powerfully influenced by Wall Street and international capital markets (Heartland 1996).

There was particular concern about the need to address the overall pattern of job growth in the U.S. and Canada, with accumulating evidence that corporate restructuring had negative effects on long-term productivity and economic stability (approximating the state Keynes famously characterized as one in which "speculation dominates enterprise"). Corporate merger activity soared in 1996, with record job cuts mounting as one of the results, a trend documented in economist Dean Baker's research presented at the first Heartland Forum. Baker also linked the decline in manufacturing jobs to a growing wage gap, heightened inequality, and a long-term rise in poverty in the U.S.

The infamous corporate raider images of the 1980s "greed decade" was replaced by one more ominous. "Corporate Killers" was one of the many magazine covers gracing Time, Newsweek, Business Week and the Economist, highlighting such "predatory" capitalists as 'Chainsaw' Al Dunlap. These new corporate barons were not necessarily industrialists who had learned the ropes from decades of climbing the corporate ladder. Rather, they were often financiers and accountants who orchestrated transactions through relationships on Wall Street or Bay Street. At the same time, government's traditional regulatory oversight responsibilities were eroded as neoliberal 'new economy' policies passed bipartisan legislatures at both federal and state levels.

These new capitalists attacked corporations externally through hostile mergers and takeovers, and internally through corporate downsizing and mass layoffs, as part of a trend toward the "low-road" economy, highlighted by Regina Markey of the AFL-CIO Housing Investment Trust and Building Investment Trust (HIT-BIT). HIT-BIT was the most active of a number of construction financing funds established by the labour federation, and capitalized by pension funds. HIT-BIT had constructed tens of thousands of housing units, mostly utilizing union labour. In her research, Markey documented how "high performance" investment strategies were generally more productive and profitable when targeting firms where workers participated in ownership or strategic workplace decisions (Heartland 1996).

The irony for workers was that their own savings were a principal source of this disruptive restructuring. Among many examples, the Oregon Teachers' Fund helped finance the record $25 billion buy-out of RJR Nabisco in 1989 (on most accounts a disastrously misguided transaction commercially, and one which resulted in thousands of layoffs. Part of the capital problem stemmed from changes in financial markets, as Tom Schlesinger of the Financial Markets Center and Regina Markey pointed out in the first Heartland Forum. Schlesinger had been active in the Financial Democracy Campaign that intervened in the savings and loan collapse in the U.S. Their research documented a series of profound changes that transformed financial markets since the 1970s. These changes included:

- the decline of banks and other traditional intermediary institutions as lenders and repositories of savings;
- a concomitant rise in non-bank credit-granting institutions; and
- explosive growth in capital market instruments derived from the packaging, unbundling and hedging of other financial products.

As banks consolidated and financial markets restructured, competitive small businesses and regional manufacturers have found themselves starved for credit, working capital, and long-term equity investments. The tyranny of the bottom line for higher profits diminished the power of communities to influence economic decisions affecting them. Concurrently, major public policy changes (statutory, regulatory and tax law revisions, expansive credit guarantee programs, etc) also helped reshape the financial system. Increased concentration, short-termism, speculation, volatility, and erratic monetary policy all tended to undermine the economic welfare of American workers (Jacobs 1992). These by-products of financial restructuring drive up the cost of capital for productive purposes, thereby distorting the nation's investment climate and deterring the creation of good jobs.

Tessa Hebb, a principal at Hebb, Knight and Associates in Ottawa, former Research Director of the New Democratic Party (NDP), and long-time friend of Gerard, has described in detail the series of events that led to the development of capital gaps for mid-sized firms in America. From the late 1980s, through the last recession, to the mid-1990s, mid-sized firms in America experienced a severe credit crunch that restricted their ability to grow and expand. The origins of this credit crunch were found in a simultaneous constriction of bank lending cited above, coupled with a reduction of available funds in the traditional markets of private placement. This was caused partly by a lack of intermediaries who bring together pools of capital and potential borrowers; a role formerly performed by large insurance companies. The result has been lost jobs in North America, lost opportunities, and lost growth (U.S. Federal Reserve Board 1993).

Hebb also reviewed the growth of Economically Targeted Investments (ETIs). Some private placement debt and equity issues are already incorporated in state public employees' pension funds through ETI programs. These funds generally target geographic preferences and pursue other covenants such as "collateral benefits." An SBA survey concluded that the impediments to pension fund investment were high risk (fiduciary responsibility) and the lack of a good fund manager in private placements (U.S. Small Business Administration 19). Some research indicates ETIs provide ancillary benefits important to a state's economic development (Levine 1997, Zanglein 1996, Calabrese 2001), while on the other hand some believe that both financial returns and "collateral benefits" could not be pursued simultaneously (Langbein 1985, Romanow 1993).

Joe Bute, then Manufacturing Director of the SVA, described the growing importance of the "middle-market" private firms among key industry sectors impacted by capital gaps. These "critical-middle" firms were overwhelmingly private closely held companies, often family-based. These firms had trouble accessing debt and equity markets to fund growth, modernization and R&D, partly due to the relative small size of these companies (annual sales of between $5 million and $100 million,) and the information-intensive process necessary to underwrite them. With the appropriate planning, technology transfer and capital, many of these companies could become world-class producers, often as part of a decentralized, but highly integrated manufacturing system. Bute reasoned that unions could and should play a central role in assisting worker-friendly middle-market firms through joint productivity and modernization efforts, and by investing union-centred and directed pension capital back into this critical and growing sector of the economy.

Rich Feldman of the Seattle Worker Center, who had experience on the board of a community development venture fund, and Tom Croft of the SVA outlined various models for investment vehicles that could finance these firms, including venture capital funds, revolving loan funds, and other investment vehicles. They provided "guidelines" for creating worker-friendly funds, modelled after many of the governance and management principles of the labour-sponsored funds.

Sherman Kreiner, President of the Crocus Fund in Manitoba, and Ken Delaney, of the Ontario First Fund, introduced the Canadian labour-sponsored funds (LSIFs). The labour funds got their start with the Solidarity Fund, initiated by the Quebec Federation of Labour in 1983. With over $4 billion in assets, it is the largest labour-sponsored fund and the largest venture capital fund in Canada. The labour funds were capitalized by workers who receive provincial and federal tax credits, thus deriving returns from the credit as well as the direct investment of the funds. Other major funds include British Columbia's Working Opportunity Fund, the Crocus Investment Fund of Manitoba, along with the First Ontario Fund and the Workers' Investment Fund (New Brunswick). Together, the labour funds are owned by over half a million shareholders, a majority of whom are union members, and in the 1990's, represented over half of all venture capital in Canada.

Professor Teresa Ghilarducci of Notre Dame University, a successful author and pension expert, explained that, during the same period that banks lost nearly half their household deposits (between 1978 and 1995), the portion of assets held by mutual funds and pension funds more than doubled, rising from 20% percent to 42%. By the early 1990s, institutions had become the dominant owners of government debt, corporate equities, and other financial assets in the U.S. Perhaps the single most dramatic aspect of this realignment is the steady institutionalization of savings. Workers' pension funds now represented the largest source of capital in the nation.

Using this body of research, the Working Group held its path-breaking two-day Heartland Labour Investment Forum in June 1996 in Pittsburgh, co-sponsored by the USWA and SVA, and HIT-BIT and the AFL-CIO Public Employees Department, featuring Rich Trumka as the keynote speaker. Among the topics presented were an analysis of the U.S. wage gap and the decline of manufacturing; an analysis of the changes in the financial capital markets and growing capital gaps; the role of workers' savings and investment in long-term job creation; U.S. models for regional sectoral investment and revitalization strategies; and an examination of the Canadian labour-sponsored funds (LSIFs). Critically, the forum showcased the potential impact of economically targeted investments (ETIs), and provided an overview of the U.S. private placement market in the 1990s. About 140 participants attended the conference, including a number of national labour and political leaders, and, importantly, pension fund advisors and managers.

A primary outcome from the intensive nine-month sessions of the Working Group, which met perhaps a dozen times in Pittsburgh in the offices of the Steelworkers, and the extensive discussions between meetings, was specific planning around the development of a national labour-capital investment strategy in the U.S. Among several plans put forward were the creation of a national fund-of-funds, which would be capitalized by a combination of pension and institutional investments. This national fund(s) would target investments through regional intermediaries. While Canadian-style tax credits were not viewed as practical, due to the right-wing control of Congress, there were proposals for "retail" investments from workers through a national pooling of a mutual fund-type vehicle.

Toward the second national conference

In 1997, following on the success of the 1996 conference, the Working Group, coordinated by Croft's efforts, obtained several prestigious foundation grants from the Ford, Rockefeller and Mott Foundations, and the McKay and Veatch Unitarian Funds to pursue further research and action. The grants were to help widen and sharpen discussion of a community-oriented labour capital strategy.

As the proposal to Ford, et al, explained, labour's capital was historically generally invested in income accounts, fixed-term securities (e.g., Treasury bonds, bills, and notes), or stock equities. In general, worker-owners had no voice in the management of pension funds and investment strategies. A virtual "pension industry complex," composed of fund managers, employer intermediaries, consultants and advisors, lawyers and actuaries, etc., generally controlled most investments.

Capped by the largest investment houses on Wall and Bay Streets, this complex has reaped over $200 billion in fees per year out of the pension system in the U.S. alone. It was not interested in "labour's involvement" in pension asset management; after all, its many functionaries—who, for the most part, invested in ways that were against the interests of worker beneficiaries—had no interest in "rocking the boat" (Baker 2001).

Due to joint trusteeship, construction unions had been successful with their Taft Hartley Funds[2] in capitalizing real estate investments. There had been limited efforts by a few state pension funds to set aside limited investments in state-level venture capital programs, and a few funds also invested in housing programs (Calabrese 2001). However, many of the practices of the venture capital firms historically were antithetical to labour interests and, due to inconsistencies in the number or selection process for labour trustees, state pension funds had not developed "worker-friendly" private capital efforts.

The industrial unions had been thwarted by the single- employer pension plans, of course, due to the fact that the funds did not permit worker trustees. But, as it turned out, a surprising number of private industry and service sector unions had, through various means and through amalgamations, inherited jointly trusted funds, similar to the construction unions.

The proposal called for efforts to explore a "labour capital strategy;" that is, a more intentional deployment of labour's capital by its owners. Early on, the Heartland Working Group realized the importance of focusing on greater capital accountability and greater capital responsibility. The former included efforts to root the control of labor's capital more firmly in the hands of its dispersed worker owners, and, more broadly, efforts to ensure investments of capital in ways that better advanced the interests of working people, while the latter ensured more responsible investments which do not hurt workers' interests over the long term.

If labour's capital was more firmly under the control of its worker owners, for example, it would be invested in ways that help foreclose the "low road" on industrial restructuring that so disrupted American labour markets and depressed family incomes, and help pave a more satisfying "high road" alternative. Additionally, it would reduce domestic investment's sensitivity to speculative international capital flows; reduce capital market volatility and impatience; and broaden the concept of enterprise shareholders to enterprise stakeholders.

Such an intentional investment strategy would not only be good for workers, but could also yield other social collateral benefits such as prudent investments in basic industries and small businesses that had been red-lined by conventional financial intermediaries. It would ease the capital gaps for such sectors; target investments in neglected metropolitan areas and abandoned industrial and mill communities; and might benefit low-income, dislocated and poor urban minority populations. Of interest to the business and labour communities alike, such changes in capital accountability would likely increase the aggregate amount of capital available for investment. This would have positive effects on economic growth, and encourage management attention to long-run capital expenditures and investments favourable to national well-being.

Heartland was willing to take on the major legal, financial, cultural, and logistical obstacles to developing a labour investment strategy. These included the historic lack of pension fund active trusteeship, the misconception of ERISA mandates, the reluctance of the financial markets to support a perceived pro-labour approach, the market's fixation on short-term liquidity, and the lack of a track record of such labour-sponsored funds. There were also institutional concerns or incapacity, including the obligation that retirement funds be available from pensions for members when they need it, or that asset growth not get in the way of growth in present wages and benefits.[3] Finally, there was a general lack of capacity among unions to manage complex investment portfolios or to do the demanding firm and industry analysis needed to make consistently profitable private placements.[4]

There were significant challenges, in short, to developing a labour/community capital strategy and longer-term investment strategy that was in any way similar to the Canadian experience. The Heartland Forum began to explore these at some length. Much more research and strategic planning was clearly required. At the same time, it was felt that there had been several developments that made the exploration of a more ambitious strategy timely, including:

- new leadership at the AFL-CIO, and among affiliates;
- discontent with traditional anti-poverty strategies among many major foundations and progressive organizations, along with regional economic democracy groups;
- new economic development strategies, including the labour federation's support for regional "high road" economic development

strategies, focused on quality jobs and small business retention and renewal, and opposed to traditional corporate subsidies;

- successful development of worker ownership and the development of ownership support networks;

- internationalization, or, more appropriately, the growing resistance to unfettered globalism, wherein a labour-capital strategy could limit some of its deleterious effects;

- market diversification: that is, the need to diversify pension portfolios so as to counter the uneasiness with the over-investment in public equities; and

- the beginnings of success: firms where CalPERs had intervened aggressively have improved their performance; housing construction trusts and socially motivated investment funds had also performed well.

These different developments together provided a rich environment for pursuing a capital strategy for labour. Clearly, there was potential to knit together a consensus program for financial institutional reform, labour revival, industry re-investment, urban and social targeted investment, and a more equitable capital system. Building on these themes, interests and coalitions, the aims of this second phase of the Heartland Project were to:

- develop research on overcoming barriers and obstacles to the ability of labor and its allies to develop a long-term capital strategy, including but not limited to replication of international success models and appropriate policy supports;

- assess current capacity, particularly in regional communities, to undertake such labour-led community-based investing;

- provide outreach to communities of interest, both at the national and regional level, on the possibilities of such a strategy; and

- connect through conferencing, networking, and other ongoing communication those interested in supporting, researching, and pursuing these strategies.

To accomplish these goals, the Heartland Working Group was expanded to include additional participants, researchers, investment analysts, regional labour and community development leaders, and religious representatives. With administration of the grants managed by the Steel Valley Authority, the Working Group established three task forces to carry out the objectives for the foundation-funded project: the Research and Policy Task Force, the Regional Network, and the Communications Task Force.

The research and policy task force

Joel Rogers, Professor of Law at the University of Wisconsin-Madison, and Director of the Center on Wisconsin Strategies, was paired with Tessa Hebb to organize the research effort. Rogers had assisted in crafting the foundation proposals. They began by organizing two colloquia to probe the economic, financial, legal, and regulatory barriers and opportunities involved in developing innovative "high road" pension investment strategies.

Rogers charged Archon Fung to assist in the preliminary research for three lengthy and extensively researched background literature reviews: "Problems in Capital Markets," "The Legal Regulation of Pension Funds," and "Social Investment: Concepts and Experiences". With these papers as background, participants at the colloquia began the process of defining the ground that a set of strategic Heartland research reports would cover.

In March 1998, the Heartland Project conducted a day-long colloquium on Capital Markets and Responsible Investing in Boston, organized around some of the most pressing economic and investment issues confronting working Americans. Convened by Project chairman Leo Gerard and hosted by Harvard University economist Richard Freeman, the event took place at the National Bureau of Economic Research in Cambridge, Massachusetts. Individuals invited to the colloquium brought a rich mix of academic expertise, trade union insight, public service, and long experience in the financial market trenches.

Gerard chaired a provocative discussion and give-and-take for hours, among some of the the foremost leaders in their field. Meredith Miller of the U.S. Department of Labour (DOL) explained that, "in 1994, we put out an interpretive bulletin (DOL 94-1) that signalled the Department's approval of alternative investments. For the first time, DOL said, 'Go ahead,' but we do not know whether pension fund trustees and money managers responded to this signal."

There was debate around a wide range of topics, covering capital markets and negative market activities, such as extreme leveraged buy-outs; capital gaps and the capital needs of small and medium-sized enterprises; high road investments and high performance work organizations; the need for trustee education, educating the consultants; responsible investments and ETIs, including the Canadian LSIFs, alternative investment fund models, social screens, and employee ownership; and defined benefit (DB) versus defined contribution (DC) plans.

The Heartland Project held a second research colloquium in April 1998 in New York City to examine the legal aspects of the possibility of regional investment strategies focused on labor's "double bottom-line" of high returns and high-road enterprise investments. Hosted by Katherine McFate of the Rockefeller Foundation, the colloquium on the *Legal Regulation of Pension Trusts and Responsible Investing* broke new ground in moving toward legal and policy frameworks. Participants included pension lawyers and advisors, academic experts on retirement law, and venture capital barristers.

"Lawyerly," yet lively and extensive discussion revolved around the ability for union trustees to craft labour capital strategies that could stand legal muster. Topics included the "whole participant," long-term value approach to pension investments; real and mythical barriers to responsible pension investing; relevant experience and models of responsible investment; and a reform agenda for a responsible ETI investment agenda. Participants such as Michael Calebrese, who later contributed a key research paper to the Heartland Project, clarified the legal aspects necessary to create worker-friendly investment vehicles that would invest in ETIs.

In addition to stimulating Heartland's research efforts, the colloquia provided an invaluable opportunity for like-minded scholars, trade unionists, legal advocates, pension practitioners, and policymakers to collaborate with one another. Scholars who were once only citations and references to each other met for the first time face to face. So did union staffers and investment professionals who manage their members' money, and advisors to pension funds.

The regional network task force

The Regional Network was coordinated by Rich Feldman, director of Seattle's Worker Center (King County AFL-CIO) and Sherman Kreiner, President and CEO of the Crocus Fund in Winnipeg. The Regional Network included organizations active in eight U.S. metropolitan areas—Baltimore, Boston, Chicago, Cleveland, Milwaukee, New York, Pittsburgh and Seattle. It also includes groups from two Canadian provinces (Manitoba and Ontario) that brought a wealth of organizing and fund-management experience to the venture.

In May 1998, the Heartland Project convened the first face-to-face meeting of its Regional Network in Pittsburgh. This meeting provided Heartland-affiliated groups with a mechanism for mutual support and technical assistance, learning from one another and collaboratively working through the development of regional investment intermediaries with a worker-friendly orientation.

Leaders of the Network compiled a tool kit providing community-based initiatives with strategic and technical assistance in three areas: creating a base of organizational support for labour investment funds; preparing effective regional market analyses; and laying the financial, legal, and marketing groundwork for fund development. Participants in the Network included a spectrum of labour organizations, community-labour alliances, and cooperative business-development groups.

Croft, Feldman and Kreiner led the discussions in this two-day session, which included Chairman Leo Gerard and a number of important speakers and guests. A second Network meeting, held in Washington, D.C. in May 1999, increased regional participation to a total of eight regions, including Baltimore, Boston, Chicago, Cleveland, Milwaukee, New York, Pittsburgh, and Seattle, as well as the Industrial Relations Center at the University of California at Berkeley.

Several Network participants had already made important strides in building the organizational support needed to begin exploring the development of regional funds. In Seattle, for example, the Worker Center won a "plank" in the King County AFL-CIO Union Cities program endorsing innovative investment strategies that may borrow from the Canadian LSIF model. In Maryland, the state AFL-CIO drafted a proposal for the state legislature calling for responsible pension-fund investing and the creation of a labour-sponsored venture fund. In Pittsburgh, the

SVA had made significant progress in actually building infrastructure for an investment fund for West Pennsylvania and surrounding states, and the Northeast Ohio group had begun to receive funding commitments to develop a regional fund.

As an article in the *Pittsburgh Post-Gazette* pointed out at the time, organized labour was already a significant investor in the Pittsburgh economy. Over a decade, union pension construction funds invested more than $158 million in Pittsburgh-area projects, generating 5,000 jobs. On the other hand, many of the corporate leaders in Pittsburgh responsible for economic development had closed plants and moved operations to Mexico.

The Regional Network meeting laid the groundwork for further regional capacity development, and began to fine-tune a number of strategy ideas for national and regional Heartland Funds, financed by a pool of labour capital, that would be targeted to worker-friendly manufacturing businesses and related industries.

The fund(s) would make investments in U.S. businesses with the objective of achieving long-term capital appreciation in the value of its investments. One investment target sector would be under-performing middle-market firms requiring operational, financial, or strategic restructuring, in cooperation with unions representing the company's employees. The fund(s) would promote meaningful workforce ownership and/or participation, utilizing high-performance and "co-determination" workforce models.

To locate and monitor suitable investments, the national Heartland Fund would utilize the Heartland regional network groups. This Network, through labour-oriented regional development authorities and corporations, would develop preliminary regional industrial and sectoral analysis and strategy, review the regional market for qualified investment opportunities, and evaluate and pre-screen such opportunities. Technical and advocacy services would include:

- marketing and shared due diligence and analysis, and ongoing monitoring services to the national fund;
- appropriate management supports, training investments, modernization financing; and
- regional public and private financing supports where possible.

Over time, national Heartland funds would invest in regional Heartland funds, which would raise matching investments in their regions or through alternative sources of labour, public and community capital. Regional funds could co-invest with the national fund or invest independently in (generally) smaller investments. The regional Heartland funds would make investments in small to medium-sized companies in their respective regions to promote and maintain capital retention and economic stability in these regions, business continuity, job retention and creation, and ownership of regional businesses, all objectives borrowed from the provincial Canadian LSIFs. The funds would also strive to provide an equitable rate of return for investors, build capital appreciation, foster economic development, and use their best efforts to promote employee ownership or employee participation in corporate governance, where appropriate.

The most significant research product created by the Network was a regional market analysis and capital gaps survey, laying the groundwork for further regional capacity development. Conducted by the Center for Labor and Community Research (CLCR), the study was organized in two sections, the first covering important and expanding economic sectors in eight U.S. metro areas, the second examining the financial status and capital needs of regionally important industries.

The Regional Network also compiled a large investment data base/inventory system for regional groups to access as part of the regional toolkit that provided resources for planning, development, seed funding, and capitalization of regional investment funds.

The communications task force

A Communications Task Force established by Tom Schlesinger and Teresa Ghilarducci was a relatively small group. It included a number of international union representatives, including union media experts, local labour activists, and community development advocates. The group organized a bi-national communications infrastructure that facilitated extensive conferencing and communications. It also created a functional "clearing-house" and website to provide multiple points of access to a broad, evolving archive of reports, data and materials regarding workers' capital.

The group set out to organize greater awareness of the national conference, and, as part of the build-up, orchestrated national and labour press articles, a newsletter, television broadcasts, publications in books and articles, and a major educational tour of the Quebec Solidarity Fund for trade union and political leaders.

The Heartland Project received an outstanding publicity launch in a nationally broadcast PBS four-part documentary on the economy, shown in over 50 cities, which featured Leo Gerard. Produced by Pulitzer Prize-winning reporter Hedrick Smith, *Surviving the Bottom Line* exposed the damages to the national economy wrought by the winner-take-all strategies driven by Wall Street money managers and corporate deal-makers. With extensive guidance from the Project, the producers visited Montreal for the final segment of the series (*"Beating the Bottom Line"*), interviewed the Solidarity Fund leaders, and described the success of workers' investment funds. The segment featured Leo Gerard, AFL-CIO Secretary-Treasurer Richard Trumka, and AFL-CIO President John Sweeney.

In January 1999, the Heartland Working Group organized an extraordinary tour of the Quebec Solidarity Fund in Montreal. Sponsored by the Steelworkers and the Solidarity Fund, the tour was organized to orient U.S. political and labour leaders to the Canadian LSIFs and develop a "cultural exchange." Twenty-one Congressional representatives and staff, labour officials and Heartland members travelled to Montreal. Two planes chartered by the USWA (Washington, D.C. and Pittsburgh) were met by representatives of the Fund, including Fernand Daoust, advisor to the President of the Fund, and Robert Dean, former Minister of Labour, Parti Quebecois, Quebec.

Presentations were made on the success of the fund, its creation and current projects. Sherman Kreiner of the Manitoba Crocus Fund also made a presentation. The tour was the beginning of ongoing pilgrimages germinated by Heartland, which led to several other trips to the Canadian labour-sponsored funds by U.S. regional groups and labour leaders, and visits to the U.S. by Canadian LSIF and labour representatives.

The Second National Heartland Conference

The "capstone" of the Heartland Project was the Second National Heartland Conference, co-hosted by the Steelworkers and the AFL-CIO Center for Working Capital (CWC), held in April 1999. It was extremely successful, and feedback from labour leaders in the working capital movement indicated it was one of the best conferences on labour capital ever held. Two hundred labour leaders and pension trustees, federal and state officials, community development and investment activists, academics and economists attended the conference from both the U.S. and Canada. Keynote speakers Rich Trumka, Secretary-Treasurer of the AFL-CIO, and Congressman David Bonior (Minority Whip) spoke at Friday's luncheon, praising the work of the Heartland Project; and Senator Paul Wellstone spoke at the Thursday reception, "firing up" the participants on a broad range of community investment issues

As part of the kick-off of the conference, Fernand Daoust explained the unheralded success on the part of the Solidarity Fund to launch the most innovative finance program in North America: "It has been a real thrill watching the Quebec Solidarity Fund come to life with more substance than we or anyone else ever imagined. It was viewed as a dream at its beginning, some sort of a Utopian idea, but now it's a reality. And it has inspired the creation of several other labour-sponsored investment funds in Canada."

Congressman Bonior, like Senator Wellstone an activist and pro-labour Democrat who went to jail on behalf of workers during the Detroit newspaper fights, started his keynote address with this statement: "It is vitally important to pursue new, sophisticated strategies to take advantage of our combined resources and to restructure our system that currently rewards irresponsible speculation and abandonment of American workers. Developing this new strategy is critical in our endeavours, and will only grow more important in the coming century."

The conference presented both the outstanding research papers completed by the Research Task Force and the goals for national Heartland funds. It hosted workshops on the development of pension trustee and regional investment education programs, and other topics. The conference unveiled investment finance public policy ideas inspired by Heartland, developed in conjunction with the Progressive Caucus of Congress. The conference set a milestone for years to come.

The Communications Task Force used the conference to help place a number of national press and media articles for Heartland. The Heartland Project attracted the attention of a number of books and publications that referenced the project, the conference, and the Canadian LSIFs over the next few years. National press for the conference or related issues included the *L.A. Times*, *Pensions and Investments Magazine*, *Steelabor* (Steelworkers), *Boston Globe*, and the Center for Working Capital Newsletter, *Working Capital*[5].

Finally, the Heartland Project went "on the road" and raised the flag at national conferences, participated in key policy discussions, and developed linkages with several important national associations, including:

- the White House Summit on Retirement Savings in June, 1998, at which Chairman Gerard made a brief presentation;
- the AFL-CIO Pension Investment Conference on September 19, 1998 in Pittsburgh (where Gerard also spoke);
- the White House briefing on community venture capital-oriented New Markets Initiative in February, 1999;
- the "High Performance Pensions Conference", in San Francisco (September, 1997); and
- the AFL-CIO Union Cities Conference in Chicago (August, 1998).

In addition, there were a number of smaller regional and local events and communications sponsored in the U.S. and Canada connected to Heartland.

Working Capital: The Power of Labor's Pensions is published

At the close of the conference in 1999, the authors of the research papers met with Leo Gerard and AFL-CIO staff to discuss their work. As a group, they felt the calibre of papers presented to the conference was sufficiently high to warrant publication and wider audience dissemination. This was particularly true in the absence of major new works on labour's capital strategy. The further work required to seek publication was supported by the USWA, AFL-CIO, and SVA. It was decided that the paper contributed by the AFL-CIO, Challenging Wall Street's Conventional Wisdom: Defining a Worker Owner View of Value (Silvers 2001), would conclude the volume and in effect generate the next stage of work in the development of labour's capital strategy.

Over the next two years, Fung, Hebb and Rogers worked with the research authors to structure the conference papers into a book for publication. The process of converting these papers was an awesome task, as the nine eventual chapters were authored and co-authored by people across the U.S. and Canada. The book was submitted to Cornell University Press, a scholarly press with a history of involvement with labour academics. In July of 2000, the editors received a green light from Cornell University Press, and Working Capital: The Power of Labor's Pensions was published in the late spring, 2001.

Working Capital: The Power of Labor's Pensions presented the findings of the Heartland Project research and documented the problems inherent in today's financial management. The work, with contributing essays by 13 academics and labour researchers, combined with a foreword by Leo Gerard, traces the thought on labour's capital strategy developed through the research colloquia, research agenda, and conference papers of the Heartland Project. The book offers new and exciting models, both in the U.S. and Canada, that advance not only ownership of labor's capital, but also its control. The result is a set of papers for pension fund trustees and others interested in using labour's power as owners of capital to advance its goals.

As with much of Heartland's work, the publication of Working Capital: The Power of Labor's Pensions can be seen as building capacity within the union movement to take on capital market issues. The book has attracted significant publicity, features and reviews since its release[6]

New directions for the labour/capital movement

Leo Gerard's vision for the labour/capital movement is to promote an alternative vision of the economy, one that is more humane and sustainable. The Heartland Project, and the Heartland Network that has grown out of this work, promotes the idea of a growing, embryonic new "labour/capital" movement in North America, focused on the democratization of capital, capital accountability, responsible investment, and regional community investment.

The broader movement is connecting labour/capital advocates around the world. The AFL-CIO, the Office of Worker Investment, and the Center for Working Capital have been working with unions from Canada, Britain, Australia, European countries, and other nations to create an international labour-capital strategy. These efforts, coordinated by the International Confederation of Free Trade Unions (ICFTU), are part of a global strategy for shareholder campaigns and pension trustee education.

The Heartland Network hopes to expand its network of progressive labour activists, pension experts and economists, development/finance advocates, social investment, religious and green leaders, connecting to regional economic democracy groups in the U.S. and the labour-sponsored funds (LSIFs) in Canada. One result may be a permanent bi-national network to explore the next steps in the development of workers' capital. These steps might include, as an extension of the pension trustee programs, the development of regional pension trustee forums.

Forums are being organized in California, New York, Boston and Pittsburgh to begin exploring long-term capital strategies around the needs of working people and their communities. The efforts of the New York trustees have led to initiatives to create affordable housing for working people in that city, utilizing the labour housing investment trusts, and to actually take a lead in developing a long-term economic recovery plan for the city. There are also a number of other states and cities in the U.S. where major new labour-capital strategies are under way, including:

- California, with the leadership of Sean Harrigan of the UFCW, State Treasurer Phil Angelides, and other active trustees such as San Francisco Mayor Willy Brown, CALPERS, the California Public Employee Retirement System, pledged to invest 2% of its total assets in poor and under-served areas in California; CalPERs is also starting an unprecedented national worker-friendly merchant bank;
- Hawaii, where a campaign to create a socially-responsible mandate for the state's pension funds and natives trusts has resulted in a "blue-green-grey" coalition that brings together blue-collar labour leaders and trustees, greens and the elders of the native people.

Just as labour needs to maintain a presence in anti-globalization resistance, as one of the few movements that have inspired students and young people to support workers' positions on issues such as sweatshops, unfair trade and anti-democratic global financial institutions (IMF, etc.), the labour-capital movement needs to forge coalitions with forces that are challenging unilateral corporate power. One context might be to explore long-term investments in profitable alternative energy companies, to lessen our dependence on overseas oil.

Again, these $7 trillion in pension funds in the U.S. and $700 million in Canada together own a plurality of corporate stock in North America. There are tremendous religious/social assets that could also be mobilized.

Workers' capital strategies will most likely have a long-lasting positive impact on society, benefiting retirees while contributing to the betterment of working families and communities. The Heartland Network, which evolved from a small "grievance committee" into an important part of the growing labour-capital movement, shows that innovative societal collaborations, particularly those involving organized labour, can create the momentum for major social change.

Notes

[1] Eminent domain powers are public powers, which allow a city to take over property. Traditionally used to build roads and other public goods, the SVA has used this provision to prevent the demolition of industrial facilities and equipment.

[2] Taft Hartley Funds, or multi-employer pension plans, were enabled by the Taft-Hartley Act, allowing union workers who worked for similar firms (such as construction companies) to pool their retirement savings.

[3] As among Chrysler workers in the 1980s, who traded pension assets for better wages and current benefits.

[4] This is so even in construction, where unions typically have higher levels of control over assets than in other sectors.

[5] Prominent references to the work of the Heartland Project include *Hijacking the Future: How Wall Street is Taking over Workers' Pensions*, an article by James Ridgeway, in a special issue of Dollars and Sense, September-October, 1999; *Economic Development: A Union Guide to the High Road*, a book by Bob Baugh, AFL-CIO Working for America Institute; *Contested Terrain: Republican Rhetoric, Pension Funds and Community Development*, an article by Gordon Clark, University of Oxford; and *Prudence, Patience and Jobs: Pension Investment in a Changing Canadian Economy*, Kirk Falconer, Canadian Labour Market and Productivity Center (January 1999).

[6] Features and reviews are in *Business Week Online*, NPR's *Marketplace*, *Business Ethics Magazine* and Social Policy Magazine.

CHAPTER 7

The role of progressive labour-sponsored funds as tools for advancing economic and social goals

The Crocus Investment Fund experience

by Sherman Kreiner

ECONOMICALLY TARGETED INVESTING IS MOST COMMONLY used to describe activities of institutional funds, including pension funds. However, labour-sponsored investment funds (LSIFs) can also be characterized as economically targeted investments (ETIs). The main distinction between them is that LSIFs utilize self-directed, rather than institutional, retirement funds.

But the activities of LSIFs meet the three-pronged definition of ETI[1].

1. Their investments are utilized to fill a capital gap: in this case, providing venture capital to small and mid-sized businesses in provinces, regions or sectors in which sources of venture capital are limited or non-existent.

2. The investments provide a collateral benefit to the community in which the investments are made. While these collateral benefits may vary from fund to fund, they almost always include job creation. They also focus on such issues as regional economic development or employee ownership.

3. The investments are designed to provide a risk- adjusted market rate of return to investors.

In fact, one of the distinctions between funds sponsored by Canadian Labour Congress affiliates across the country, including the five funds in the Labour-Sponsored Investment Funds Alliance,[2] and the "rent-a-union" funds[3] is that many of the rent-a-union funds are not designed to provide a collateral benefit, and in that respect do not meet the three-pronged ETI definition which the Alliance funds meet.

LSIFs also provide a platform for more conventional ETIs because they offer a track record of experienced proven local management managing within an ETI mandate. One of the challenges often faced by institutional funds in considering ETIs is that they do not have the internal management capability to make the investment decisions associated with the ETI mandate. They would prefer to place that investment responsibility in a local manager, but in many communities there are no such experienced managers. LSIFs offer that management capability, at least in the area of venture capital. Many LSIFs, including the Crocus Fund, now manage institutional capital in sectoral or regional funds, along with the individual investment capital which makes up the bulk of their investment assets.

The Crocus Fund was the first, and is the largest, labour-sponsored investment fund in Manitoba. Its corporate mission, however, extends beyond the narrow venture capital mandate; Crocus's mission is to be the pre-eminent economic development organization in Manitoba. The Fund attempts to achieve that mission through three major areas of activity: first, the core venture capital fund itself, which has both financial and social policy objectives; secondly, through the creation and management of other sectoral venture capital funds; and thirdly, through a variety of initiatives designed to facilitate downtown and core area development, including the True North Project, the Manitoba Property Fund, and the not-for-profit enterprise development corporation called Community Ownership Solutions, all of which will be described in greater detail below.

The Crocus Fund was the first LSIF initiative in a small-population province. It accounts for the majority of available venture capital in Manitoba and has been the catalyst for the creation of other venture capital pools in that province. It achieves its capital formation through a multi-track sales network which has grown its asset base to close to $170 million. Its more than 30,000 individual shareholders represent approximately one-tenth of all Manitoba RRSP holders.

The Fund was initiated as a community and labour response to the 1989 U.S./Canada Free Trade Agreement, and evolved in response to the question as to whether employee ownership might be an effective strategy to mitigate the economic dislocations associated with free trade. While the ultimate answer to that question was "No, large plant shutdowns are not good candidates for employee ownership," its exploration revealed some significant challenges, including ownership challenges, within the Manitoba economy.

Manitoba was starved for institutional venture capital. Once businesses grew beyond the financial resources of their founders, friends, family and angel investors, access to capital became a daunting challenge. Many businesses simply stopped growing. Others, often those led by the most entrepreneurial members of the business community, sourced capital elsewhere in Canada or in the U.S., too often at the price of moving corporate headquarters to the capital source. This resulted in companies leaving the province, just at the time they were becoming large enough to become meaningful corporate citizens.

The ownership challenge was equally daunting. Much of the local economy was not locally owned. Much of the portion which was locally owned was owned by entrepreneurs with succession challenges. If they had children, in many instances, they were no longer in Manitoba, or, if they were, they were still in-province: they were now doctors or lawyers, or in other professions, and had no interest in taking over the business.

Because Manitoba is so far from commercial centres, prospective purchasers of those businesses, if any, were primarily interested in market share and not operating capacity. So, at the first opportunity for a rationalization, they would shut the Manitoba operations down while maintaining the customer lists for production at facilities outside of Manitoba. In many cases there would be no prospective buyers at all, and the business would simply shut down on the day that the entrepreneur/ founder retired.

The people most likely to maintain the business as an operating business were the people who worked there: the managers and employees of the business. But no one treated them as serious purchasers because they were not deemed to have sufficient personal wealth to buy the business. The Fund was designed to provide equity capital to help private Manitoba businesses grow, to complement sources of equity of workers and managers should an employee or management buyout ultimately be pursued, and to begin the process of transition to employee ownership well in advance of the owner's retirement.

The Fund concept was endorsed by the Manitoba Federation of Labour in 1991 and enacted into law as the Manitoba Employee Ownership Act in the same year. The Fund was supported by the federal and provincial governments, each of which provided seed equity as well as tax credits to individual investors, and the Fund began seeking individual investors in January of 1993.

The Fund had five objectives at the outset:

1. to facilitate capital retention in Manitoba;
2. to promote the growth of small and mid-sized businesses and to ensure their continuity from one generation to the next;
3. to retain existing jobs in small and mid-sized companies and to create new jobs;
4. to foster employee ownership and employee part in corporate governance and management; and
5. to provide a competitive rate of return to the Fund's investors.

As noted above, start-up capital was provided by government seed equity,[4] with $2 million invested by both the provincial and federal governments. The Fund has also raised institutional investment from a variety of local sources, including Credit Union Central of Manitoba, the Workers' Compensation Board, the Manitoba Government Employees' Union Strike Fund, Manitoba Blue Cross, and the Garment Manufacturers and Garment Workers' Pension Fund. The early commitment of these organizations to provide capital to the fund helped increase the Fund's credibility in the financial services community and was a key factor in fostering the early rounds of individual investment.

Because the Fund is in a small-population province, it was decided to utilize a multi-track sales network to maximize sales. Essentially, the plan was to make the Fund available in a broad range of venues so that, wherever an investor was comfortable purchasing, the Fund would be available for sale. The Fund is sold by brokers and mutual fund dealers. It is also sold in credit unions and it is sold by Crocus Capital Inc., a wholly-owned Fund subsidiary.

Crocus Capital is staffed by volunteer union members who are seconded to the Fund to sell Crocus shares. They are trained in a course developed by Crocus and approved by the Manitoba Securities Commission, and are supervised by a broker with the highest level of supervisory designation, the PDO designation.

The sales network is a hybrid of the approaches taken across Canada. In Quebec, the initial LSIF, the Solidarity Fund, makes all of its sales through seconded representatives, utilizing a Crocus Capital type model. In English-speaking Canada, prior to the Crocus initiative, sales were made exclusively through the conventional financial services community, brokers, and mutual fund dealers. In order to maximize sales in a small-population province, Crocus utilized both sales networks.

This model has subsequently been adopted by the First Ontario Fund and the Workers' Investment Fund in New Brunswick. However, of the more than two dozen—now rapidly increasing to three dozen—labour-sponsored funds in Canada, only four, the Solidarity Fund and the three funds previously identified in English-speaking Canada, utilize seconded reps to make a portion of their sales.

There are benefits to this model in terms of maximizing sales, but there are also benefits that flow to the labour union. From the Fund's perspective, the use of seconded representatives removes the sole dependency on the traditional financial services specialists. Their commitment may be fickle and dependent on the performance of the Fund and the performance of competing products.

The model also generates a knowledge base in the labour movement which did not previously exist. This knowledge is both in the area of investment and investment vehicles and provides benefits for a broad range of personal investment decisions made by the secondees. It also develops a broad expertise in finance, reading and understanding financial statements, and financial management, which secondees can take back to their place of work. This expertise can increase their effectiveness in a variety of contexts, including collective bargaining.

The Fund is now, and has been for many years, the primary source of venture capital in Manitoba. There was such a shortage of venture capital in the province that, as early as 1996, when the Fund had approximately $50 million in assets, it accounted for more than two-thirds of all available institutional venture capital in the province. While the growth in Fund assets has continued to be dramatic, the percentage of institutional venture capital which it represents has declined slightly as other participants, encouraged by the Fund's positive experience, have entered the field. These have included a number of sectoral funds, focused primarily in the bio-tech and information technology sectors, and another labour-sponsored fund.

The Fund has invested approximately $130 million in 60 small and mid-sized Manitoba businesses. The diversity of the investment portfolio reflects the diversity of the Manitoba economy. Approximately 32% of the portfolio is invested in the manufacturing sector, 18% in entertainment and hospitality, 24% in science, medical and technology, 10% in financial services, 9% in the service sector, and 7% in the transportation sector.

The Fund assures that it maintains its commitment to a range of social policy objectives by piggybacking a unique social audit component onto its conventional due diligence when it evaluates an investment in a particular company. The conventional due diligence looks to determine whether there is a strong management team largely in place, whether the company has growth potential, evaluates the strength of its balance sheet, and looks at its history of profitability. The primary focus in this part of the work is on the evaluation of management, because, first and foremost, the Fund invests in people.

But this conventional due diligence is supplemented by a social audit which evaluates the practices of the prospective investee company in the areas of health and safety, environment, employment equity, and labour relations. In utilizing this social audit instrument, the Fund is not just an economically targeted investor; it is also an ethical or socially responsi-

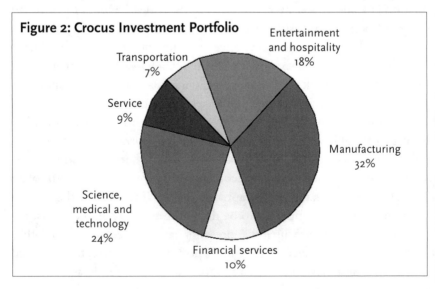

Figure 2: Crocus Investment Portfolio

Transportation 7%
Service 9%
Science, medical and technology 24%
Financial services 10%
Manufacturing 32%
Entertainment and hospitality 18%

ble investor. Unlike some SRI funds, the social audit is not primarily used to create a negative screen, although, in egregious cases involving environmental degradation or consistently poor health and safety practices, the social audit will be a reason for the Fund not to invest. Rather, the Fund looks to use the social audit to create a positive screen to provide the opportunity to invest in best-of-sector businesses. This approach is similar to the approach taken by Michael Jantzi Research Associates in developing the Jantzi Social Index[5] for public Canadian companies.

One example of the Fund's best-of-sector approach is its investment in Dynamic Pork, a Manitoba-based hog processing operation. Manitoba has experienced a dramatic increase in hog production in the past half-dozen years, and a number of hog producers approached the Fund for investment. The Fund's social audit suggested that, if the environmental practices being utilized by the companies that approached the Fund were maintained in an industry that grew from one million to nine million hogs in Manitoba, the industry would not be environmentally sustainable. As a consequence, the Fund made a decision to make no investments in that sector.

Dynamic Pork, however, reflected a very different approach to environmental compliance. It committed to the construction of all new facilities. The company made a decision to comply immediately with environmental regulations that were not scheduled to be implemented by the province until four years later. It imposed a requirement that any sub-contractor also comply with the yet-to-be-implemented environmental regulations, and it funded an internal environmental compliance position to ensure aggressive internal monitoring of environmental compliance. The Fund believed that, if these practices were implemented across the industry, industry growth could be sustained at the anticipated levels without creating permanent long-term environmental damage. The Fund therefore made a decision to invest in Dynamic Pork as the best-of-sector operator and to try to increase that company's market share, putting increasing pressure on other competitors to raise their performance to the environmental bar set by the Fund's investee company.

The Fund has also used the best-of-sector approach in making decisions regarding investments in traditionally low-wage sectors in which labour is treated as a commodity and profit margins are maximized by driving down labour costs. The Fund has looked, by contrast, to invest in companies which believe that the most important determinate of a quality service is a quality job and which have striven to increase market share through a differentiation based on high quality rather than low cost. The Fund's investments in a restaurant management company, a security company, and a collision repair consolidator have been driven by the "employer of choice" commitment made by their entrepreneur/ leaders.

The Fund also has as an objective the facilitation of employee ownership and participative management. The Fund has a variety of reasons for pursuing this objective. Employee ownership maintains local ownership of Manitoba businesses and assures that business decisions affecting those businesses are made locally. As described more fully above, employee ownership also provides a mechanism for inter-generational transfer of business in retiring-owner scenarios where there is no family-based succession plan. Employee ownership also creates wealth for workers, and in doing so provides a counter-point to the growing wealth disparity between rich and poor in North America.

U.S. employee ownership trade associations report that the average worker in an ESOP (Employee Stock Ownership Plan) company accrues value in the plan, over 10 years, which is equivalent to twice his or her average annual earnings[6]. Employee ownership improves productivity in companies that have plans in combination with participative management programs[7]. In short, the Fund promotes employee ownership because it both facilitates several important policy objectives and because it fosters improved productivity and performance compared to conventional companies, giving Manitoba companies which implement such plans a competitive advantage in the global economy.

The Fund supports employee ownership in a variety of different ways. Discussions of employee ownership with prospective partners are incorporated in the Fund's due diligence. As part of its social audit, Fund staff evaluate the predisposition of senior managers to implement participative management programs in their companies. The Fund has designed a variety of innovative models to create broad-based ownership plans in its investee companies, including models which utilize a deferred profit-sharing plan structure and models which utilize a group RRSP structure.

The Fund has also created a CEO Roundtable in which the CEOs of all investee companies participate. The Roundtable has a broad agenda, covering many issues of concern to the CEO's. Included within that agenda is the introduction by the Fund to the CEOs of principles of employee ownership and participative management. This discussion, within a peer setting, promotes a frank conversation of fears, concerns, perceived benefits and risks. Investee companies are not mandated to implement plans. The concepts are simply introduced to them in an environment where they, along with other CEOs, can explore options, identify issues of concern, and ask blunt questions.

Companies implementing or considering the implementation of employee ownership plans have set up working groups within the Roundtable, and recently undertook and completed a comprehensive manual for investee companies comparing and contrasting their various employee ownership plans. The purpose of the manual was to provide companies considering employee ownership with a range of options they might consider, the pro's and con's of the decision that they might make with regard to particular structural elements, and detailed information on plan design so that companies implementing employee ownership plans do not have to "re-invent the wheel" each time, with the considerable accounting and legal costs involved. The Fund also supports employee ownership by offering a range of customized and more general educational programs for both managers and rank-in-file workers, which may cover such topics as financial education, the details and structure of an employee ownership plan, and strategies for implementing effective participative management programs in employee- owned companies.

The Fund has created employee ownership opportunities for more than 30% of all employees within its investee companies. One powerful testament to the impact of employee ownership comes with the early 2000 sale of the Angus Reid Group to Paris-based IPSOS, the world's ninth largest market research company. The sale serves as a glowing testament to the benefits of employee ownership. Unlike most Canadian companies, a broad-based group of employees own a significant portion of the business. Close to half the company's ownership is vested in its employees, and more than half of the company's full-time employees are worker-owners.

Employee ownership was a significant factor in the company's extremely strong pre-acquisition performance. In a recent letter to the Fund, Reid noted:

> [The employee ownership plans] *have been extraordinarily powerful tools, and one of the most important factors underlying our success in recruiting and retaining the very best talent in the*

industry. In addition ... we now produce quarterly and annual financial reports with commentary, commensurate with being a public company, and we educate employees as to the balance sheet, our financial plans, and the key drivers of our profitability (and therefore share price). The success of this program is best illus-trated by the high level of enthusiasm and the fact that we now have 132 employee shareholders, with a clear focus on what it takes to make this company a continuing economic success.

Now, post-acquisition, the employee owners will be reaping the ben-efits through significant wealth creation. Some stand to triple their in-vestment, while others will achieve a five- or six-fold increase.

As described in detail above, research data are quite strong in suggest-ing that performance benefits of employee ownership require a contem-poraneous implementation of participative management programs. In their absence, while performance improvements may be associated with the implementation of employee ownership plans, those performance improvements are not maintained. Many Roundtable CEOs have recog-nized this need and have sought a forum to which other senior managers in their companies could receive comprehensive training in implement-ing participative management. To respond to that need, the Fund worked closely with the University of Manitoba Program in Continuing Educa-tion and the Asper School of Business to create a Certificate Program in Participative Management which is offered jointly by the University of Manitoba and the CEO Roundtable. The 200 contact hour program pro-vides instruction in subject areas relevant for developing a participative management style and workplace environment. The first seven gradu-ates of the program, all from Crocus investee companies, completed the course in the spring of 2001. The second course commenced in the fall of 2002 with 15 enrollees, including participation from Crocus investee companies, non-investee companies, and community-based non-profit organizations.

Employee ownership is much less prevalent in Canada than in the United States, where close to 10% of all corporate equity is owned by employees. This is in part because, since 1974, American tax and em-ployee benefit law has enabled the creation of tax-advantaged trusts called employee stock ownership plans (ESOP) designed for the sole purpose of acquiring employer securities for the benefit of a broad-based em-ployee group. These trusts can leverage the employer's corporate assets to borrow acquisition capital that is repaid in pre-tax dollars. Employees thus become owners, through a leveraged buy-out mechanism that requires no employee out-of-pocket investment. Complementary tax incentives have been provided to shareholders that sell 30% or more of company shares to employees.

Canada does not have ESOP legislation. As a result, companies have modified other employee benefit structures (not specifically created for employee ownership) to create employee ownership plans. In some circumstances where companies want to create employee ownership, existing law flatly prohibits them. In other cases, the structures used are unnecessarily complex.

As a consequence, the Fund, often working closely with its investee company CEOs, has been a tireless advocate for federal legislation to create a Canadian stock ownership plan as an analogue to the U.S. ESOP.

Lastly in the area of employee ownership, the Fund is working with a number of employee-owned Manitoba companies to create a Centre for Excellence in Employee Ownership at the University of Manitoba. Modelled on the Ohio Employee Ownership Center at Kent State University, the centre would provide research, education and technical assistance for employee-owned companies or companies considering the implementation of employee ownership plans.

As noted above, job retention and job creation are also primary Fund objectives. As of September 30, 2001, the Fund's investments in 60 small and mid-sized Manitoba businesses had created[8], saved[9], or maintained more than 11,200 jobs and had resulted in the creation of more than 4,000 new jobs. Fund investments create or save one new job for each $20,740 invested. This is twice the number of jobs created or saved per dollar invested as the venture capital industry average.

The Fund's core activities, which are described above, are now being supplemented in several areas, including the creation of sectoral venture capital funds. The Fund's first foray into this area was the creation of the Manitoba Science and Technology Fund (MS&T). This is a $10 million fund which invests in emerging science and technology companies. The Fund is structured as a limited partnership, with a wholly-owned Fund subsidiary acting as the general partner and managing the investments. Capital is sourced from the Fund itself, as well as from local and non-local institutional and individual sources. The Fund plans to use the MS&T fund as a template to develop a broad range of new sectoral funds with total assets under management in excess of $100 million. These new sources of venture capital for investment in Manitoba will primarily be capitalized by Manitoba institutional funds; that is, by the creation of conventional ETI investment opportunities.

In early 2002, the fund announced the creation of the Springboard Fund, which will provide capital for early-stage commercialization for research developed by University of Manitoba researchers. This early-stage investment can be later supplemented by investment from the Manitoba Science & Technology Fund and, if the companies grow, ultimately by investment from the core Crocus Investment Fund. Other sectoral funds are being developed in the areas of value-added agriculture, environmental technology and alternative energy, and Aboriginal-owned businesses. The Fund is also developing a technology carve-out fund for non-U.S. rights for the manufacture of products developed by Minnesota-based Fortune 500 companies, which include committed supply contracts and licences from the Fortune 500 companies and their affiliates.

In addition to the creation of a broad range of sectoral funds, the Fund is fulfilling its economic development mandate through a range of downtown and core area development initiatives. The Fund has significant investment in a broad range of businesses that are committed to Winnipeg's downtown development. These include the Winnipeg Goldeye's Baseball Team, CanWest Global Park, a number of high-end downtown restaurants managed by the WOW Hospitality Group, a downtown nightclub called the Mezzo Partnership, one of Manitoba's leading IT service providers (On-Line Business Systems), and Manitoba's leading local brokerage firm, Wellington West Capital.

The Fund has also recently moved its office to the downtown historical Exchange District, Winnipeg's commercial centre at the early part of the 20th Century. The Fund's participation as the anchor tenant in an old six-storey hardware/department store has given that building, which was slated for demolition, a new life. The Fund's commercial lease has made it possible for the balance of the building to be occupied by a range of arts organizations, including the Manitoba Music Conservatory, Contemporary Dancers Institute, and the Winnipeg Folk Festival, as well as the Manitoba Arts Stabilization Fund. The Fund hopes to use the Crocus building as a model for mixed-use development in Winnipeg's downtown.

The Fund has also fostered downtown activity through its support for the Manitoba Theatre for Young People's capital campaign, which brought a new performing arts centre for young people to the Forks where the Red and Assiniboine rivers converge in downtown Winnipeg. In addition, the Fund sponsors Crocus Thursday Night Live at the Forks, bringing live jazz, blues and big-band music downtown each week throughout the summer.

The Fund is also a primary proponent of the True North Project, an effort to build a new sports and entertainment complex in the heart of Winnipeg's downtown, replacing the more than 50-year-old Winnipeg Arena. While the project has generated some controversy because of its proposed location at the site of the abandoned Eaton's department store, it is viewed by the Fund as a critical linchpin for downtown development. It will be the home of Winnipeg's American Hockey League Manitoba Moose team, the site for a range of large and small concerts, as well as a retail and commercial centre, including a number of street-level restaurants, combined with local streetscape enhancement. The $135 million project is a true public/private partnership involving all three levels of government with very significant private sector equity investment and debt financing provided by a syndicate of local lending institutions.

The Fund is also attempting to foster downtown development through the creation of a real-estate fund with a downtown investment focus. The Fund will invest in renovated mixed-use facilities like the newly-renovated Crocus building, as well as more mainstream downtown commercial real-estate investments. It will be capitalized primarily by economically targeted investing, by pension funds, and Crown Corporations. Its initial capitalization target is $20 million, although a larger capital pool is ultimately desired. In many respects, the Manitoba Property Fund is modelled on the B.C.-based Concert Properties Real Estate Development Corporation, but, unlike Concert which is focused almost exclusively on affordable housing, the Manitoba Property Fund will have a wider range of real estate investments in its portfolio because the scope of the real estate capital gap in Winnipeg and Manitoba is much broader than the capital gap that was experienced in British Columbia at the time that Concert was being formed.

Finally, in the area of core area development, the Fund has created a not-for-profit enterprise development corporation called Community Ownership Solutions (COS) and has obtained charitable status from

Revenue Canada. This corporation, which is governed by a board which includes individuals from other community development corporations, labour leaders, business leaders, university presidents, and other community leaders, is designed to create high-quality jobs for individuals from low-income communities through the creation of relatively large-scale business enterprises. The approach is market-driven and is based on the quality job/quality service linkage described above: that is, the belief that the most important determinate of a quality service is a quality job. COS defines a quality job as one which offers good wages and benefits, career advancement opportunities, empowerment through participation, and financial security through ownership.

Companies which offer such jobs can differentiate themselves from their competitors who offer low-quality jobs in terms of the quality of service which they provide. If they are successful in providing that higher quality service, that form of market differentiation will increase their revenues and their market share. As they become market leaders, pressure will be put on their competitors to move away from treating labour as a commodity and match the wages and benefits being offered to the employees in the successful companies. Otherwise competitors will find their best workers leaving to join the company which has raised the bar in terms of job quality. This model has been extremely successful in childcare, homecare, home-cleaning and temporary services sectors in the United States, and Community Ownership Solutions is designed to replicate those successful models in Winnipeg's core area.

The core of the Crocus Fund's business remains its unique venture capital fund, which fosters business continuity and growth, job creation, and employee ownership, through investments in ethical Manitoba businesses. However, in order to effectively meet its economic development mandate, the Fund has broadened its approach to foster the creation of new venture capital pools, real estate development funds, sports and entertainment facilities, and other downtown amenities and enterprise development corporations in low-income communities. Many of these initiatives are designed to be catalysts for dramatically increased levels of local investment by local individual and institutional sources, and ultimately to lever significant investment of outside capital in the province.

Notes

[1] The three-pronged definition of economically targeted investing was established by the US Department of Labour in Department of Labour Interpretive Bulletin 94-1 on Economically Targeted Investments, 59 Fed. Reg. 32,606 (June 23, 1994.)

[2] The five funds in the Labour Sponsored Investment Funds Alliance are the Quebec Solidarity Fund, the Workers Investment Fund (New Brunswick), the First Ontario Fund, the Crocus Investment Fund (Manitoba) and the Working Opportunity Fund (British Columbia).

LSIFA has an agreed set of progressive principles, which ensure not just labour sponsorship of the capital pool, but control by a legitimate labour organization, a commitment to making economic and social goals in making investments, including a commitment to job retention and job creation, a commitment to regional economic development, a commitment to the use of a social audit as part of investment due diligence focusing on workplace health and safety, sound environmental practices, ethical employment practices and cooperative labour relations; and a commitment to changing labour-management relations within investee companies which may focus on employee ownership participative management or financial education for workers. LSIFA Funds are also committed to: participation by a broad base of average working people; the provision of venture capital within a diversified portfolio, cooperation between labour and business, and the provision of a competitive rate of return to shareholders.

[3] Rent-a-union funds are non-Canadian Labour Congress Funds, sponsored by professional associations or small renegade labour organizations who cede effective control of their funds to conventional venture capital fund managers in exchange for a fee based on the amount of assets under management.

[4] The Provincial Government investment was structured as non-redeemable equity with detachable warrants permitting the government to purchase up to 200,000 shares of the Fund at $10 per share (the original share price) at any time after the year 2000. The Federal Government investment was structured as a contribution with annual repayment obligation of $200,000 in years in which particular profit thresholds were surpassed. The seed equity was designed to cover the Fund's anticipated operating losses in the years prior to the Fund reaching a breakeven size (approximately $30 million in assets) without causing a reduction in the Fund's share price.

[5] "MJRA is Canada's leading provider of social and environmental research for institutional investors. The JSI is a socially screened, market capitalization-weighted common stock index modeled on the S&P/TSE 60. The JSI consists of 60 Canadian companies that pass a set of broadly based social and environmental screens. MJRA created the JSI to be a benchmark for money managers and other investors against which they can measure the performance of socially screened portfolios. From its inception on January 1, 2000 through January 31, 2002, the JSI lost 8.78%, while the S&P/TSE 60 lost 9.64%, the TSE 300 lost 7.02% over the same period." (Taken from the Michael Jantzi Research Associates News Release, dated February 15, 2002.)

[6] See also, Kardas, Peters; Scarf, Andria; Keogh, Jim (1998). Wealth and Income Consequences of Employee Ownership, a comparative study from Washington State, Washington State Community Trade and Economic Development. This study explored the relationship between ESOP company performance vs. Non-ESOP company performance and benefits accruing to employers and concluded that: wages at ESOP companies grew 8% higher than the comparison group at the median, 4% higher at the 10th percentile and 18% at the 90th percentile; total compensation for employee owned company employees is approximately 20% higher, with ESOP companies more likely to provide comprehensive benefits to all employees: and the value of pension and retirement plans was $32,000 in ESOP companies compared to $12,500 in comparison companies which also had a much lower participation rate.

[7] For discussion, see the following:

General Accounting Office (1987). *Employee Stock Ownership Plans, Little Evidence of Effects on Corporate Performance.* GAO/PEMD-88-1

Quarry, Michael and Rosen, Corey (1987, updated 1997), *Employee Ownership and Corporate Performance.* Reprinted in National Centre for Employee Ownership, 1998

Rosen, Corey; Klein Katherine; and Young Karen (1986). *Employee Ownership in America: the equity solution.* Lexington, MA: Lexington Books

Winther, Gorm (1993). *Employee Ownership in New York: A Comparative Analysis of Growth Performance.* In NCEO 1998

Maxwell, Jill, Rosen, Corey, and Weeden (1998) *Open Book Management and Corporate Performance.* In NCEO 1998

Kardas, Peter; Sommers, Paul; Winther, Gorm; Marens Richard; and Gale Katrina (1993). *Employment and Sales Growth in Washington State Employee Ownership Companies: a comparative analysis.* Washington State Department of Community Development

Kardas, Peter (1994). *Comparing Growth Rates in Employee Ownership Companies to their Participatory Competitors.* Washington State Department of community Development

[8] The Fund defines a job created as a full-time permanent or full-time equivalent new job created within one year of the Fund making an investment or an add-on investment.

[9] The Fund defines a job saved as a job which but for the Fund's investment would have been lost. There are few jobs in this latter category. An example, involves a manufacturing company, which was to be sold to a multinational company, which had a publicly stated intention to close a significant portion of the Manitoba operations. The Funds investment facilitated a management/employee buyout, which maintained all Manitoba operations. The jobs which would have been lost had the multinational buyer been successful are categorized as jobs saved

CHAPTER 8

Economically targeted investments

Doing well and doing good

by Sean Harrigan[1]

ECONOMICALLY TARGETED INVESTMENTS (ETIS) ARE PROFITABLE. ETI opportunities, when properly identified and sought out, can be prolific. And, without question, they have a proper place in your investment portfolio.

It may help to explain why I am such an advocate of ETIs if I start by telling the story of a woman I'll call Ann. It starts back in the late 1980s, when she was a legal secretary at the California Department of Transportation, the agency that builds that state's roads and highways.

Ann was a single mom, with a young child to raise on her own. As an entry-level worker, she brought home a modest living wage—but it was just enough to put a roof over their heads. One day she came home and found a letter taped to her door. It was from the landlord. She opened it with a feeling of dread: yes, the rent was going up, and Ann was devastated.

When she sat down and penciled things out, she realized she couldn't afford the increase in rent. But she figured out she could do better if she went out and bought a condominium. In fact, her mortgage payment might even be less. But she had two strikes against her. She didn't have money for a down payment. And she doubted she could get a loan, because it was the beginning of a recession in California, and many banks weren't lending.

Shortly afterward, Ann mentioned her dilemma to her boss over lunch one day. Her boss listened sympathetically and agreed with her: it was a darn shame. But he got to thinking that night, not only about how fortunate he was to have purchased a home, but also about what might be done to assist hard-working public employees. After all, these are people with good jobs, who are good credit risks, and who shouldn't be charged an arm and a leg to borrow for their home.

So, he wondered, could CalPERS—the California Public Employees' Retirement System—help her out? Could a program be set up to allow her to borrow against her own retirement contributions for the down payment? Could we somehow see to it that she got an affordable home loan? Closing costs? Now, trustees of the CalPERS pension fund weren't going to finance an investment unless it met its own risk/return profile. But, depending on how it was structured, maybe it could. Maybe, just maybe, there was a win-win opportunity here.

Was there a good investment opportunity there for CalPERS? Could CalPERS get into the home loan business? And if CalPERS backed these residential loans, would that help stimulate new housing construction, provide jobs, and strengthen communities? And wouldn't new housing communities need goods and services? And isn't CalPERS providing capital for just these types of new businesses that are needed in new communities?

Well, it didn't take long for that idea to come before the CalPERS Board of Administration. You see, Ann's boss, in addition to being an attorney at the California Department of Transportation, had been elected to the CalPERS Board of Administration and was chair of the pension fund's Investment Committee.

The CalPERS Board came to the conclusion that not only could it get a good risk/adjusted rate of return by getting into the residential mortgage financing business, but it could make a difference in the lives of thousands of state employees like Ann, help stimulate jobs, and thereby strengthen the California economy. A strong California economy was in the best financial interests of CalPERS' 1.2 million members.

From that premise, the CalPERS Member Home Loan Program was born in 1989. It has helped many public employees like Ann. Since then, more than 71,000 families have been able to live the dream of owning their own home. More than 60 lenders across the state participate in the CalPERS Member Home Loan Program. We've provided some $9.6 billion in mortgages. In the last quarter alone, we provided more than $911 million in loans, a 308% increase over the previous quarter.

The investment for CalPERS comes from the purchase of Ginnie Mae and Fannie Mae[2] mortgage-backed securities. Our holdings in these securities to date have returned nearly 12%.

Many other stories of this type could be told. There are examples involving every kind of company, from across every major industry sector, that span every region of the state. They will, I hope, set you thinking about the gold mine of ETI opportunities here and throughout Canada.

There is a growing interest in labour, management, and public policy circles about the role institutional investors could play in the Canadian economy. Indeed, pension funds form the second largest pool of capital in Canada's financial system, after the banks. Some Canadians may be unsure of how ETIs could work in their country, and it's true that some obstacles exist that have to be hurdled. But if you seek out the right investment opportunities, and exercise due diligence, you will find that these investments can stand on their own, and that the benefits are well worth making the effort.

I will share with you the nature and focus of CalPERS policy on economically targeted investments, our commitment to such investments, and the reasons we are able to make them. Together, we will explore the methodologies CalPERS uses to maximize returns and minimize risks. And I'll provide some examples of investments we have made in our private equity and real estate asset classes, in the hope that you will be able to use our experience as a guide.

We at CalPERS and you in Canada have much in common. Many of you who will be reading this book are trustees of pension funds. We share that sacred trust and responsibility important for watching over working families' retirement security. Every one of us is affected by the economic strength of both of our respective countries, provinces, and states.

California and Canada are about the same size in population, with about 30 million people each. Even our growth rate—1% a year—is nearly the same. Our patterns of productivity and living standards are similar.

Both California and Canada have a diverse economy, with a high number of knowledge-based jobs. Each country is dominant in the high value-added manufacturing and service sectors.

California's Gross State Product (GDP) accounts for approximately 13% of the U.S. GDP. According to data provided by the World Bank Development Center, we are both in the top ten of the world's largest economies.

The 1989 U.S.-Canada Free Trade Agreement and the 1994 North American Free Trade Agreement (NAFTA) have touched off a dramatic increase in trade and economic integration between Canada and the United States. According to the World Fact Book, more than 84% of Canada's exports come to the U.S. And Canada is also the third largest purchaser of exports from California.

I think our experience with economically targeted investments can, if applied properly, have a tremendous and positive impact on Canada's future. In fact, one wonders, with all of our similarities, if you can't properly replicate the positive CalPERS experience in your country.

Before I go into our own success stories, I would like to tell you a little more about CalPERS: who we are and what drives us. CalPERS is the largest public employee retirement system in the United States and the second largest in the world. We have approximately $147 billion in our trust fund. The fund is administered by a Board of Administration whose 13 memberas serve as the fiduciaries for more than 1.2 million members. Included in our membership are active and retired public servants: state government workers, local government workers, and non-teaching school employees.

Six of our board members are elected by our active and retired membership. Three are appointed: two by the Governor of California and one by the California legislature. The remaining four members are ex-officio members, including California's Controller and State Treasurer, the director of the Department of Personnel Administration, and my position as a representative of the State Personnel Board. I also serve as Vice-Chairman of CalPERS Investment Committee.

The California Constitution assigns us the plenary authority and the sole and exclusive fiduciary responsibility for investment of monies and administration of the system "in a manner that will assure prompt delivery of benefits and related services to participants and their beneficiaries."

The constitution requires that my colleagues and I on the Board discharge our duties solely in the interest of and for the exclusive purpose of providing benefits to participants and their beneficiaries, minimizing employer contributions, and defraying reasonable expenses of administering the system.

Our Board fully understands the requirements of the California Constitution, one of which is that each member of the Board must exercise the utmost care, skill, prudence and diligence in carrying out their fiduciary responsibilities. CalPERS operates under an investment policy designed to generate the best possible total return on a long-term basis at an acceptable level of risk. Because the comparative performance of different sectors invested by CalPERS varies extensively over any given length of time, our portfolio is well diversified.

At the end of our fiscal year (June 30, 2001), public equities, or stocks, represented approximately 59% of CalPERS assets. Fixed income, or bonds, represented 28% of the system's assets, real estate 8%, and private equity investments represented 5% of assets. Returns in the form of income and capital gains are determined by the level of activity and profitability of the economic sectors in which investments are made, both domestically and internationally.

Economically targeted investments (ETIs) are most commonly defined as investments "designed to produce a competitive rate of return commensurate with risk, as well as to create collateral economic benefits for a targeted geographic area, group of people, or sector of the economy." Some investors will argue that ETIs are no more than "social investments" which would not be made by prudent fiduciaries because they are based partially on considerations other than those in the immediate best interests of the assets. It is clear to us at CalPERS, however, that the present and future financial health of our trust fund is inextricably linked to the economic health of California.

Beyond the obvious microeconomic analysis that is required to make specific investment decisions, isn't it also necessary for us, as prudent fiduciaries, to simultaneously consider macroeconomic conditions? I believe the answer to that question is a resounding Yes! It is also necessary to consider the macroeconomic implications of our investments.

In other words, it is not acceptable just to consider what are referred to as the collateral economic benefits of any investment; it would be imprudent not to include such considerations in the investment decision-making process.

CalPERS Board of Administration adopted an ETI policy in April 1993. The geographic area of focus in the policy's definition is, of course, California. Our policy spells out the parameters.

For example, for the sake of an ETI, we will not make a concession of risk-and-cost-adjusted return. We won't distort established asset allocation and geographic diversification guidelines, either. We don't have a separate ETI asset class with a specific asset allocation or a separate target rate of return. There is no downgrading of investment quality contemplated, implied or assumed. Rather, ETIs can be in any asset class as long as they can be made with risk-adjusted market rate of return expectations.

After an ETI can demonstrate the investment meets the Board's duties under the California Constitution, we can consider the benefits of the investment—in this order—to:

- the CalPERS members,
- residents of the state,
- investments that benefit, support or create jobs for residents of the state; and
- investments that address the economic and social need of U.S. residents with unique major representation in the state.

As a practical matter, the impact of this policy has been, and probably will continue to be, in just two asset classes: private equity and real estate. The Canadian Labour and Business Centre has already compiled some case studies on innovative investment strategies for pension funds in Canada designed to have high investment returns and economic impacts. CalPERS venture capital investment vehicle, called California Emerging Ventures, is highlighted in this research.

However, I want to share with you a few other examples to help you fully appreciate the financial soundness and the potential benefits ETI investments have had in California. Four examples of ETIs in the private equity arena come to mind, all of which I believe demonstrate their value.

Delimex—retail foods

In 1997, we were approached by a rapidly growing producer and distributor of high-quality frozen ethnic foods: Delimex, a company with $27 million in revenues and $15 million in cash flow. The company was founded in 1984, and was headquarterd in San Diego with manufacturing facilities in San Diego and Monterey, Mexico. They were the leading supplier of frozen tequitos, tamales, and rice bowls to two large California wholesale foodchains.

It looked like a good investment, when you consider that ethnic foods are among those in the fastest growing market segment of the frozen food industry. In fact, Mexican food is replacing the hamburger as the third most popular hot food for school lunches. In addition, Delimex had a proven track record in its warehouse club market; it had been well managed, and to expand, obviously, it needed a partner.

So we invested $25 million—$5 million as a co-investment and $20 million with Fenway Partners, a New York-based private investment firm. As a result, Delimex was able to expand, adding a 122,000-square-foot production plant, and they have subsequently built two new additions. The company doubled sales to over $160 million, and tripled its profitability. This was good for them, good for the San Diego economy, and I think you will agree it was really good for our trust fund. Delimex was recently purchased by the big H.J. Heinz Company for $63 million. It was a win/win for all concerned, including the city of San Diego, the state of California, and certainly for CalPERS.

Zhone Technologies—telecommunications technology

The opportunities aren't just in San Diego, or Los Angeles or San Francisco. My second example is a company based in a blighted area of downtown Oakland, California.

In October 1999, we took a $50 million investment in a company called Zhone Technologies. Not a household word, since it only started up in 1999, but take my word for it: it is likely to be as big as an IBM or Microsoft some day. With the evolution of the Internet, the demand for faster, higher-quality communication networks is resulting in a massive growth and change for the telecommunications equipment industry. As you know, the average home has multiple incompatible networks for phone, voice, and Internet. They are built by competing suppliers, resulting in a lack of choice, high prices, and multiple bills for the consumer.

There are many companies focusing on building equipment for the next generation core of networks. While the backbone networks are becoming fast, the next "Holy Grail" is technology-agnostic "last-mile" equipment. "Last-mile" is that part of the network from the switching centre into your home or business. Zhone is focused on becoming the industry leader in that "last-mile" access equipment segment.

When we were approached to join others in financing this ambitious strategy, we were attracted by the likelihood that it could revitalize jobs in a downtown urban area, and had the potential for creating literally hundreds of new jobs. But it mostly was an opportunity with an excellent return/risk ratio.

In fact, the founding management team is the same team that built Ascend Communications into one of the most successful telecommunications equipment companies in the world, growing it over a 10-year period from a startup to a company that was sold for $24 billion to Lucent Technologies.

Our investment in Zhone comes with a strong alignment of interest. The management team contributes $30 million and they agreed they would receive no value from the company until the investors received twice the money or approximately a 30% internal rate of return. Today, Zhone Technology officials—who met with us in 1999 with nothing more than an idea on a flip chart—have three new buildings in downtown Oakland. The company stands tall and proud in the re-development district of Oakland, takes advantage of local re-development tax breaks, has 500 employees, and $100 million in revenues. Zhone even enjoys an exit off the major interstate with the company's name.

It is forming technology alliances with a variety of communications hardware and software vendors to speed its time to market with products that extend intelligence through the local access network, including Ericsson, Hughes Electronics, Qwest, and Texas Instruments.

The California Initiative—urban and rural economic development

My third example is quite unique and one that I'm very proud our Board supported. This is not just one investment, but rather an investment vehicle. We call it the California Initiative. Last summer, our private equity staff came to the Board with a proposal. They wanted to invest $500 million in "underserved markets" located in California. Now, the term "underserved market" may not sound appealing, and you might wonder how you can make money in an underserved market. But what I mean by the term "underserved markets" is an urban and rural area that has limited access to needed goods and services.

Our staff found that underserved markets largely offer companies untapped assets, such as large labour pools, low real estate costs, and underutilized infrastructure. Potentially, they are a gold mine for companies wishing to expand and grow and tap underutilized resources. There are unmet needs in California's urban and rural markets, and we believe our initiative represents a golden opportunity for CalPERS and the state. We could get superior returns for our Fund and our members, while fuelling the growth of jobs, businesses, and stronger communities.

CalPERS Board agreed with the concept, and our staff set out to find firms that could make this happen. They recommended that the California Initiative use five different investment approaches, each employing a different type of partner. These five are corporate partnerships, investments through already established CalPERS' general partners, mid-sized private equity funds, fund-of-funds (a fund that invests in other funds), and innovative new funds that focus on smaller companies and venture opportunities. We hired 11 private equity firms for the California Initiative, and their investment strategies cover a broad range.

For example, we gave $200 million to Yucaipa Corporate Initiative Fund, a firm renowned for its ownership role in grocery chains such as Fred Meyer, Ralph's, Food 4 Less, and Dominicks. The firm has been able to unlock value by adding operational expertise, unique partnerships, and managerial oversight. Ron Burkle, who runs the Yucaipa fund, is well regarded by unions and company management for his track record of adhering to fair business practices. Yucaipa's role in the California Initiative will be to build corporate partnerships with retail, distribution, food, manufacturing, and commercial product companies that are interested in expanding operations in underserved communities.

At the other end of the scale, we gave $10 million to American River Ventures, which is located just outside of our state's capital in Folsom, California. Their investment focus is to target new and start-up companies in the area located between San Francisco and Reno, Nevada. American River believes there are attractive investments in Central California for two reasons:

- there is an increasing number of high technology start-up companies in the targeted area: and
- the region is served by many "angel" investors—a few local branch offices of multi-state venture capital firms, and a few small local venture firms that have access to limited resources. These angel investors have acted as the primary source of capital in this area, and American River Ventures hopes to capture part of the market segment.

Biotechnology fund

This next private equity investment takes advantages of business strengths that already exist in California—in biotechnology. In fact, biotechnology was invented in California. In the late 1990s, biotechnology was the most underexposed area ripe for investment in California. But, between 1992 and 1999, no one wanted to touch it. And, while many folks were investing in dot-coms, we were quietly researching the strengths of investment in this area. What did we find? That the industry needed long-term patient capital. It was poised for tremendous growth, given recent technological breakthroughs. Over long periods of time, the industry has delivered and would likely continue to deliver superior returns.

The advent and convergence of powerful new technologies—like genomics, bioinformatics, and combinatorial chemistry—is leading to faster discovery and development of better therapies for patients. The likelihood of developing new therapies over the next five to 20 years include everything from gene therapies and cell therapies to immunotherapies, engineered tissues, and on and on. Not to mention the aging population, which will require or desire safer, more effective therapies to treat conditions brought on by old age.

So we worked carefully, methodically, over an entire year to find an appropriate and successful way to participate. And in June of 2001, we approved a biotechnology allocation of up to $500 million. Our biotechnology fund is set up to develop partnerships with leading pharmaceutical companies and to work with leading universities, as well as public and private laboratories, to incubate new businesses coming out of research and development.

Our goal is also to build new vehicles that other public and private investors can join, so CalPERS can participate in the economics as the vehicles grow over time. While our fund is new, we believe the benefits to California are many—housing, jobs, secondary industries—and we hope the results will help our own members lead healthier lives.

Now' let me turn to our real estate portfolio and give you a few examples of ETIs in the real estate market.

Single Family Housing Program— residential development

CalPERS real estate portfolio for California is very diverse. We have millions of dollars invested in office and industrial buildings, apartments, and retail business spaces. We also partner with local real estate developers to make investments in housing. In 1992, CalPERS committed $475 million to establish a Single Family Housing Program. We believed that we could invest responsibly on behalf of our members and still help build communities at the same time.

But what prompted CalPERS to sink $475 million in residential development in the midst of California's recessionary cycle? The answer was a capital shortage. Not a cyclical shortage, but a real fundamental change in the suppliers of capital in the housing investment arena.

In the early 1990s, although California's population continued to grow, building permits and funding for construction from the bank and the savings and loan industry was significantly down. Housing to us began to look very interesting from an investment point of view. We began by partnering with eight real estate developers. One of those firms is Institutional Housing Partners (IHP), out of Southern California. IHP has many housing projects under their belt, but one important example of an ETI comes to mind.

In Simi Valley, California, a 4-village development of 4,000 homes began to take shape in 1982. It was located on land that used to be a working cattle ranch. In fact, for many years, a windmill has pumped water for the ranch, and still stands as a historical link to the past for the community and housing development. The original developer left in the 1990s when his cash flow dried up. The local school superintendent asked the developer to make good on his promise to build an elementary school. So the developer signed over the deed to 1,400 acres of land to the School District.

IHP entered the picture shortly thereafter and purchased the school district's land and the housing development with monies funded through CalPERS Housing Program. It was a CalPERS investment that eventually built the school, where 500 kindergarten through 5th graders are now receiving a good education. Since ground was broken in 1997 for the fourth and final housing phase of the development, 416 families have moved into their new homes. About 236 homes are left to be completed. The barbed wire fence that stood around the cattle ranch is gone, and several acres of open space have been made available to the public. Many cycling and walking trails are now used by the community at large. I know that the people who live there and the kids that grow up there will benefit from CalPERS investment in the community for years to come.

It's projects like this that have brought CalPERS investment returns above 20%. Today, we have committed more than $1 billion to our housing program and built more than 40,000 homes for Californians.

Investment in urban redevelopment

One of the more recent initiatives in our real estate portfolio was to expand our investments in real estate investments in California's urban areas. Our California urban real estate initiatives have a history that can be traced back as far as 1991. One of our first steps was when we committed nearly $28 million to two Trusts run by the AFL-CIO.

CalPERS allocated $25.3 billion to AFL-CIO's Building Investment Trust (BIT)—a pooled real estate investment program that invests in institutional quality commercial real estate in California. More than $2 million was invested in the AFL-CIO Housing Investment Trust (HIT) for investment in mortgage-backed securities, construction, and long-term mortgage loans.

The AFL-CIO Housing and Building Investment Trusts are helping the state achieve important goals for housing production and economic development. Most of the 1,300 California housing units financed by the HIT are located in San Francisco, Los Angeles, and San José. They include projects like the House of Unity, a $6 million apartment complex for families who were once homeless in Los Angeles. And there's Los Esteros, an affordable housing unit complex in San José, which received $10 million from HIT.

The BIT has financed 2.9 million square feet of office, industrial, and retail development in 22 California projects. BIT is financing $20 million toward the Hilton hotel in Santa Clara, which will serve the city's local convention centre. In San Francisco, the Holiday Inn Express received $30 million from BIT to help fill the needs of business and tourist travellers to the city's Fisherman's Wharf district.

For the last 10 years, average annual rates of returns for HIT and BIT have averaged approximately 10%. In 2001, we expanded the program to harness the investment opportunities created by the growth of California's population and the shortage of affordable housing and general development in California's urban locations.

We hired four urban real estate investment partners and gave them $200 million to develop and redevelop multi-family units, single family houses, industrial, office and mix-used properties in urban settings. Today, we have more than $1 billion committed to California urban real estate initiatives.

Merchant banking for unions and workers

I'd like to provide you one final example of an ETI in our investment portfolio. Earlier I referred to our investment with Yucaipa in our California Initiative Program. Recently, we formed a strategic financial relationship with Yucaipa to create a worker-friendly merchant bank that partners with unions and their workers to earn outstanding financial returns.

Yucaipa has built a strong track record by working in partnership with organized labour in companies in which it invests, rather than in opposition to them—hence the term "worker-friendly." This has been a key to their investment success. The objective of our relationship is to profit alongside Yucaipa as it expands its existing private equity franchise and builds a leading integrated, broad-based worker-friendly merchant bank.

The relationships Yucaipa has built with union leaders and workers have given them a unique competitive advantage. The firm's ability to work with unions to avoid work stoppages, strikes, and inefficient labour agreements has enabled Yucaipa's portfolio companies to excel.

The worker-friendly merchant bank will attract and manage the private equity investment capital of union pension funds, commonly referred to as Taft-Hartley plans. Today, Taft-Hartley plans control over $400 billion in assets, but invest approximately one-tenth of one percent in private equity. Given the scale of Taft-Hartley plan assets, even modest investments in private equity would represent tens of billions of new capital. For CalPERS and its members, we get outstanding financial returns. For Taft-Hartley funds, they are able to place the dollars of their workers in the hands of a firm with a strong track record of investment success that is sensitive to the goals and needs of workers, such as job preservation, fair wages and sound business practices. We expect to finalize our relationship with Yucaipa soon, and Yucaipa will soon be reaching out to Taft-Hartley funds to talk about this exciting investment opportunity.

As you can see, we have been very successful in our efforts to incorporate ETIs in our investment portfolio. What I've discussed here is really only the tip of the iceberg. Today, CalPERS has more than $20 billion— or 13%—of its investment portfolio invested in California. In a survey of state and local government employee retirement systems conducted by the Government Finance Officers' Association Research Center, CalPERS ranked the highest state retirement system investing in-state.

CalPERS capital infusion in California is far-reaching, and no one really knows the true impact of our investments across the state. What we do know is that our investments have brought life to more than 438 emerging California companies. More than 40 of these have gone public. We own 41 industrial buildings, 15 office complexes, and 23 shopping centres in California. Three of these shopping centres were once dilapidated buildings in the heart of urban Los Angeles and today stand as new signs of growth and urban redevelopment. We have more than $740 million invested in California corporate bonds, and we are a stock owner in 750 publicly-traded companies headquartered in California.

We also know that capital helps to jump-start the economy. It helps companies grow and expand, it creates jobs, strengthens communities, and stimulates the need for supporting goods and services. According to the California Technology, Trade and Commerce Agency, international investment in California topped $3 billion last year. The flow of international capital in our state created approximately 8,200 jobs. Given this statistic, one could estimate that CalPERS $20 billion investment in California created more than 54,000 jobs.

The future for ETI investment in our Golden State looks bright. California has long been recognized for its entrepreneurial spirit and innovation. This reputation continues and has fuelled increased confidence of venture capital investments in California. Internet-related investments continue to be popular, including software, electronics, information services, communications, and networking. And there is renewed interest in biotechnology that has spurred investment in medical software and biopharmaceuticals.

Our researchers, world-class universities, and laboratories are playing a significant role in the expansion of medical technology.

Continued economic expansion has increased demand for housing, as job opportunities draw more people to California. Our real estate construction has remained strong. Residential home and multi-family construction increased by more than 8% in the last year. Industrial construction had double-digit growth. There is no shortage of ETI investment in California.

I hope I've been successful in sharing with you CalPERS perspective on ETIs and our experience with them in our investment portfolio. As I said at the start, there's plenty of room for ETIs in a well-diversified public pension fund portfolio.

I wish you the best in your search for ETI investments here in Canada. I have no doubt that your country holds the ETI opportunities that have been afforded to us, and my hope is that you will have success in incorporating them as you deem appropriate.

Undoubtedly, CalPERS will continue to seek out opportunities provided by the markets in the future. And we will do so in ways that generate favourable risk-adjusted market returns while hitting economic targets in the bull's-eye.

Notes

[1] Sean Harrigan isVice Chairman of the Investment Committee of California Public Employees' Retirement System (CalPERS). This speech was presented at the conference of the Canadian Labour and Business Centre—'Capital that works!' on January 16, 2002, in Montreal, Quebec

[2] Fannie Mae was chartered by the U.S. Federal Housing Department in 1938. The impetus for creation of Fannie Mae was twofold: to meet a national commitment to housing and to fill the gap caused by the inability or unwillingness of private lenders to ensure a reliable supply of mortgage credit throughout the country. The primary purpose of Fannie Mae was to purchase, hold, or sell FHA-insured mortgage loans that had been originated by private lenders. The Charter Act of 1954 provided the basic framework under which Fannie Mae operates today but did not remove it from direct federal control. The 1968 Charter Act split Fannie Mae into two parts: Ginnie Mae and a reconstituted Fannie Mae. Ginnie Mae would continue as a federal agency and be responsible for the then-existing special assistance programs, and Fannie Mae would be transformed into a "government-sponsored private corporation" responsible for the self-supporting secondary market operations. The 1968 Act provided the authority to issue Mortgage-Backed Securities (MBS).

Bibliography

American Federation of Labor and Congress of Industrial Organizations. (2000). *Investing in our future: An AFL-CIO guide to pension investment and proxy voting*. Washington: AFL-CIO Employee Benefits Department.

American Federation of Labor and Congress of Industrial Organisations. (1993). *Pensions in changing capital markets*. AFL-CIO Publication #0-248-637-0393-2.

Ambachtsheer, Keith & Ezra, Don. (1998). *Pension fund excellence*. Toronto: John Wiley and Sons Inc.

Asmundson, Paul and Foerster, Stephen R. (2002). Socially responsible investing: Better for your soul or your bottom line? *Canadian Investment Review*, winter. *www.investmentreview.com/archives/winter01/social.html*

Atkins, Ralph and Lewis, William. (2000). Triumph for Vodafone as Mannesman gives in. *Financial Times*. London.

Baker, Dean and Fung, Archon (2000). Collateral damage: Do pension fund investments hurt workers? In Fung, Archon, Hebb, Tessa and Rogers, Joel. (2000). *Working capital: The power of labor's pensions*. Ithaca: cornell University Press. Pp. 13-43.

Baldwin, Bob, Ted Jackson, Michael Decter, and David Levi. (March,1991). *Worker investment funds: Issues and prospects*. Ottawa: Report prepared for the Canadian Labour Congress.

Barber, Randy.(1982). Pension Funds in the United States: Issues of Investment and Control. *Economic and Industrial Democracy*, vol.3, p. 31-73.

Barber, Randy & Ghilarducci, Teresa. (1993). Pension funds, capital markets, and the economic future, in eds. Dymski, Gary, Epstein, Gerald & Pollin, Robert, *Transforming the U.S. financial system*. Pp. 287-319. New York: M.E. Sharpe.

Barber, Randy. (May, 1997). *Retirement, Pension and Capital Strategies: An Inventory of Major Issues Confronting Labor*. Centre for Economic Organizing. Unpublished Research Paper.

Beggs, Darcy. (1993). *Control of pension funds*. Toronto: Paper presented to the conference on Financial Capital for Economic Renewal (December).

Board of Trustees v. City of Baltimore, 562 A.2d 720 (Md. 1989).

Bruyn, Severyn. (1987). *The Field of Social Investment*. Cambridge: Cambridge University Press.

Business and Society. (1997). Socially irresponsible and illegal behaviour and shareholder wealth. Vol. 36, #3, pp. 221.

Calabrese, Michael. (2000). Building on success: Labor-friendly investment vehicles and the power of private equity. In Fung, Archon, Hebb, Tessa and Rogers, Joel. (2000). *Working capital: The power of labor's pensions.* Ithaca: Cornell University Press. Pp. 93-127.

CalPERS. (2000). CalPERS Statement of Investment Policy for Economically Targeted Investment Program. 14 February. Available at *www.calpers.ca.gov/* invest/policies/pdfs/ economicallytargetedinvestmentprogram.pdf.)

Campbell, Beverley Ross, and Josephson, William. (1983). Public pension trustees" pursuit of social goals. *Journal of urban and contemporary law,* Vol 24:3, pp. 43-120.

Canada, Standing Senate Committee on Banking, Trade and Commerce. (1998). *The governance practices of institutional investors: Report of the standing senate committee on banking, trade and commerce.* November.

Canada Business Corporations Act, R.S.C. 1985, s.137, c. C-44, as amended *S.C. 2001, c. 14.*

Canada Business Corporations Regulations. (2001).

Canada Council for International Cooperation. Mission based investing: A financial strategy for foundations, endowments and NGOs. Ottawa, Ont.: CCIC, 2001. (Available at http://www.ccic.ca/volsect/MBI/ mbi1_introduction2.htm.)

Canadian Democracy and Corporate Accountability Commission. The New Balance Sheet: Corporate Profits and Responsibility in the 21st Century. Toronto: Thistle Printing, 2001. (Available at *www.corporate-accountability.ca.*)

Canadian Labour and Business Centre. (1995). *Access to capital resources in Canada.* Ottawa: author.

Canadian Labour and Business Centre. Capital That Works!: Pension Funds and Alternative Strategies for Investing in the Economy. Ottawa: CLBC, 2001. (Discussion paper available at www.clbc.ca).

Canadian Labour Congress. (1993). *Towards democratic control of our economy: The case for a national investment fund.* Ottawa: Social and Economic Policy Department of the Canadian Labour Congress Working Papers (June 16).

Canadian Union of Public Employees. (2002). *"Pension Talk": Bringing Union Values to Pension Investing*

Carmichael, Isla. (1996). *The development and control of occupational pension plans by workers in Canada: The Ontario Public Service Employees' Union Pension Trust.* Toronto: Unpublished research paper.

Carmichael, Isla. (1998). *A survey of union pension trustees.* A joint project of the Canadian Labour Market and Productivity Centre and the Ontario Public Service Employees" Union.

Carmichael, Isla. (2000). Union pension funds. Worker control and social investment in Canada: Implications for labour education. Doctoral thesis.

Carmichael, Isla, Thompson, Shirley and Quarter, Jack. (2003). Transformative education for pension fund trustees. *Canadian Journal for Studies in Adult Education.* May 17(1).

Casselton, Valerie. (1988). The Hard-Hat Capitalists. *The Vancouver Sun,* May 14, D10-12.

Cordery, Adam. (1994). Foreign Capital Flows and Latin America; A Perspective on Recent Trends. *Business Economist*, vol. 25, # 2, spring.

Council of Institutional Investors.(2000). Investment Policies. Available through CII at (202) 822-0800.

Cowan v. Scargill. (1984). 2 All, E.R., 750.

Crocus Investment Fund. (2002). About Crocus: Mission, vision and values. Winnipeg: http://www.crocusfund.com/about/mission.html (January 26).

Davis, E. P. (1997). *Can Pension Systems Cope? Population Ageing, and Retirement Income Provision in the European Union.* London, Royal Institute of International Affairs.

Deaton, Richard Lee. (1989). *The political economy of pensions: Power, politics and social change in Canada, Britain, and the United States.* Vancouver: University of British Columbia Press.

Diltz, J. David. (1995). The private cost of socially responsible investing. *Applied Financial Economics*, vol. 5, no. 2, April, pp. 69-78.

Drucker, Peter. (1976). The Unseen Revolution: How Pension Fund Socialism Came to America. New York: Harper & Row.

Ellmen, Eugene. (1989). *Profitable ethical investment.* Toronto: James Lorimer.

Ellmen, E. (1996). Reforming Capitalism. *Canadian Forum*, January-February, 1996. pp.9-14.

Financial Times. (1998). Lessons of the Asia crisis. 12 December.

Falconer, Kirk. (1998). *Pension barriers to financing small and medium-sized business in Canada*. Notes for a presentation to the Pension Investment Association of Canada.

Falconer, Kirk. (1999). *Prudence, patience and jobs: pension investment in a changing economy*. Ottawa: Canadian Labour and Business Centre.

Falconer, Kirk. (2002). Private equity expansion. *Benefits Canada*. April. P. 13.

Farrar, J.H. & Maxton, J.K. (1986). Social investment and pension scheme trusts. *Law Quarterly Review*, vol 102, no.32.

Fung, Archon, Hebb, Tessa and Rogers, Joel. (2001). *Working Capital: The Power of Labor's Pensions*. New York: Cornell University.

Ghilarducci, Teresa. (1994). U.S. Pension Investment Policy and Perfect Capital Market Theory. *Challenge*. July-August, pp. 4-10.

Gindin, Sam. (1989). Playing a capital game: The Québec Solidarity Fund, *Our Times*, (March), 24-25.

Government of Manitoba. (1991). The Manitoba Employee Ownership Fund Corporation Act. Winnipeg: July 26.

Greifer, Nicholas.(2001). Pension Investment Policies: An Evaluation of the State of the Art Prepared for January 2002 meeting of Committee on Retirement Benefits and Administration of the Government Finance Officers Association. Available at *http://www.gfoa.org/* committees/corba/Pen.Inv.Policies.pdf.

Grossman, Blake & Sharpe. (1986). Financial implications of south africa divestment. *Financial Analysts Journal*, July- August 1986.

Guerard, John B. Jr. (1997). Additional evidence on the cost of being social responsible in investing. *The Journal of Investing*, Winter, pp. 31-35.

Hamilton, Sally, Jo, Hoje, & Statman, Meir. (1993). Doing well while doing good? The investment performance of socially responsible mutual funds. *Financial Analysts Journal*, November-December 1993.

Hawley, James P. and Williams, Andrew, T. (2000). *The Rise of Fiduciary Capitalism*. Philadelphia: University of Pennsylvania Press.

Hebb, Tessa. (2000). Introduction: The challenge of labor's capital strategy. In Fung, Archon, Hebb, Tessa and Rogers, Joel. (2000). *Working capital: The power of labor's pensions*. Ithaca: Cornell University Press. Pp. 1-13.

Her Majesty's Treasury & The Department for Work and Pensions (2001). *Myners Review: Institutional Investment in the UK, The Government's Response*. *www.actuaries.org.uk/* finance_invest/Myners_gov_resp.pdf.)

Holzmann, Robert. (1997). Pension reform, financial market development and economic growth: preliminary evidence from Chile' International Monetary Fund Working Paper WP/96/94.

Hutchinson, James, & Cole, Charles G.(1980). Legal standards governing investment of pension assets for social and political goals. *University of Pennsylvania Law Review*, vol. 128, pp. 1340-1388.

Hutchinson, Moira. (1996). *The promotion of active shareholdership for corporate social responsibility in Canada.* Toronto: Paper prepared for the Canadian Friends Service Committee (November).

Interfaith Centre on Corporate Responsibility. *2002 ICCR Proxy Voting Checklist* (2002). (Available at www.socialfunds.com/sa/status.cgi.)

International Finance Corporation. (1996). Emerging Stock Markets Fact Book. Washington: World Bank, IFC.

International Finance Corporation. (1998). Emerging Stock Markets Fact Book. Washington: World Bank, IFC.

International Monetary Fund. (1997). International capital markets: Developments, prospects and key policy issues. Washington: IMF.

International Monetary Fund. (2001). World Economic Outlook. Washington: IMF. October.

International Network of Pension Regulators and Supervisors (2001). *Fifteen Principles for the Regulation of Private Occupational Pension Schemes.* 25 April.

Jackson, Andrew. (1993). *A national investment fund.* Paper presented to the conference on Financial Capital for Economic Renewal, Toronto: York University (December).

Jackson, Edward T. and Francois Lamontagne. (1995). *Adding Value: The Economic and Social Impacts of Labour-Sponsored Venture Capital Corporations and Their Investee Firms.* Ottawa: Canadian Labour and Business Centre.

Jackson, Ted. (1996). ETIs: A tool for responsible pension fund investment, *Making Waves* 8, (2), 2-3.

Just Pensions Project (2001). *Just Pensions: Socially Responsible Investment and International Development: A Guide for Trustees and Fund Managers.* May. www.justpensions.org.

Kelsey, Jane. (1995). *Economic fundamentalism.* London: Pluto Press.

Kinder, Lydenberg and Domini. (1998). *The Domini Social Index.* http://www.kld.com

Kurtz, Lloyd, & DiBartolomeo, Dan. (1996). Socially screened portfolios: an attribution analysis of relative performance. *Journal of Investing*, Fall.

Lane, Patricia. (1991). Obstacles to the use of union pension funds as social capital. Proceedings of the conference *Strategies for responsible share ownership: Implications for pension and other investment funds*. Sponsored by the Centre for Corporate Social Performance and Ethics and the Task Force on the Churches and Social Responsibility, pp. 49-53.

Lane, Patricia. (undated). Ethical investment: Towards the best interest of everyone. *The Advocate*, pp. 171-182.

Langbein, John H. & Posner, Richard A. (1980). Social investing and the law of trusts. *Michigan Law Review*, vol. 79, pp 72-112.

Lawson, Gary. (1995) Are pension funds being bullied into investing in etis? *Pension Management*. June.

Longstreth, Bevis. (1986). *Modern investment management and prudent man rule*. New York: Oxford University Press.

Lowry, R. (1991). *Good money: A guide to profitable social investing in the 90s*. New York: W.W. Norton and Co.

Luck, Christopher & Pilotte, Nancy. (1993). Domini social index performance. *Journal of Investing*, Fall.

Manitoba Federation of Labour. (1983). Resolution M-6 from the Manitoba Federation Of Labour 28th Convention. Winnipeg: September.

Manitoba Federation of Labour. (1990). The Manitoba labour-sponsored investment fund: A proposal to the Special Labour Market Initiatives Program of the Canada Employment & Immigration Commission. Winnipeg: author.

Manitoba Law Reform Commission. (1993). *Ethical investment by trustees*. Manitoba: Office of the Queen"s Printer.

Megarry, Robert. (1989). Investing pension funds: The mineworkers" case. In ed. Youdan, T.G., *Equity, Fiduciaries and Trusts*. Toronto: Carswell.

Mercer, William Ltd. (1997). *The Mercer Pension Manual*. Toronto: Carswell.

MiningWatch Canada (2000, February 17). Shareholders demand placer dome disclose environmental risk. Press Release. *www.miningwatch.ca*

Minns, Richard. (2001). *The cold war in welfare: Stock markets versus pensions*. London: Verso.

Minsky, Alan. (1988). Introduction to trust responsibility. In eds. *Canadian Employee Benefit Plans*, pp. 81-90.

Mortgage Fund One. (1999). Business plan summary 1999-2003: Investing today and tomorrow. Vancouver: Mortgage Fund One: ACM Advisors Ltd.

Moye, Melissa. (1997). A Review of Studies Assessing the Impact of Labour-Sponsored Investment Funds in Canada. Unpublished paper.

Myners, Paul.(2001). *Institutional Investment in the UK: A Review.* UK: HM Treasury, March. *www.hm-treasury.gov.uk/mediastore/otherfiles/31.pdf.*

National Union of Public Government Employees. *Its Our Money: What Workers Need to Know About Pension Governance and Control. www.nupge.ca/ pdf/its_our_money.pdf.*

Office of the Superintendent of Financial Institutions. (April 2000). *Guideline for the Development of Investment Policies and Procedures for Federally Regulated Pension Plans.* Ottawa: OSFI. *www.osfi-bsif.gc.ca/eng/pensions/guidelines/pdf/ penivst.pdf.*

Ogden, S.G., (1995). Transforming Frameworks of Accountability: The Case of Water Privatisation. *Accounting, Organisations and Society,* vol. 20, #2/3, pp. 193-218.

O'Grady, John. (1993). *Financial capital for economic renewal.* Paper presented to the conference on Financial Capital for Economic Renewal, York University (December).

Ontario Arts Council, (1997). Assessing the local economic impact of the arts: A handbook. Ontario Arts Council. Prepared by Informetrica. November.

Opler, Tim C. and Jonathan Sokobin. (October 1995). *Does Coordinated Institutional Activism Work? An Analysis of the Activities of the Council of Institutional Investors. http://fisher.osu.edu/fin/journal/dice/papers/1995/95-5.pdf*

OPSEU Pension Trust. (1996). *Annual Report.* Toronto: author.

Organisation for Economic Cooperation and Development. (1997). *Financial Market Trends,* # 68, Paris: OECD.

Organisation for Economic Cooperation and Development. (1998). *Maintaining prosperity in an ageing society.* Paris: OECD.

Ontario Public Service Employees' Union. (1987). *Our Pension, our future.*

OPSEU Pension Trust. (1997). Annual report.

Palmer, Geoffrey. (1986, June). Trustee investment: The relative merits of the legal list and prudent man approaches to trustee investment. Report by the New Zealand Joint Working Party. Wellington: Government PrinterPalmer, 1986;

Pearce, P. & Samuels, A. (1985). Trustees and beneficiaries and investment policies. *Conv,* 52

Pension Benefits Standards Regulations. (1985). C.R.C., section 7.1.

Quarter, Jack. (1992). *Canada's social economy: Co-operatives, non-profits and other community enterprises.* Toronto: James Lorimer.

Quarter, Jack. (1995). *Crossing the line: Unionized employee ownership and investment funds.* Toronto: James Lorimer.

Quarter, Jack. (2000). *Beyond the bottom line: Socially innovative business owners.* Westport, Conn.: Quorum.

Quarter, Jack, Carmichael, Isla, Sousa, Jorges, and Elgie, Susan. (2001). Social investment by union-based pension funds and labour-sponsored investment funds. *Industrial Relations.* 56 (1): 92-114.

Ravikoff, Ronald and Myron Curzan. (1980). Social responsibility in investment policy and the prudent man rule, *California Law Review*, 68, 530-536.

Reder, Alan. (1995). *In pursuit of principle and profit: Business success through social responsibility.* New York: Jeremy P. Tarcher/Putnam.

Rehfeld, Barry. (1997). Worldly-wise asset allocation. *Institutional Investor.* New York; January,vol. 31, #. 1; pps. 41-46.

Romano, Roberta. (1993). Public pension fund activism in corporate governance reconsidered, *Columbia Law Review*, 93 (4), 795-853.

Rubenstein, Daniel. (1989). Black oil, red ink. *CA Magazine*, Toronto. November, pp.30-35.

Scane, Ralph E., Q.C. (1993). Occupational pension schemes: is the trust an adequate form of provision? In ed. Waters, Donovan W.M., *Equity, Fiduciaries and Trusts*, pp. 359-382. Toronto: Carswell.

Scott, A.W. (1987). *The law on trusts.* 4th Edition. Boston, Toronto: Little, BrownScott.

Sethi, 1995 Sethi, S. Prakash, (1995). Introduction to *AMR"s* special topic forum on shifting paradigms: Societal expectations and corporate performance. *Academy of Management Review*, vol. 20, no. 1, 18-21.

Shareholder Association for Research and Education. (2002). *Prospectus 2(1).* Spring/Summer. *www.share.ca.*

Shareholder Association for Research and Education. (2001a).*Prospectus 1(2).* Fall/Winter. *www.share.ca.*

Shareholder Association for Research and Education. (2001b). *2001 Key Proxy Vote Survey.* Vancouver: SHARE. *www.share.ca.*

Social Investment Forum. (2001). *Report on socially responsible investing trends in the United States.* Toronto: SIO, 28 November. www.socialinvest.org

Social Investment Organization. (2000). *Canadian Social Investment Review.* Toronto: Social Investment Organization, December. *www.socialinvest.ca*

Sparkes, Russell. SRI Comes of Age. *Pension Investor.* July.

Statistics Canada. *Quarterly Estimates of Trusteed Pension Funds.* vol. 29, # 2. Ottawa: Minister of Industry, 2001. (Catalogue no. 74-001-XIB)

State Pension Review Board, Texas. *Written investment policies for public pension systems. http://www.prb.state.tx.us*

State Pension Review Board, Texas. T*rustee outline for developing a written investment policy. http://www.prb.state.tx.us*

Singh, Ajit. (1996). Pension reform, the stock market, capital formation and economic growth: A critical commentary on the World Bank's proposals. *International Social Security Review*, vol. 49, #3.

Singh, Ajit and Bruce A Weisse. (1998). Emerging stock markets, portfolio capital flows and long-term economic growth: Micro- and macroeconomic perspectives. *World Development*, vol. 26, # 4, April.

Smith, Michael P. (1996). Shareholder activism by institutional investors: Evidence from CalPERS, *The Journal of Finance*, 51 (1), 227-252.

Social Investment Organization. (1998). SRI fund performance, *Forum*, 8 (5) (September/October), 3.

Stanford, Jim. (1999). *Paper boom.* Ottawa: Canadian Centre for Policy Alternatives and James Lorimer.

Statistics Canada. 2001. *Quarterly estimates of trusteed pension funds (second quarter).* Ottawa: Income Statistics Division.

Sullivan, Leon. (1999). *The Global Sullivan Principles. http://www.chevron.com/newsvs/pressrel/*

U.S. Department of Labor (2001). Interpretive Bulletin 94-2, codified at 29 C.F.R. pt. 2509.94-2.

Suret, Jean Marc. (1993). *The fonds de solidarité des travailleurs du Québec: A cost/benefit analysis.* Quebec City: Unpublished paper.

Taskforce on the Churches and Corporate Responsibility. (2002). About us: TCCR's history. January 26. *http://www.web.net/~tccr/*

Task Force on the Investment of Public Sector Pension Funds. (1987). *In Whose Interest?* (Chaired by Malcolm Rowan). Toronto: Queen's Printer.

Trades Union Congress. (1996). *Pension fund investment: A TUC Handbook.*

United Church of Canada. (1989). *Corporate responsibility guidelines issued by the Investment Committee of the United Church of Canada.* Toronto: March.

Wahal, Sunil. (1996). Pension fund activism and firm performance, *Journal of Financial and Quantitative Analysis* 31 (1): 1-23.

Waitzer, Edward. (1990). Pension fund trustees as shareholders. In *Proceedings of the conference, Strategies for Responsible Share Ownership: Implications for Pension and Other Investment Funds*, 7-12. Centre for Corporate Social Performance and Ethics and the Task Force on the Churches and Corporate Responsibility (December).

Waitzer, Edward. (1991, November-December). The bishop of Oxford and ethical investment. *The Corporate Ethics Monitor*, pp. 95-96.

Wall Street Journal Europe. (1999). 1 September.

Warner, Alison. (1998).Behind the hedges. *Banker*, November, pp. 24-5.

Wilshire and Associates. (1994). Performance of companies targeted by CalPERS between 1987-1992. California: Santa Monica.

Wilshire and Associates. (1995). The CalPERS Effect. California: Santa Monica.19 July.

Working Opportunity Fund. (2001). Annual report. Vancouver: author (August 27).

Working Opportunity Fund. (2002). Ethics Review. Vancouver: author

World Bank. (1994). *Averting the old-age crisis: Policies to protect the old and promote growth*. New York: Oxford University Press.

World Bank. (1998). *Global Development Finance*. Washington:World Bank.

Yaron, Gil. (2000). The responsible pension trustee: Reinterpreting the duties of prudence and loyalty in the context of socially responsible investing. *Estates, Trusts and Pensions Journal*. P. 305.

Yaron, Gil. (2001). The responsible pension trustee. *Estates, Trusts & Pensions Journal* June 20(4):305.

Yaron, Gil. (2002). Institutional shareholder activism in Canada. *UBC Law Journal* (forthcoming). Also at *www.share.ca*

Zadek, Simon, Peter Pruzan, and Richard Evans. (1997). *Building corporate accountability*. London: Earthscan Publications.

Zanglein, Jayne, E. (1995). High performance investing: Harnessing the power of pension funds to promote economic growth and workplace integrity. *Labor Lawyer*, 11, 59. pp. 59-150.

Zanglein, Jayne, E. (1998). From Wall Street walk to Wall Street talk: The changing face of corporate governance. *DePaul Bus. L.J.* 11): 43.

Zanglein, Jayne, E. (2000). Overcoming institutional barriers on the economically targeted investment superhighway. In Fung, Archon, Hebb, Tessa and Rogers, Joel. (2000). *Working capital: The power of labor"s pensions*. Ithaca: Cornell University Press. Pp. 181-202.

Biographies of contributors

Dr. Isla Carmichael is Senior Research and Education Officer with the Ontario Public Service Employees' Union, the provinces' second largest union. She recently completed her doctorate at the Ontario Institute for Studies in Education of the University of Toronto. The subject of her dissertation was worker control of pension funds and social investment in Canada, to be published by University of Toronto Press. She developed a method of evaluating investments, taking into account criteria other than the rate of return. In November 2000, her research was recognized through the Graduate Prize for Outstanding Research by the Policy Research Initiative of the Government of Canada. For twelve years, as Negotiator, Coordinator of Education and Campaigns, and Chief Executive Assistant at OPSEU, Isla Carmichael has specialized in strategic policy in workers' rights, workplace democracy, equity and the social value of work. She is also a program director of the Trustee Education Program, sponsored by OISE and the Centre for the Study of Training, Investment and Economic Restructuring at Carleton University. She holds a Master's degree in Adult Education and an M.A. in Moral Philosophy and Logic and Metaphysics and teaches at the graduate level at the Faculty of Social Work and OISE, of the University of Toronto.

Thomas Croft is the Director of the Heartland Labour Capital Network, a binational working group in the U.S. and Canada leading the development of new "stakeholder" and responsible investment strategies for workers' capital. The Network commissioned *Working Capital: The Power of Labor's Pensions*, published by Cornell University Press in 2002, an effort that has received extensive international acclaim. Through the Network, he has also supported the development of a new national network of worker-friendly private capital funds in the U.S., and is President of a regional investment fund-in-formation in the Pittsburgh area. His primary responsibility is as Executive Director of the Steel Valley Authority, a regional development authority in Pittsburgh that is a model for regional economic democracy and revitalization, and business retention. He founded, in 1985, the Seattle Worker Center, and also established the first program for dislocated timber workers on the West Coast. Thomas Croft has been involved for twenty years in designing new economic policies and programs that have been adopted at the municipal, state or federal levels, and has recently completed a U.S. Department of Labor National Guidebook that provides guidance for states in addressing economic transition. His efforts have been featured in two national PBS documentaries, including "Surviving the

Bottom Line" by Pulitzer Prize-winner Hedrick Smith. Tom received a Masters Degree in Public Affairs from the University of Washington in 1992, and a BA in Political Science from Humboldt State University. He has been a member of the USWA and two other unions. He is the proud father of two daughters.

Sean Harrigan, a member of the State Personnel Board (SPB), serves as its representative to the CalPERS Board of Administration. He was appointed to the seat by the SPB in December 1999. He is the Vice-Chair of the Investment Committee and a member of the Benefits and Program Administration and Health Benefits committees. Mr. Harrigan brings to CalPERS a wealth of experience in the labor field. In addition to his post on the State Personnel Board, he is currently the International Vice-President and Regional Director of the Food and Commercial Workers International Union (UFCW) Region 8 – Western. He has more than 30 years' experience in the food industry. For seven years, he worked for Safeway Supermarkets in various capacities before joining Richland Retail Clerks Local 1612 as a Union Representative. In 1991, he was appointed Executive Assistant of UFCW Region 8 – Western in California, and in 1993 he became Assistant to the Director of Organizing in Washington, D.C. He holds a Bachelor of Arts degree in economics from Whitman College in Washington State.

Tessa Hebb is a Visiting Scholar with the Faculty of Public Affairs and Management and Director of Capital Strategies for CSTIER, where she is a program director of the Trustee Education Program. She is an independent economic consultant and President of Hebb, Knight and Associates. Ms. Hebb's extensive background in public policy research includes work with trade unions both in Canada and the United States, with a particular focus on investment and pension funds. She recently completed a major project in the U.S. as Research Chair for the Heartland Labour-Capital Project, a three-year project funded by the Ford and Rockefeller Foundations. She co-edited *Working Capital:The Power of Labor's Pensions* (Cornell University Press, 2001). Ms. Hebb is a graduate of Harvard University and is a doctoral candidate at Oxford University. She holds a Master's Degree in Public Administration, with a concentration in international finance.

Freya Kodar is a doctoral student at Osgoode Hall Law School, York University. She articled and practised in the legal aid clinic system in British Columbia, and has worked as a researcher for a number of non-profit organizations, including the Shareholder Association for Research and Education. Her current research interests are in the areas of pension regulation and policy, corporate law, labour law and social welfare law. She is an active member of CUPE Local 3903.

Sherman Kreiner is the President and CEO of the Crocus Fund. He worked with the Manitoba Federation of Labour to design the Fund, and has been responsible for successfully guiding the growth of the Fund from its initial public offering in 1992 to an established venture capital corporation with over $170 million in assets and 31,000 Manitoba shareholders. Prior to joining the Fund, Mr. Kreiner had 15 years experience working with the labour movement, government and community organizations in the strategic development of employee ownership and related investment banking, business planning and legal structural design. He is a Regent of the University of Winnipeg, a member of the Premier's Economic Advisory Council and the Business Council of Manitoba, and an advisor to the Investment Committee of the Workers' Compensation Board. He also serves on the Boards of the Winnipeg Folk Festival, several Crocus investee companies, and as Chair of Community Ownership Solutions Inc., an enterprise development corporation serving low-income Winnipeg communities.

Jack Quarter is a professor at the Ontario Institute for Studies in Education of the University of Toronto, specializing in the study of non-profits, co-operatives, workplace democracy, social investment, and community development. His recent books include: with Laurie Mook and Betty Jane Richmond, *What Counts: Social accounting for non-profits and cooperatives* (Prentice Hall, 2002); *Beyond the Bottom Line: Socially innovative business owners* (Greenwood/Quorum; 2000); with Uriel Leviatan and Hugh Oliver, *Crisis in the Israeli Kibbutz* (Greenwood/Praeger; 1998); with Paul Wilkinson, *Building A Community Controlled Economy: The Evangeline co-operative experience* (University of Toronto Press; 1996); *Crossing the Line: Unionized employee ownership and investment funds* (James Lorimer; 1995); and *Canada's Social Economy* (James Lorimer; 1993). His current research, funded by the Social Science and Humanities Research Council of Canada and the Canadian Centre for Philanthropy, is on calculating the value added of volunteer contributions in non-profits, the social investment of union-based pension funds, and the conversion of public housing to non-market co-operatives.

Gil Yaron is the Director of Research, Law and Policy for the Shareholder Association for Research and Education. SHARE is a national not-for-profit organization helping pension funds to build sound investment practices, to protect the interest of plan beneficiaries, and to contribute to a just and healthy society. SHARE represents institutional investors, including union pension funds, with total assets of more than two billion dollars on pension investment matters. He holds a Master's in Law from the University of British Columbia and has been a member of the bar of British Columbia since 1998. Mr. Yaron has most recently authored a leading article on pension trustee fiduciary duties and socially responsible investing published in the Estates, Trusts and Pensions Journal.

Index